ABORTION
AND THE
CHURCH

> For behold, the LORD is about to come out from His place
> To punish the inhabitants of the earth for their iniquity;
> And the earth will reveal her bloodshed
> And will no longer cover her slain.
>
> *Isaiah 26:21*

EVANGEL PRESBYTERY

WARHORN MEDIA
BLOOMINGTON, INDIANA

WARHORN MEDIA
2401 S Endwright Rd.
Bloomington, IN 47403
WARHORNMEDIA.COM

© 2022 by Evangel Presbytery. All rights reserved.
Paperback redesign published 2023.

Unless otherwise indicated, all Scripture quotations are from the NEW AMERICAN STANDARD BIBLE®, © 1960, 1962, 1963, 1968, 1971, 1972, 1973, 1975, 1977, 1995 by The Lockman Foundation. Used by permission.

ISBN-13
Paperback: 978-1-940017-54-9
Spiral: 978-1-940017-46-4
PDF: 978-1-940017-47-1
EPUB: 978-1-940017-48-8
Kindle: 978-1-940017-49-5

Library of Congress Control Number
2023910951

Electronic versions of this book are available for free online at
abortion.evangelpresbytery.com

Listen for free at
abortion-and-the-church.transistor.fm

The paperback edition can be purchased online at
warhornmedia.com

For more information on Evangel Presbytery, please visit
evangelpresbytery.com

Contents

Preface   vii
Summary Introduction   1

CHAPTER 1

The Bloodshed of the Twentieth Century   3

A Grim Progression   4
   War   4
   Targeting Civilians   4
   Rulers Killing Citizens   5
   Parents Killing Children   6

Abortion's Consequences   9
   Sex-Selective Abortion   9
   In Vitro Fertilization: Babies in the Fridge   12
   Fetal Cell Lines: Cannibalization of Unborn Babies' Body Parts   15

The Church's Response to Abortion   24
   Protestants and *Whatever Happened to the Human Race?*   25
   Pro-Life Protestants and the Growth of Chemical Abortions   26

The Truth about Hormonal Birth Control   28
   IUDs, the Pill, and the Prevention of Implantation   29
   The Significance of Our Lord's Incarnation   36

The Body Count   39
   Surgical and Chemical Abortions   40
   Accounting for Hormonal Birth Control and IUDs   41
   Accounting for In Vitro Fertilization   44
   The Total   45

Conclusion: Genocide   46

CHAPTER 2
Abortion's Assault upon God's Character and Law   50

Moral Arguments   50
   Overthrowing Our Creator's Command against Murder   51
   Denial of the Right to Life   51
   The Removal of Woman's Moral Agency   52
   The Death of the Conscience   56

Natural Law Arguments   57
   Man as Unique Creation   59
   Personhood from the Beginning   59
   SLED Arguments   61

Societal Arguments   63
   Man as Social Being   63
   The Loss of Potential   65
   Economic Considerations   66
   Devaluing One Devalues All   70
   The History and Destruction of the Unborn's "Right to Life" in the West   71

The Witness of Church History   78

The Testimony of Scripture   84
   Imago Dei   84
   "Your Hands Formed Me"   88
   Woman as Life-Giver   89
   God as Sanctifier of Birth   92
   Children as Gift from the Lord   93
   Murder Incompatible with God's Character   94
   Man Accountable to God for the Shedding of Blood   94
   God's Hatred for the Shedding of Blood   95
   God's Particular Hatred for the Shedding of the Blood of Children   97
   The New Testament's Condemnation of *Pharmakeia*   100

Dealing with Common Justifications for Abortion   109
   Rape and Incest   109
   Health of the Mother   119
   Clinical Callousness   125

CONTENTS

CHAPTER 3
Applications 128

The Duty of Civil Authorities 128
   The Civil Ruler and God's Law 129
   Keeping Our Eye on the Ball:
      Understanding the Dangers of Incrementalism 134
   Zeal Tempered by Knowledge: Prudent Policies 137
   The Accountability of Civil Rulers 141

The Duty of Church Authorities 143
   The Church and Abortion: Success Followed by Failure 143
   The Church's Bloodguilt 148
   The Necessity of Repentance 151
   The Church's Public Witness against the Killing 153
   Instructing the Civil Magistrate 157
   The Civil Authority and the Power of the Keys 160
   Walking alongside Our Sheep in the Death of the Unborn 161

The Duty of Individuals 163
   Male Leadership in Fighting Abortion 164
   Christian Witness at the Killing Places 167
   Christian Witness on the Job 171
   Christian Witness in the Public Square 172
   What about the Babies of Pagans? 176
   Dedication to Life in the Face of Congenital Anomalies and Disabilities 177

Two Challenges 179
   Challenge 1: Restoring Our Depleted Understanding
      of the Image of God in Man 179
   Challenge 2: Maintaining the Unity of the Body of Christ 184

The End of Abortion:
Reclaiming God's Blessing of Fruitfulness 189

Epilogue 209

Preface

Evangel Presbytery is a group of churches who have joined together to confess the historic orthodox, Christian, Protestant and Reformed faith. Evangel provides for our mutual fellowship and instruction, but also serves as an ecclesiastical court adjudicating the inevitable disagreements and conflicts which every church has faced since the Council of Jerusalem recorded in Acts 15. Evangel has produced a Book of Church Order[1] by which we govern the proceedings of our individual congregations and presbytery.

From time to time, Evangel writes and adopts statements addressing contemporary doctrinal and moral challenges mounted against God and His truth by the world in which we live. One previous statement titled Declaration of Doctrine and Policies Concerning Sexuality[2] condemns the world's attack upon God's gift of the diversity of sexuality by which He makes every man either male or female. Two statements addressing matters related to Covid also were adopted by Evangel: the Statement on Sphere Authority, Worship, and COVID-19 Quarantines (2020)[3] and the Statement on Conscience and COVID-19 Vaccine Mandates (2021).[4]

---

1. https://bco.evangelpresbytery.com. The BCO includes a Directory for Worship by which we govern our worship (https://bco.evangelpresbytery.com/preface.html).
2. https://bco.evangelpresbytery.com/form-of-government.html#declaration-of-doctrine-and-policies-concerning-sexuality.
3. https://evangelpresbytery.com/wp-content/uploads/2020/06/STATEMENT-ON-SPHERE-AUTHORITY-WORSHIP-AND-COVID-19-QUARANTINES.pdf.
4. https://evangelpresbytery.com/wp-content/uploads/2021/10/Conscience-and-COVID-19-Vaccine-Mandates_Evangel-Presbytery.pdf.

This statement on abortion was written by members of Evangel Presbytery in response to a petition by the session of Sovereign King Church[5] requesting that Evangel Presbytery address the sin of abortion. In response to that petition, at its stated meeting on October 8, 2021, Evangel appointed a committee to study and write a report on abortion. This report was presented to Evangel Presbytery for their action at the stated meeting held on June 2, 2022. The Presbytery received this report titled *Abortion and the Church*, voting to commend it to our member churches and the church catholic around the world.

When the committee began its work, there wasn't a hint of the Supreme Court of the United States taking any action to reverse its 1973 ruling in *Roe v. Wade*. Then, on May 2, 2022, *Politico* shocked the nation by releasing a draft majority opinion by Justice Alito in the case *Dobbs v. Jackson Women's Health Organization*. Reading Alito's draft opinion, it seemed apparent a majority of the court was poised to overturn *Roe v. Wade*.

On June 24, 2022, the Supreme Court of the United States issued their decision in *Dobbs v. Jackson Women's Health Organization* in which they did, indeed, reverse *Roe v. Wade*.[6]

Evangel Presbytery thanks God for causing the Supreme Court to overturn *Roe v. Wade*. *Roe*'s forty-nine years of oppression represent a bloody rebellion against God's Sixth Commandment, our nation's Constitution, and the fundamental rule of law. The court's 1973 ruling fueled the greatest denial of basic human rights in our history, as well as the most enduring and highest conflict our nation has experienced since its founding in 1776. The court's formal repudiation of their former wicked decision is joyful news for the righteous across our nation, as well as those who fear God across the watching world.

Infinitely more important, though, is the hope this brings that the millions of little ones who have been slaughtered during the genocidal holocaust perpetrated against this class of defenseless persons may finally be recognized and mourned as victims of murder, so that, in time, our nation may come to full repentance for this bloodshed we have committed individually and as a nation.

We have addressed *Abortion and the Church* to "the church of the living

---

5. https://www.sovereignkingchurch.com/.
6. *Dobbs v. Jackson Women's Health Organization*, No. 19-1392 (US June 24, 2022).

PREFACE

God, the pillar and ground of the truth" (1 Tim. 3:15, KJV). It is our prayer that, first, the church herself will repent of her own murders committed against the little ones given her by God as His individual blessings placed in the wombs of His daughters. This statement does its most exhaustive work naming and proving the church's own bloodguilt in this matter. This is only right given God's words, "For it is time for judgment to begin with the household of God; and if it begins with us first, what will be the outcome for those who do not obey the gospel of God? And if it is with difficulty that the righteous is saved, what will become of the godless man and the sinner?" (1 Pet. 4:17–18).

Still, the end of all things is near and soon the King of kings and Lord of lords will return in power and glory to judge the whole earth. On that day, the Creator of all things will not render His judgments concerning only His own people, the Christian church. Rather, He will judge all men who will then learn the truth of Scripture that "it is a fearful thing to fall into the hands of the Living God" (Heb. 10:31, KJV). Concerning our slaughter of many millions of little ones, we must face our Lord Jesus' warning concerning those who harm children:

> He called a child to Himself and set him before them, and said, "Truly I say to you, unless you are converted and become like children, you will not enter the kingdom of heaven. Whoever then humbles himself as this child, he is the greatest in the kingdom of heaven. And whoever receives one such child in My name receives Me; but whoever causes one of these little ones who believe in Me to stumble, it would be better for him to have a heavy millstone hung around his neck, and to be drowned in the depth of the sea. (Matt. 18:2–6)

The Father Almighty sees everything. Nothing can be hidden from Him who has warned us He hates the bloodshed of innocents. Whether the murder of His little ones is accomplished with drugs very early or surgically very late, every abortion is the bloodshed of innocents. Will the people of God repent? Will those who have no faith in Jesus turn and repent, fleeing to His cross for the forgiveness of their bloodguilt?

The reversal of *Roe v. Wade* may lead to some decrease in the slaughter, but it will not bring this slaughter to an end. The end of this horror will arrive only when God works among us to cause men to repent and turn to the Lord Jesus, restoring the love and honor of woman as the life-giver God created her to be. The bloodshed will end only when man[7] once more receives with joy those little ones God blesses us with when He places them in woman's womb.

Genesis records that Adam "called his wife's name Eve, because she was the mother of all the living" (Gen. 3:20). To love woman is to love the fruit of her womb. In springtime, this is the beautiful opening and awakening cried out by all creation.

May God cause the heart of man to return to woman, the heart of husband to return to wife, and the heart of father and mother to return to the little child who is the fruit of their love, knit together by God in the secret place.

> For You formed my inward parts;
> You wove me in my mother's womb.
> I will give thanks to You, for I am fearfully and wonderfully made;
> Wonderful are Your works,
> And my soul knows it very well.
> My frame was not hidden from You,
> When I was made in secret,
> And skillfully wrought in the depths of the earth;
> Your eyes have seen my unformed substance;
> And in Your book were all written
> The days that were ordained for me,
> When as yet there was not one of them.
>
> (Ps. 139:13–16)

---

7. This usage of "man" as a gender inclusive will be constant in this document. God Himself named our race (both male and female together) "man" (Hebrew *'āḏām*) after the male of the species (Genesis 5:2). The usage of "man" to refer to both male and female of the species therefore honors God's naming in a way the more common "human," "human being," "humanity," "humankind," and "person" obscure.

PREFACE

Evangel Presbytery Study Committee on Abortion

Brian Edward Bailey[†]
JD (Maurer School of Law, Indiana University)
Elder, Trinity Reformed Church (Bloomington, Indiana)

Rev. Joseph T. Bayly[†]
BDiv (New Geneva Academy)
Pastor, Christ Church Cincinnati (Mason, Ohio)

Rev. Timothy B. Bayly[*]
MDiv (Gordon-Conwell Theological Seminary)
Pastor, Trinity Reformed Church (Bloomington, Indiana)

Rev. James Brown Jr.
Pastor, Holy Trinity Reformed Church (Camby, Indiana)

Joshua Congrove[*]
PhD (Classical Studies; Indiana University)
Elder, Trinity Reformed Church (Bloomington, Indiana)

Rev. Andrew Dionne[†]
MDiv (Covenant Theological Seminary), DM (Jacobs School of Music, Indiana University)
Pastor, Trinity Presbyterian Church (Spartanburg, South Carolina)

Rev. Jürgen von Hagen[†]
PhD (Economics; University of Bonn)
Pastor, Free Evangelical Church (Mülheim, Germany)

Abram Hess
DDS (Indiana University School of Dentistry)
Elder, Clearnote Church (Indianapolis, Indiana)

Devin Maddox
Elder, Holy Trinity Reformed Church (Camby, Indiana)

Kenneth Patrick
Elder, Christ Church Cincinnati (Mason, Ohio)

Renton Rathbun
PhD (Apologetics; Westminster Theological Seminary), ThM (Theology; Puritan Reformed Theological Seminary)
Elder, Trinity Presbyterian Church (Spartanburg, South Carolina)

Rev. Joseph Spurgeon[†]
MDiv (Southern Baptist Theological Seminary)
Pastor, Sovereign King Church (Jeffersonville, Indiana)

[*] Principal writer   [†] Supplemental writer

We wish to thank those listed below for their generous help in this work:

Nathan Alberson
Church of the King (Evansville, Indiana)

Ben Burlingham
PhD (Chemistry; Indiana University)
Elder, Trinity Reformed Church
 (Bloomington, Indiana)

Chris Connell
PhD (Mathematics; University of Michigan)
Trinity Reformed Church
 (Bloomington, Indiana)

Daniel Coughlin
PhD (Biochemistry; University of
 Michigan),
JD (The University of Toledo
 College of Law)
Trinity Reformed Church
 (Bloomington, Indiana)

Rev. Alex McNeilly
BDiv (New Geneva Academy)
Pastor, Christ Church Cincinnati
 (Mason, Ohio)

Eric Rasmusen
PhD (Economics; Massachusetts
 Institute of Technology)
Trinity Reformed Church
 (Bloomington, Indiana)

Caleb Starr
PhD (Biochemistry; Indiana University)
Trinity Reformed Church
 (Bloomington, Indiana)

**Rev. and Mrs. Benjamin
 (Megan) Sulser**
BDiv (New Geneva Academy)
Pastor, Church of the King
 (Evansville, Indiana)

Benjamin Walker
PhD (Biochemistry; Indiana University)
Deacon, Trinity Reformed Church
 (Bloomington, Indiana)

Summary Introduction

In chapter 1, we outline the historical context for the spread of abortion in the twentieth century. We show how world wars and Communist tyranny set the stage for genocide in our very own homes. In addition to seeing the staggering number (billions) of souls who have been sacrificed in this most recent holocaust, readers may be shocked to see how dependent our society is on abortion's bloodshed. Perhaps the most difficult matter for Christians to accept will be the true nature of hormonal birth control, IUDs, and in vitro fertilization. To those who have ears to hear, we explain that many, if not most, of our little ones are being destroyed, not by surgeon's instruments late in pregnancy, but before our babies are even allowed to attach themselves to their mothers' wombs.

After building an understanding of how and to what extent we have given ourselves to this destruction, we then lay out in chapter 2 the many arguments which exist against the practice of abortion. Several sections of this chapter are very technical, drawing on research from a wide range of academic fields. We thank God for blessing Evangel Presbytery with godly brothers who are experts in the disciplines of economics, biochemistry, law, classical studies, and medicine. These brothers' careful and faithful labors unequivocally demonstrate abortion's vileness. The arguments assembled from their work build up to and conclude with Scripture's authoritative, clear, and multifaceted teachings against the practice of murdering our children.

In chapter 3, we lay the biblical foundation of what it looks like for (1) civil authorities, (2) church authorities, and (3) individuals to act and speak faithfully regarding the slaughter of the unborn. We answer many common questions and objections, but not all, since the work of application is necessarily specific to each person's unique calling, relationships, location, gifts, weaknesses, and so forth. Walking in obedience to God's will in these matters will require Christians to live together, counsel one another, and submit to one another in the fear of Christ (Eph. 5:21).

The thrust of the work before you is unavoidably negative. Our primary objective here is to awaken consciences to the depth of our bloodguilt. When we as a people have given ourselves to such evil for so long, we absolutely must do the painful work of exposing our unfruitful deeds of darkness (Eph. 5:11). We all must hear the condemnation of God's law. And then we must *repent*. To do so is to flee the wrath to come, and we know that God's wrath is certainly coming upon murderers, whose part will be "in the lake that burns with fire and brimstone, which is the second death" (Rev. 21:8). When we repent of murder, we run away from this second death.

Repentance, however, is more than just turning away from death. The repentance which our merciful God grants us is not just repentance *from death*, but repentance *unto life* (Acts 11:18). We flee *from* God's wrath and *towards* the eternal life promised in Christ Jesus. Then, as possessors of life eternal, we embrace God's gift of life here and now. This is why we conclude our work by showing that the end of abortion is not simply the denouncing of murder, but the embracing of God's beautiful blessing of fruitfulness, especially in His giving of woman to be the giver of life.

CHAPTER 1

The Bloodshed of the Twentieth Century

When the record of our time is written, it will be a record of bloodshed on a scale previously unimaginable across the history of mankind. The heart of that bloodshed is the war carried out by the born against the unborn. The victims of this war are a class of persons constrained within the wombs of their mothers, and they live without sight, sound, or voice. The disability that unites them is their incapacity to lift a finger in their own defense.

Other great moral evils exist, of course, but abortion is unique in targeting the most helpless members of our society. Our bloodlust has never before found a class of victims so utterly vulnerable. For this reason abortion's bloodshed dwarfs every other bloodshed. How we repent of this bloodshed is thus the greatest moral issue of our time, and this repentance or its absence will be predictive of our repentance of a multitude of other moral evils of our age. Infanticide, euthanasia, and physician-assisted suicide are of the same moral fabric as our slaughter of little ones.

Some speak of this genocide as being on the decline today. This is false. Across the world, abortions are not falling, but rising. The United Kingdom's premier medical journal *The Lancet* reports abortions currently stand at 73.3 million per year.[1] Based on that figure alone, we are killing 1 percent of the world's population each year—but we note this estimate *excludes*

---

1. Jonathan Bearak et al., "Unintended Pregnancy and Abortion by Income, Region, and the Legal Status of Abortion: Estimates from a Comprehensive Model for 1990–2019," *The Lancet Global Health* 8, no. 9 (September 1, 2020): e1152–e1161, https://doi.org/10.1016/S2214-109X(20)30315-6.

those babies aborted in their first week of life. To facilitate the murder of these babies, our medical authorities have (as we will see) declared that babies in the first week of life are not yet living beings.

Abortion's slaughter is staggering. Reading such estimates, we ask if it is possible we have murdered billions of babies? How can this be? Why did we not know this number? How did we get here? Who is responsible? What can be done about it?

The beginning of answering these questions is to take a step back.

A Grim Progression

War

The twentieth century—what would become history's bloodiest century—began with war between many nations. The warfare's scale, tactics, and techniques were unprecedented. World War I's trench warfare was so dehumanizing and the killing so sustained that many declared their optimism this horror would force a sea change in governments' ability to send their men into war. Thus H. G. Wells named World War I "the war to end all wars."

He was wrong. World War II followed hard on the heels of World War I so that, during the first half of the century, fatalities from these two world wars reached 77 million. But cloaked within this number was a detail foreshadowing the trajectory massive killing would take as the century continued.

Targeting Civilians

Until the twenty-first century, Christendom had condemned the killing of civilians during warfare. Since the Middle Ages, the Western world had held to the necessity of *jus in bello*, and three commitments stood out among just war principles: soldiers who surrendered were not to be killed; suffering was to be minimized; and the indiscriminate killing of noncombatants was prohibited.

But at the turn of the twentieth century, Christendom itself was, in a sense, on the wane. Atheism and rebellion against God's moral law had grown in the centuries since the Enlightenment, and civilization was about to pay the price. Sadly, of the 17 million fatalities of the First World War, 7 million were civilians. The Second World War was worse: of an estimated 60 million fatalities, 40 million were civilians. Note that these numbers don't even include the tens of millions who died from secondary causes like disease and famine.

Thus, from the start, the twentieth century was exceedingly bloody. The wars were worldwide, the killing was beyond anything imaginable, and civilians were intentionally targeted so that the elderly, women, and children made up the majority of the wars' casualties. By the end of the Second World War, targeting civilians was a major strategy of both Axis and Allied forces. Both sides of the conflict used conventional bombs to kill the civilian populations of their enemies.

Speaking only of our Allied air forces' attacks on Japan, on March 9 and 10, 1945, the air raid called Meetinghouse sent 300 bombers to drop 1,665 tons of bombs on Tokyo, leaving close to 16 square miles destroyed and 100,000 dead. United States forces later dropped nuclear warheads on Hiroshima and Nagasaki, killing 105,000 men, women, and children.

By the end of World War II, Allied bombing had damaged or destroyed over one-quarter of German homes, killing or injuring 1 million German civilians. The relentless nature of Allied bombing of civilians is demonstrated by the fact that 50,000 tons of bombs were dropped on the city of Cologne alone.[2]

In the end, during the first half of the twentieth century, war claimed 77 million souls, of whom 47 million were civilians. Just war principles had been cast aside. In its conduct of war, the Western world had sown the wind. In the justice of God, we would now reap the whirlwind.

Rulers Killing Citizens

As the century continued, the killing turned from nations killing nations to rulers of nations killing their own people.

---

2. *The Effects of Strategic Bombing on German Morale*, The United States Strategic Bombing Survey (Morale Division, May 1947), 1:7–8, https://isr.umich.edu/wp-content/uploads/historicPublications/Effects_300_.PDF.

The Soviet Union's great prophet Aleksandr Solzhenitsyn estimated Joseph Stalin was responsible for the deaths of more than 60 million. Chairman Mao's Great Leap Forward, Great Famine, and Cultural Revolution claimed somewhere between 40 and 100 million lives. The death toll of Pol Pot's Khmer Rouge in Cambodia was only 2 million, but these 2 million souls comprised one-quarter of his nation's population.

First, World Wars I and II killed 77 million souls. Then Communism killed at least 100 million souls; and this was bloodshed in service, not to national boundaries defended as patriotism, but pure ideology. As Solzhenitsyn wrote documenting Stalin's death toll in the Soviet Union, "Thanks to *ideology*, the twentieth century was fated to experience evildoing on a scale calculated in the millions. This cannot be denied, nor passed over, nor suppressed."[3]

First, soldiers killed soldiers. Then, soldiers killed civilians. Then, rulers killed their own people.

The prophet Hosea warned that bloodshed begets bloodshed,[4] and so it was that the killing next turned inward to the home and family; fathers and mothers killed their own sons and daughters.

Parents Killing Children

Domestic slaughter began with birth control.[5] The first abortions were not surgical, but chemical and hormonal. Before women became willing to pay for their child to be cut out of their wombs, they began using birth control methods that had an abortifacient agency. As we will discuss in greater detail later, these methods include intrauterine devices (IUDs) and the Pill.

This was well-known and presented a problem the medical establishment felt the need to resolve. There was no debate in the scientific and medical world that the moment sperm and egg joined, a new life came

---

3. Aleksandr Solzhenitsyn, *The Gulag Archipelago*, trans. Thomas P. Whitney (HarperCollins, 2007), 1:174.
4. Hosea 4:2.
5. Note the use of the term "birth control" for what would almost always be labeled "contraception" across scientific and medical literature. In our usage, "contraception" will refer only to methods of birth control which actually prevent conception, defined as the fertilization of the egg producing an embryo. On the other hand, "birth control" will include contraceptive agents and methods, but also abortifacient agents and methods which, properly speaking, do not prevent conception, but the little one's implantation, development to full term, and birth.

into existence.[6] Nor was there any question this preborn life had a rightful claim to all the protections accorded life outside the womb.

These truths, though, stood squarely in the path of the mid-century explosion of the practice of birth control so that, midway through the century, the American medical establishment undertook the project of denying these little ones were living human beings. Every scientist, physician, and mother knew conception was the beginning of life, so what was to be done?

The story is recounted by the American College of Pediatricians who report that, back in 1959, a physician with ties to Planned Parenthood named Bent Böving "argued for . . . moving the date of conception from when fertilization occurs to when implantation occurs."[7] Böving suggested "the social advantage of [birth control] being considered to prevent conception rather than to destroy an established pregnancy could depend upon something so simple as a prudent habit of speech."[8]

A few years later, Dr. Böving's "prudent habit of speech" was formally adopted by the American College of Obstetricians and Gynecologists who, in 1965, issued a bulletin changing the definition of conception from fertilization to implantation.[9]

Consider the significance of this subterfuge promulgated by the American medical establishment. By redefining conception, the killing of babies during their first week of life by means of birth control methods was no longer "abortion," but "contraception." The baby was not aborted, because he was never conceived. The baby never died, because he never lived.

Never mind that these little ones are God's own image-bearers having unique DNA and needing nothing more than the sustenance and protection of their mother's womb to be born and live threescore and ten. Who could ever have imagined then, eight years before *Roe v. Wade*, the monstrous death toll that would result from this lie adopted as merely a "prudent

---

6. See testimony of Dr. Jerome Lejeune in *Davis v. Davis*, as reproduced in pt. 1 of *A Symphony of the Preborn Child* (National Association for the Advancement of Preborn Children, 1989), 18, https://naapc.org/wp-content/uploads/2010/05/symphony.pdf. We will quote extensively from Dr. Lejeune's testimony when addressing in vitro fertilization below.
7. "When Human Life Begins," American College of Pediatricians, March 2017, https://acpeds.org/position-statements/when-human-life-begins.
8. Bent Böving, "Implantation Mechanisms," ch. 7 in *Mechanisms Concerned with Conception*, ed. C. G. Hartman (MacMillan, 1963), 386.
9. The American College of Obstetricians and Gynecologists (ACOG) Committee on Terminology, "Terms Used in Reference to The Fetus," *Terminology Bulletin*, no. 1 (September 1965): 1. For more on this change, see https://acpeds.org/position-statements/when-human-life-begins.

habit of speech"? This saying is true: "What a tangled web we weave, when first we practice to deceive."

We can't be reminded often enough that murderers lie. In his book *Aborting America,* Dr. Bernard Nathanson confesses the history of his work legalizing abortion in the late sixties and early seventies. He speaks candidly of the lies he and his Abortion Rights Action League co-belligerents told. He writes:

> I confess that I knew the figures were totally false. . . . But in the "morality" of our revolution, it was a useful figure, widely accepted, so why go out of our way to correct it with honest statistics? The overriding concern was to get the laws eliminated, and anything within reason that had to be done was permissible.[10]

The legalization and growth of the practices of birth control and abortion are inseparable. This fact must be faced squarely by the people of God. The use of birth control would not have spread as it did without the lie that life doesn't begin at conception. This wicked lie has metastasized across the past seventy years, and now the life of the unborn is denied during all three trimesters.

Abortifacient birth control methods that killed children in their first days of life gave birth to abortions throughout pregnancy so that, today, in some places late-term abortions are legal even as the baby is in the birth canal about to take his first breath outside the womb.

Thus, in the decades following 1950, abortion came to dwarf every other killing field of the twentieth century.

Today, it is commonly thought, at least in the United States, that the slaughter of abortion was unleashed by the Supreme Court's 1973 decision *Roe v. Wade.* This is factually wrong. Birth control of an abortifacient agency as well as surgical abortions were widely practiced prior to the Supreme Court's *Roe v. Wade* ruling. In 1972 alone, the year prior to *Roe v. Wade,* the death toll of unborn babies surgically aborted in the United States was 586,760.[11]

---

10. Bernard Nathanson and Richard Ostling, *Aborting America* (Doubleday, 1979), 193.
11. Willard Cates Jr., David Grimes, and Kenneth Schulz, "The Public Health Impact of Legal Abortion: 30 Years Later," *Perspectives on Sexual and Reproductive Health* 35, no. 1 (January/February 2003): 25–28, https://www.guttmacher.org/sites/default/files/article_files/3502503.pdf.

Abortifacient birth control methods propped up by scientists and physicians redefining conception and life make no sense outside a world that had become inured to the bloodshed of innocents. World wars and Communist ideologies had killed their hundreds of millions. Now the bloodthirst turned inward, and the home became the killing field.

Not surprisingly, this intimate familial bloodshed was first normalized behind the Iron Curtain within the Soviet Union where Russians and Eastern Europeans began killing their unborn children in the early fifties. But it didn't take many years for this horror to spread to Western Europe and North America; and now, most of the world. Violence begets violence.

We become proficient at killing, thinking we have it under control. But actually, the bloodshed has us under its control, and its appetite is voracious and growing.

Abortion's Consequences

The destruction caused by the spread of abortion becomes more clear as we examine some of its additional consequences.

Sex-Selective Abortion

Across South Asia, sex-selective abortion is now widespread. It was first practiced in South Korea, producing in certain cities a sex ratio at birth (SRB) of 125 boys to 100 girls.[12] China copied the practice so that, now, a number of provinces have an SRB of 130 boys to 100 girls. Soon, the practice spread to India where several states now have an SRB of 120 boys to 100 girls. The National Library of Medicine of the National Institutes of Health gave the following report concerning China:

> The SRB across the country for first-order births is 108, for second-order births it is 143 and for the (albeit rare) third-order births it is 157.[13]

---

12. Therese Hesketh, Li Lu, and Zhu Wei Xing, "The Consequences of Son Preference and Sex-Selective Abortion in China and Other Asian Countries," *Canadian Medical Association Journal* 183, no. 12 (September 6, 2011): 1374–1377, https://doi.org/10.1503/cmaj.101368.
13. Ibid., 1375.

In 2012, Planned Parenthood's research arm, The Guttmacher Institute, reported:

> The Chinese Academy of Social Sciences predicts that by 2020, China will have 30–40 million more boys and young men under age 20 than females of the same age. India, too, is facing a national crisis with its sex ratios. The Indian census does not publish sex ratios at birth, but rather child sex ratios, expressed as the number of females below age seven for every 1,000 males. The last four census surveys point to rapidly increasing disparities: The child sex ratio dropped from 962 (girls to 1,000 boys) in 1981 to 945 in 1991 to 927 in 2001, and according to the latest census, in 2011, the ratio decreased further, to 914.
>
> . . . The northern Indian states of Haryana and Punjab are notorious for their exceedingly disparate ratios, at 830 and 846, respectively, with some districts dipping into the 770s.[14]

The Guardian reports, "India is estimated to have 63 million fewer women since sex determination tests took off in the 1970s."[15]

A decade ago, *The Economist* reported:

> China alone stands to have as many unmarried young men—"bare branches," as they are known—as the entire population of young men in America.[16]

More recently, *The Economist* did a piece on gendercide in the Caucasus states, especially Georgia, Azerbaijan, and Armenia:

> But in Armenia and Azerbaijan more than 115 boys are born for every 100 girls and in Georgia the ratio is 120. These are bigger distortions than in India. In all three the figure has risen sharply since 1991. . . . In 2010, reckons Marc Michael of New York University's Abu Dhabi campus, the number

---

14. Sneha Barot, "A Problem-and-Solution Mismatch: Son Preference and Sex-Selective Abortion Bans," *Guttmacher Policy Review* 15, no. 2 (2012): 19, https://www.guttmacher.org/gpr/2012/05/problem-and-solution-mismatch-son-preference-and-sex-selective-abortion-bans.

15. Amrit Dhillon, "Selective Abortion in India Could Lead to 6.8m Fewer Girls Being Born by 2030," *The Guardian*, August 21, 2020, https://www.theguardian.com/global-development/2020/aug/21/selective-abortion-in-india-could-lead-to-68m-fewer-girls-being-born-by-2030.

16. "Gendercide," *The Economist*, March 4, 2010, https://www.economist.com/leaders/2010/03/04/gendercide.

of girls born was 10% lower than it would have been had the ratio been normal. The gap is second only to China's.[17]

Enlightened Westerners condemn this killing of unborn girls for its "sexism." They are rightly horrified at the denial of the equality of the sexes it demonstrates. The image of God is the foundation of our personhood and is equally shared by man and woman, so any denial of woman's equal worth is an assault on God Himself.

Yet if we place this practice under scrutiny, it becomes clear something much worse than the denial of the equality of persons is motivating this gendercide. Consider feminist women who argue in defense of the right of women to have gender-selective abortions. In *Gendercide: The Implications of Sex Selection*, the late Mary Anne Warren, philosophy professor at San Francisco State University, argued against any legal prohibition of gender-selective abortion. Dedicating her book "To utopian feminists, who dream of alternative futures," Warren wrote:

> I will argue that the objections to sex selection are insufficient to show that it is inherently immoral to preselect the sex of a child.[18]

Speaking of the need to "resist prohibition" of gender-selective abortion in her chapter titled "The Case for Freedom of Choice," Warren writes:

> There is great danger that the legal prohibition of sex selection would endanger other aspects of women's reproductive freedom [including] the right to choose abortion.[19]

In her book's conclusion, Warren states:

> We must not accept the argument that women who opt for sex selection [abortion] ... are not making *real* choices.[20]

---

17. "Gendercide in the Caucasus: Sex-Selective Abortion," *The Economist*, September 21, 2013, https://www.economist.com/europe/2013/09/21/gendercide-in-the-caucasus.

18. Mary Anne Warren, *Gendercide: The Implications of Sex Selection* (Rowman & Allanheld, 1985), 5. Warren is slippery in stating specific arguments, but her book is a defense of gender-selective feticide.

19. Ibid., 183.

20. Ibid., 197. Emphasis original.

Warren's foundational principle is women's self-determination. It must take precedence over the life of the unborn child. The liberation of women is of such importance and the ability to abort one's child is so central to that liberation that even the killing of unborn children based on their sex must be legitimated to serve this commitment. Women must have the right to kill any unborn child they do not want, even if the mother doesn't want that child because she's a girl.

This same underlying commitment is shared by all those who kill their unborn children. Regardless of why she is unwanted, an unwanted child is an unwanted child, and that's the end of it.

When we justify the murder of our little ones by talk of self-determination and our desires and goals being foiled by this baby in our womb, what does it really matter what those desires and goals are, so long as our ability to kill the child remains unimpeded? So, as to the sex-selective feticides of the East killing unborn baby girls particularly, the West has no reason to express concern or moral disapproval. Those in the West who declare that unwantedness of any sort justifies a mother killing her child have no basis to say the unwantedness of a child in the East is morally reprehensible. To each her own.

But really, did anyone anticipate the normalization of sex-selective abortion in India alone would result in 63 million sons unable to marry because their fathers and mothers murdered 63 million daughters?

In Vitro Fertilization: Babies in the Fridge

A further consequence of the normalization of abortion is the growth of in vitro fertilization (IVF; literally, "fertilization in glass").[21] This procedure removes eggs from a woman's ovaries to fertilize them with sperm outside the body in a laboratory dish.[22] Normally, several eggs at a time are taken from the mother in order to fertilize them and have several children on hand from which to select the one or two who will be implanted in their mother's womb. Not every embryo will successfully attach himself to his

---

21. See European Society of Human Reproduction and Embryology (ESHRE), "More Than 8 Million Babies Born from IVF Since the World's First in 1978," *Science Daily*, July 3, 2018, https://www.sciencedaily.com/releases/2018/07/180703084127.htm.

22. "In vitro fertilization (IVF)," Mayo Clinic, https://www.mayoclinic.org/tests-procedures/in-vitro-fertilization/about/pac-20384716.

mother's womb, so fertility clinic doctors make a habit of fertilizing several eggs at a time.[23]

Those embryos not given the privilege of implantation in their mother's womb are cryogenically frozen and stored for usage later by their parents in another IVF cycle (if the child's sibling doesn't survive[24] implantation), donated for scientific research (requiring the child's death), offered to another infertile couple, or simply destroyed.

Note here precisely what it is under discussion. IVF companies conceive image-bearers of God in a test tube, freeze them, make utilitarian calculations about how many babies they need, and so on.

In August 1989, world-renowned geneticist Jerome Lejeune testified in a Tennessee court concerning what he refers to as "little ones kept in the fridge." He opened up the ghoulish premises and procedures at the heart of the in vitro fertilization business. We quote extensively from Lejeune's testimony because of the close application of his testimony to those babies aborted at the same early stage of development through birth control. The human life that Dr. Lejeune testifies exists after conception is the same stage of embryonic life of those little ones prevented from attaching themselves to their mother's womb by IUDs and hormonal methods of birth control. Those babies imprisoned and killed by IVF procedures are the same age as those killed by IUDs and hormonal birth control.

The following is from Dr. Lejeune's court testimony:

> Each of us has a unique beginning, the moment of conception.... As soon as the program is written on the DNA, there are twenty-three different pieces of program carried by the spermatozoa and there are twenty-three different homologous pieces carried by the ovum. As soon as the twenty-three chromosomes carried by the sperm encounter the twenty-three chromosomes carried by the ovum, the whole information necessary and sufficient to spell out all the characteristics of the new being is gathered....
>
> ... Now, I know that there has been recent discussion of vocabulary, and I was very surprised two years ago that some of our British colleagues invented the term of pre-embryo. That does not exist, it has never existed.

---

23. Ibid.
24. Notably, even the scientific literature refers to embryos' ability to *survive* the freeze-thaw cycle. Ibid.

I was curious, and I went to the encyclopedia, to the French encyclopedia, the one I inherited from my great father so it was fifty years ago it was printed.

And at the term of embryo it was said: "The youngest form of a being," which is very clear and simple definition, and it stated: "it starts as one fertilized cell, (fertilized egg, which is called also zygote), and when the zygote splits in two cells, it is called a two-cell embryo. When it split in four it is called a four-cell embryo." Then it's very interesting because this terminology was accepted the world over for more than fifty years by all the specialists of the world, and we had no need at all of a sub-class which would be called a pre-embryo, because there is nothing before the embryo. Before an embryo there is a sperm and an egg, and that is it. And the sperm and an egg cannot be a pre-embryo because you cannot tell what embryo it will be, because you don't know what the sperm will go in what an egg [*sic*], but once it is made, you have got a zygote and when it divides it's an embryo and that's it. . . .

If we stop the process, if we slow down the movement of the molecules, we progressively come to a relative standstill, and when the embryo is frozen, these tiny human beings, they are very small, one millimeter and a half of a dimension, a sphere a millimeter and a half, you can put them in canisters by the thousands. And then with the due connotation, the fact of putting inside a 19 [degree] very chilly space, tiny human beings who are deprived of any liberty, of any movement, even they are deprived of time, (time is frozen for them), make them surviving, so to speak, in a suspended time, in a concentration can. It's not as hospitable and prepared to [give] life as would be the secret temple which is inside the female body that is a womb which is by far much better equipped physiologically, chemically, and I would say intellectually than our best laboratories for the development of a new human being. . . .

. . . There is no, no difficulty to understand that at the very beginning of life, the genetic information and the molecular structure of the egg, the spirit and the matter, the soul and the body must be that tightly intricated because it's a beginning of the new marvel that we call a human.

In response to the question, "What ethical considerations do you have about freezing?" Dr. Lejeune responded:

I think love is the contrary of chilly. Love is warmth, and life needs good temperature. So I would consider that the best we can do for early human beings is to have them in their normal shelter, not in the fridge.[25]

It's natural to sympathize with those who desire to have children and are unable to do so naturally. In God's Word, there are a number of women who longed for children and mourned their empty wombs. In this connection, Scripture says repeatedly that it is God who opens and closes the womb.[26] Yes, children are a gift from the Lord, but when God has closed the womb, is it right for those mourning their barren wombs to take matters into their own hands at the cost of most of their children conceived at IVF businesses being kept in a concentration can, or killed?[27]

"You shall not murder" is true even if murdering will allow you, finally, to have a baby of your very own.

Fetal Cell Lines: Cannibalization of Unborn Babies' Body Parts

A further consequence of the normalization of abortion is the global traffic in baby parts. This has been known and documented for a number of decades, although mostly in specialist literature. More recently, though, some of this trafficking has been brought to the attention of the broader population through the work of the Center for Medical Progress which received broad news coverage back in 2015 when they published videos of conversations they had with abortionists arranging the purchase of body parts from babies the abortionists had murdered. Then, more recently, because of Covid-19, there has been a surge in the discussion (limited mostly to Christians) of the use of fetal cell lines in the development and/or testing of vaccines.

---

25. Lejeune, in *A Symphony of the Preborn Child*, 14, 18, 19–20, 24, 26.
26. See Genesis 20:18; 29:31; 1 Samuel 1:6; Psalm 127:3; Isaiah 66:9; among others. From Eve, to Sarah, to Rachel, Hannah, and so on, Scripture is full of instances proclaiming that God opens the womb. And conversely, it also teaches that God closes the womb: e.g., Abimelech's household, Rachel, Hannah, etc.
27. The authors know of a couple who used IVF to produce a number of embryos. Determined to use each of them, they delivered multiple sets of twins and singles. Eight years after their last pregnancy, they were convicted that the final two embryos were still in limbo. So at the age of 42, with a house already quite full of children, the wife was implanted with the final embryos and brought two more souls into the world.

Both appearances of public discussion of this horror received their fifteen minutes of attention, and were quickly gone. The roots of this horror go very deep, though, and those profiting from this business work to keep it hidden.

In 2015 *Nature* ran an article by Meredith Wadman titled "The Truth about Fetal Tissue Research," with the subheading, "The use of aborted fetal tissue has sparked controversy in the United States, but many scientists say it is essential for studies of HIV, development and more."[28] Wadman explained the context for her article:

> An explosive climate has surrounded US research with fetal tissues since July, when an anti-abortion group called the Center for Medical Progress in Irvine, California, released covertly filmed videos in which senior physicians from the Planned Parenthood Federation of America bluntly and dispassionately discussed their harvesting of fetal organs from abortions for use in research.[29]

The article began:

> Every month, Lishan Su receives a small test tube on ice from a company in California. In it is a piece of liver from a human fetus aborted at between 14 and 19 weeks of pregnancy.
> Su and his staff at the University of North Carolina at Chapel Hill carefully grind the liver, centrifuge it and then extract and purify liver- and blood-forming stem cells. They inject the cells into the livers of newborn mice, and allow those mice to mature. The resulting animals are the only "humanized" mice with both functioning human liver and immune cells and, for Su, they are invaluable in his work on hepatitis B and C, allowing him to probe how the viruses evade the human immune system and cause chronic liver diseases.
> "Using fetal tissue is not an easy choice, but so far there is no better choice," says Su, who has tried, and failed, to make a humanized mouse with other techniques. "Many, many biomedical researchers depend on

---

28. Meredith Wadman, "The Truth about Fetal Tissue Research," *Nature* 528, December 10, 2015, https://doi.org/10.1038/528178a.
29. Ibid., 179.

fetal tissue research to really save human lives," he says. "And I think many of them feel the same way."[30]

Medical research made great progress during the twentieth century, and the benefits have been remarkable. Yet the cost of this progress has often been the cannibalization of body parts of the unborn, as Wadman describes. Those opposing Covid vaccinations have described a part of this research to their constituents, explaining the development of these vaccines is dependent upon fetal cell lines largely derived from the bodies of babies killed through elective abortions. However, their explanations have been very limited concerning the origin, history, and present pervasive use of these cell lines.

Fetal cell lines go by esoteric names like HEK 293, WI-38, MRC-5, and Walvax-2. They are valued by scientists because of their ability to reproduce in great numbers while still being genetically and functionally normal, making them useful for a variety of purposes.[31] They are developed from tissue—often the lungs—from aborted babies.

These cell lines have been under development since the 1960s, and the amount known about the aborted babies used to create them varies. Some of the babies whose tissue was used were aborted by the mother for psychological reasons. Other babies whose tissue was used were aborted for reasons that aren't known. It is possible some of these babies were not killed by elective, but rather spontaneous, abortions. Due to the research methodology, though, it's clear the vast majority of the babies died through elective abortions.[32]

As mentioned above, it was the political ferment over Covid-19 vaccines that led to a discussion of these cell lines recently, largely among Christians. Vaccine development is one of the original-use cases for fetal cell lines. Rather than growing attenuated viruses in animal cells such as chicken

---

30. Ibid., 178.
31. For a discussion of biotherapeutic proteins manufactured in different cell lines, including HEK 293 cells and their derivatives, see Jennifer Dumont et al., "Human Cell Lines for Biopharmaceutical Manufacturing: History, Status, and Future Perspectives," *Critical Reviews in Biotechnology* 36, no. 6 (November 2016): 1110–1122, https://www.ncbi.nlm.nih.gov/pmc/articles/PMC5152558/. There are other cell lines developed from cancerous cells that also replicate themselves in great numbers but have whatever genetic/functional changes that made them cancerous.
32. "Fetal Tissue Research: Focus on the Science and Not the Politics," *The Lancet Respiratory Medicine* 7, no. 8, June 24, 2019, https://doi.org/10.1016/S2213-2600(19)30222-X.

eggs, it is beneficial that the environment these viruses replicate in is of human origin.[33] This is nothing new, nor is it unique to Covid-19 vaccines.

The cell line called MRC-5 was developed in 1966 from the lung tissue of a 14-week-gestation male who was aborted for psychiatric reasons by a healthy 27-year-old mother.[34] The MRC-5 cell line is broadly used for the production of vaccines used against diseases such as chickenpox, shingles, rabies, hepatitis A, and polio. A variety of other fetal cell lines have been used in the development of a variety of other vaccines, and such research is ongoing. For decades, without question or ethical opposition, Christians have used these vaccines for themselves and their children.

New cell lines continue to be created. One named Walvax-2, for example, was released in 2015 after four years of work. This cell line is an attempt to improve on other cell lines already in use for vaccine development in China. Walvax-2 "was derived from fetal lung tissue (similar to WI-38 and MRC-5) obtained from a 3-month old female fetus aborted because of the presence of a uterine scar from a previous Cesarean birth by a 27-year old healthy woman."[35] Nine aborted children were used in the process, each carefully selected. Their parents gave what was purported to be a proper substitute for their baby's informed consent. The parents themselves had to be healthy and employed in careers that didn't involve any exposure to chemicals. The location of the abortion was prescribed so the "freshly aborted" body could be "immediately sent to the laboratory for the preparation of the cells."[36] The method of abortion was also specified: in order to protect the baby's body from harm during the process of his birth, labor was to be induced by breaking the mother's water.

Given the emphasis on speed and freshness of tissue, it is not cynical to ask whether these babies were truly deceased before their lungs were removed from their bodies. If these babies were living while their tissue

---

33. "The primary cell lines, which are obtained from animals, introduce potentially risky exogenous agents. In contrast, human diploid cell strains (HDCSs), acquired from embryos or other tissue cells of human origin, possess identical chromosome sets that are free of all known adventitious agents." Bo Ma et al., "Characteristics and Viral Propagation Properties of a New Human Diploid Cell Line, Walvax-2, and Its Suitability as a Candidate Cell Substrate for Vaccine Production," *Human Vaccines & Immunotherapeutics* 11, no. 4 (2015): 999, https://doi.org/10.1080/21645515.2015.1009811.

34. See AG05965-D, "Fibroblast from Skin, Lung," product from Coriell Institute for Medical Research, https://catalog.coriell.org/0/Sections/Search/Sample_Detail.aspx?Ref=AG05965-D.

35. Bo Ma et al., 999.

36. Ibid., 1006.

was taken, this would be consistent with many precedents documented in the pages of the literature of the fetal medical research industry.

Still, vaccine research and development is merely one small area of medical research and product development that depends upon the ongoing supply of tissue and body parts harvested from living little ones ripped from their mother's womb.

Alvin Wong, MD, describes the many uses of the fetal cell line HEK 293:

> The human embryonic kidney (HEK) 293 cell line is widely used in laboratory research. HEK 293 was derived from the kidney cells of a human embryo, as its name denotes. A student or fellow involved in life sciences research would almost inevitably encounter this cell line in the course of his work. A common use for it is in the field of gene therapy, where it is used to propagate adenovirus. Adenovirus is a common vehicle used to deliver experimental genes. There are also other derivatives of HEK 293 used in this field.[37]

For several reasons, the fetal cell line HEK 293 is a special case. First, both researchers who developed this line have stated they have no knowledge whether the unborn baby they used died from a spontaneous or elective abortion.[38] This might be the only cell line where this information is *not* known.

HEK 293 is also unique because it has been "immortalized," meaning the cells can keep undergoing division without losing their useful properties. This makes the cells less useful for vaccine development, but they

---

37. Alvin Wong, "The Ethics of HEK 293," *The National Catholic Bioethics Quarterly* 6, no. 3 (Autumn 2006): 473–474, https://doi.org/10.5840/ncbq20066331.

38. See Frank Graham, whose work was responsible for the first transformation of the fetal cells into a perpetual line: "Abortion was illegal in the Netherlands until 1984 except to save the life of the mother. Consequently I have always assumed that the HEK cells used by the Leiden lab must have derived from a therapeutic abortion." Ivan Couronne, "How Fetal Cells From the 1970s Power Medical Innovation Today," *Courthouse News Service*, October 20, 2020, https://www.courthousenews.com/how-fetal-cells-from-the-1970s-power-medical-innovation-today/. See also Alex Van der Eb, in whose lab Dr. Graham worked: "The fetus, as far as I can remember was completely normal. Nothing was wrong. The reasons for the abortion were unknown to me. I probably knew it at that time, but it got lost, all this information." Vaccines and Related Biological Products Advisory Committee, Advisory Committee Meeting, May 16, 2001, transcript by Neal R. Gross, United States of America Food and Drug Administration Center for Biologics Evaluation and Research 81, https://wayback.archive-it.org/7993/20170404095417/https://www.fda.gov/ohrms/dockets/ac/01/transcripts/3750t1_01.pdf.

are widely used in other categories of research. As Dr. Wong indicated, HEK 293 is so widely used it's unlikely any student or researcher can avoid it. But beyond students and researchers, it's practically impossible for the average person to avoid benefiting from HEK 293 research in his day-to-day life.

Christian, stop and think about this. If we're going to battle against abortion and its surrounding industries, we must count the cost. Certainly many will declare us enemies of women's dignity and value, but those involved in science will also denounce us, saying, "You're going to hinder medical research everyone benefits from, often in ways that protect human lives!" Are we prepared to respond, "Yes, our resolve is firm. It is more important to defend babies' lives than to defend the availability of their body parts for research and development, even if those body parts are used in the development of lifesaving procedures and products."

Can Christians really sustain one more accusation of being "against science"? Having delved deeply into the literature of this grisly practice and trade in fetal parts beyond the limited area of the development of cell lines, we assure readers we have avoided recording here the most awful acts imaginable committed against some of these little ones. These crimes have been documented for many decades now, even in the pages of our own US government publications,[39] and we will not elaborate here other than to say the church has no excuse for how long our eyes have been blind. Pro-life is as pro-life does, and pro-lifers have only done what is obvious—what smacks us in the face and stays there mocking us.

The recent popular exercise of Christian conscience in opposing the relationship of abortion to fetal cell lines has been selective. Covid vaccines were fortuitous in allowing some to raise the issue of the cannibalization of our unborn children's bodies for Covid vaccines specifically, but this present awakening appears to have been quite limited in its scope. It has not matured into any parallel awakening of Christian conscience in the abuses of unborn children's bodies (not related to cell lines) which are ubiquitous in the developed world and have been for decades.

Many opposed Covid vaccinations, saying, "Fetal cells have been used

---

39. For more, see U.S. Department of Health, Education, and Welfare, "Appendix: Research on the Fetus," The National Commission for the Protection of Human Subjects of Biomedical and Behavioral Research (1976), https://archive.org/details/researchonfetusa00unit/page/n3/mode/2up.

to develop and test these vaccines, and I'll have no part of it." This led to the assumption that Covid vaccines were unusual in this regard, representing a new tyranny extending into our lives by requiring this participation in abortion's bloodshed.

Now, though, we have presented a larger picture demonstrating that Covid vaccines are a small aspect of medical and corporate scientific dependence on the body parts of aborted babies. Whether we know or admit it, we participate.

In retrospect, the internal logic of the thing is inevitable. With the slaughter of babies in the billions, why not salvage some value by utilizing body parts as the little one's non-consensual donations to the well-being of the larger human community? As some medical ethicists might put it, "Do these little ones not have a duty to contribute their own legacy to our social contract? Ought we not to assume they would affirm their own moral obligation to make some small contribution to the lives of others?"[40]

During the half century that has passed since *Roe v. Wade*, God's people have learned the intense difficulty of reversing this bloody decision. It has been a long, hard political battle with almost none of us anticipating this late victory recently gained here in 2022.

Yet now, with the reversal of *Roe v. Wade*, we come to recognize the relative insignificance of this reversal for the protection of our little ones. It seems likely the majority of abortions will continue unabated as chemical abortions in the first weeks and days of life predominate. Thus, faced with the now-present reality of a post-*Roe* world, we have died to the previously widely held conviction that *Roe v. Wade*'s reversal would restore protection under the rule of law to preborn babies. This conviction has proved to be as illusory as any parallel hope that the reversal of *Roe v. Wade* would also bring an end to the trafficking in body parts on which modern medical research is dependent.

The genocide of the preborn has become so integral to Western society that it's hard to conceptualize a path forward that would provide any substantive hope of bringing it to an end. Across the developed world, society

---

40. Readers might gasp at this argument, thinking it can't possibly be what anyone would write or say. Your writers, though, have read a significant amount in the literature of medical ethics dealing with the question whether preborn babies are proper subjects of experimentation and can be surmised to have given their informed consent, and this summary is accurate.

has become dependent upon the systematic extinction of all preborn life judged to be inconvenient. Add to this our medical-industrial complex's dependence on the bodies of this holocaust's victims for many of the raw materials needed for their research and development, and the near impossibility of restoring the protection of every child's right to life, liberty, and the pursuit of happiness from the moment of conception becomes clear.

Repentance and reform are always difficult, though, and we must confess publicly that this world was created by the God who is truth, and truth is its own justification.

Now then, to make any claim to democracy is to make a parallel claim to the value of each individual. Do each of these little ones robbed of life while nestled safely in the body of their mother not have a right to be born, to live, to work, to study, to play, to laugh, to cry, to marry, to have their own children; and as they die, to leave an inheritance to their grandchildren?

Yet here we are, the Great American Empire spreading democracy around the world while robbing these little ones of every one of their human rights. The little ones don't even get a vote on the use of their leftover body parts by medical science and product development.

All of the ghoulish trafficking and research happen behind laboratories' closed doors, so it's easy for us to claim ignorance, trotting out a modicum of knowledge only when it is useful politically, to further some other more expedient end. Are we wrong, then, to force the church to see the extent of this horror? Would it not be better to allow our brothers and sisters in Christ to continue to live in ignorance, or at least plausible deniability?

Surely not. It is the duty of God's servants to tell the whole bloody truth. Until we see this truth, we will never know what is being done to our little neighbors, and our love will never extend to these particular "least of these" of our Lord. The traders in the body parts of preborn babies might think they're getting away with it—and humanly speaking they are. But across Scripture, God speaks the same truths He spoke to the prophet Ezekiel:

> The iniquity of the house of Israel and Judah is very, very great, and the land is filled with blood and the city is full of perversion; for they say, "The LORD has forsaken the land, and the LORD does not see!" But as for Me, My eye will have no pity nor will I spare, but I will bring their conduct upon their heads. (Ezek. 9:9–10)

The bloodshed associated simply with researchers' constant need for fetal body parts runs so deep, and is so pervasive, that readers may wish us to be specific in our guidance here, providing particular steps we should take to begin to oppose it. But here, we think it best to refrain from doing so.

Remember, fetal research encompasses a very broad sphere of scientific investigation involving far more than the development of cell lines. Keep in mind also that in this more encompassing area we are referring to as "fetal research," the church at large is very limited in its understanding. As God's people are taught and grow in our knowledge of this evil, consciences will be awakened to the multifaceted nature of this thorny issue and choose this or that method of defending these lives too. Likely there will be those who decide they will not allow any vaccinations in their family, whether for children or adults, whether for diseases similar to polio or to this year's flu. Others will decide to work toward the growth of scientific research that displaces the continued need for dependence on present cell lines for valuable testing and research. Many voices will produce a variety of places of conscience and witness, as God leads each of us.

But wherever this or that person or congregation chooses to stand, every effort must be taken to avoid making that standing place a test of orthodoxy or Christian faith. We must avoid such division and schism. Where one conscience has been awakened and pricked on such matters, there is also the potential for judging another conscience that does not share that person's precise convictions. And of course, we know that every man thinks every other man should share his convictions, so on an issue with such weight as the bodies of little babies, the possibility of censoriousness is great.

The firestorm in the church over Covid has recently shown the great potential for schism over secondary and tertiary matters, but it has also shown that a variety of Christian responses can be within the bounds of Scripture and according to godly principles.[41] For example, on the question of vaccines and fetal research, Cardinal Ratzinger's letter on the use

---

41. For more on this issue, a helpful place to start is Evangel Presbytery, "Conscience and COVID-19 Vaccine Mandates: In Defense of Sphere Authority," October 8, 2021, https://evangelpresbytery.com/wp-content/uploads/2021/10/Conscience-and-COVID-19-Vaccine-Mandates_Evangel-Presbytery.pdf. See also Evangel Presbytery, "Statement on Sphere Authority, Worship, and COVID-19 Quarantines," June 2020, https://evangelpresbytery.com/wp-content/uploads/2020/06/STATEMENT-ON-SPHERE-AUTHORITY-WORSHIP-AND-COVID-19-QUARANTINES.pdf.

of vaccines prepared from cells derived from aborted babies shows but one way of approaching the topic in a careful and Christian way.[42] Other such evaluations could and should be written, and it is our hope that God through His Spirit grants the church an increasing knowledge and wisdom on how to address these matters with courage, wisdom, and unity.

The Church's Response to Abortion

Back in the fifties when what was called "birth control" was first normalized in conjunction with the change of definition of "conception" and "life," this change in definitions had the inevitable result of allowing abortion to throw off its guilt and shame. Christians and pagans together grew used to employing birth control technology to prevent children so that, as surgical abortions came forward and began to increase in frequency, Christians were desensitized. The horror of doctors taking money to cut apart and remove infants from their mother's womb didn't register among the people whose practice of birth control depended upon conception not being conception and life not being life.

---

42. Cardinal Elio Sgreccia wrote a public letter to Mrs. Debra L. Vinnedge, June 9, 2005, which included a study on vaccinating children with vaccines prepared using cell lines derived from aborted human fetuses that concluded as follows:

- there is a grave responsibility to use alternative vaccines and to make a conscientious objection with regard to those which have moral problems;
- as regards the vaccines without an alternative, the need to contest so that others may be prepared must be reaffirmed, as should be the lawfulness of using the former in the meantime insomuch as is necessary in order to avoid a serious risk not only for one's own children but also, and perhaps more specifically, for the health conditions of the population as a whole—especially for pregnant women;
- the lawfulness of the use of these vaccines should not be misinterpreted as a declaration of the lawfulness of their production, marketing and use, but is to be understood as being a passive material cooperation and, in its mildest and remotest sense, also active, morally justified as an *extrema ratio* due to the necessity to provide for the good of one's children and of the people who come in contact with the children (pregnant women);
- such cooperation occurs in a context of moral coercion of the conscience of parents, who are forced to choose to act against their conscience or otherwise, to put the health of their children and of the population as a whole at risk. This is an unjust alternative choice, which must be eliminated as soon as possible.

Accessed at https://www.immunize.org/talking-about-vaccines/vaticandocument.htm. The study was later published as "Pontifical Academy for Life Statement: Moral Reflections on Vaccines Prepared from Cells Derived from Aborted Human Foetuses," *The Linacre Quarterly* 86, no. 2–3 (May–August 2019): 182–187, https://doi.org/10.1177/0024363919855896.

As pointed out earlier, the explosion of surgical abortions preceded 1973's *Roe v. Wade* decision. Nevertheless, *Roe v. Wade* threw the door open in a way the previous laws of the fifty states had not done.

Protestants and *Whatever Happened to the Human Race?*

How did the church respond to *Roe v. Wade*?

Roman Catholics didn't waver in their longstanding, historical opposition to contraception and abortion, but Protestants—including Evangelicals—simply accepted *Roe v. Wade* as the law of the land. The Supreme Court was the standing civil authority and Evangelicals believed God required them to honor this Supreme Court ruling.

Undoubtedly some readers survey the contemporary disrespect for authority, and particularly the opposition to surgical abortion which is now so characteristic of conservative Protestant churches in North America, and have trouble believing the same disrespect and opposition to the Supreme Court's *Roe v. Wade* ruling was not present in 1973 and years following.

In the wake of *Roe v. Wade*, it's a tragic fact that Evangelicals were silent and compliant. This can be demonstrated in many ways, but the most obvious way is the national barnstorming tour of C. Everett Koop and Francis Schaeffer showing their films and giving lectures based on their jointly authored book *Whatever Happened to the Human Race?*

It wasn't until 1979 that Koop and Schaeffer toured the country's major cities calling attendees to wake up to the horrors of surgical abortions, and their attendees were exclusively Evangelicals. At the time, Koop (later to become surgeon general under President Reagan) and Schaeffer complained to their Denver audience[43] that they had contacted fifteen or so Evangelical leaders in Wheaton, inviting them to attend their Chicago series, but none of them had been willing to come. This, they explained, was one more proof of the lack of concern over abortion on the part of Evangelicals, and particularly Evangelical leaders.

Nevertheless, Koop and Schaeffer were respected within Evangelicalism's rank and file, and their prophetic witness of 1979 single-handedly woke Evangelicalism up so that conservative Protestant Christians still

---

43. One of our authors was present there in Denver and heard Schaeffer's lament.

today view opposition to abortion as a fundamental part of Christian ethics.[44] Since 1979, therefore, pro-life commitments have been a fundamental component of Christian political witness and action.

But notice that *Roe v. Wade* was issued in 1973, and Koop and Schaeffer did not publish their book and give their lectures until 1979—six years later.

Pro-Life Protestants and the Growth of Chemical Abortions

It is God's kindness that the conservative Protestant church has mostly been firm in her opposition to abortion since 1979, but that opposition has been focused almost exclusively on surgical abortion. More recently, there has been some opposition to later chemical abortions that are committed up until the tenth week of pregnancy by means of the drugs mifepristone (RU-486) and misoprostol, but the pro-life commitments and witness which grew out of Koop and Schaeffer's witness never matured into opposition to abortifacient birth control methods not involving surgery or mifepristone and misoprostol.

Even as we write, IUDs and hormonal birth control methods like the Pill continue to be widely used by conservative Protestants who consider themselves pro-life. Most of them remain oblivious to the abortifacient nature of their hormonal methods and IUDs.

Meanwhile, surgical abortions are in decline and chemical abortions have taken over.

In 2019, one medical journal co-sponsored by The Faculty of Sexual & Reproductive Healthcare of the Royal College of Obstetricians & Gynaecologists estimated "medication (or medical) abortion accounts for at least half of all abortions in the majority of countries."[45] Again, keep in

---

44. In *First Things* back in 1998, Richard John Neuhaus commented on the influence of Koop and Shaeffer's book and film series: "Through his films and lectures, Schaeffer dramatically posed the question of what was becoming of the human race and almost single-handedly alerted evangelicals to the significance of the abortion debate. He did not use the language of John Paul II about 'the culture of death' versus 'the culture of life,' but that was the gist of his message, and his effective delivery of that message was a critical factor in bringing about the ever-growing alliance between evangelicals and Catholics in the great cultural tasks of our time. As our evangelical friends do not usually say, *Requiescat in pace*." "A Tacit Admission of Defeat: The Public Square," *First Things* 82, April 1998, 60–75.

45. Anna Popinchalk and Gilda Sedgh, "Trends in the Method and Gestational Age of Abortion in High-Income Countries," *BMJ Sexual & Reproductive Health* 45, no. 2 (April 2019): 95–103, https://doi.org/10.1136/bmjsrh-2018-200149.

mind that this estimate excludes the abortion of little ones by birth control methods that have an agency preventing the child's implantation in his mother's womb. When the Royal College's obstetricians and gynecologists speak of "medication abortions," they are only referring to later abortions committed by means of the drugs mifepristone and misoprostol up through ten weeks of gestation.

Remember that the scientific and medical communities redefined "conception" and "life" in order to normalize the mid-century birth control pill known to have an abortifacient agency. Largely by means of these redefinitions almost sixty years ago, the word "abortion" has never been associated with the Pill, the IUD, or any other hormonal birth control.

Within the broader pro-life community, there has been some opposition to later-term mifepristone and misoprostol abortions. Some have recognized the peculiar danger of these drugs due to the perception that they are a kinder, gentler way of killing than scalpels and suction machines. But what about the abortifacient agency of IUDs and hormonal drugs and devices? Shouldn't our pro-life witness be consistent?

The child conceived by his father's fertilization of his mother's egg takes six or seven days to wend his way to his mother's uterus and attach himself to her uterine wall. Rightly understood, chemical abortions are not just mifepristone and misoprostol given later in pregnancy, but they include IUDs and drugs that obstruct the child's attachment to the wall of the uterus, denying him the nurture and protection of his mother's womb.

Note carefully: the deaths of children caused by IUDs, by early birth control methods with a hormonal component, by later birth control methods utilizing mifepristone and misoprostol, and by surgical abortions all break the Sixth Commandment. But all these killings are not equally visible and felt.

The blood, body parts, and shame of surgical abortions are hard to hide, but it's easy to hide the tiny little ones killed by IUDs and the Pill. Thus with surgical abortion's decline, the emotional and spiritual toll of abortion has grown increasingly hidden.

Unlike the death-camp victims of World War II, aborted babies who are also the victims of genocide have not been liberated, and their pictures have not been taken. No holocaust museum recounts their chemical tortures and deaths. As abortions continue to move toward the first weeks of pregnancy and the chemical removal of the child, it will become ever more difficult to see and oppose this bloodletting. Mothers will hide their murders at home, inside their wombs, and this secrecy will make it exceedingly difficult to protect the little victims in any court of law.

Nevertheless, God sees these murders, and all the blood will be brought to His bar of justice. It will not remain hidden:

> They even sacrificed their sons and their daughters to the demons,
> And shed innocent blood,
> The blood of their sons and their daughters,
> Whom they sacrificed to the idols of Canaan;
> And the land was polluted with the blood.
> Thus they became unclean in their practices,
> And played the harlot in their deeds.
>
> Therefore the anger of the LORD was kindled against His people . . .
> (Ps. 106:37–40)

The Truth about Hormonal Birth Control

To come to some awareness of the scale of this bloodshed, we must reckon with the many abortions caused specifically by IUDs and hormonal birth control. This is a very difficult question for many Christians today. How can the default birth control methods used by Christians within the church for the past seventy years be called into question? Surely the medical establishment (and particularly Christians who are a part of that establishment) would have warned us if their birth control methods were aborting our children, right? Is the goal here simply to condemn all forms of birth control? Are the authors of this document Roman Catholic?

Good questions, and no, your authors are not condemning all use of birth control. Although we believe most practices of birth control today are not morally justified, there are occasions where pregnancy prevention is justified, and in such cases there are methods of pregnancy prevention which are truly and only pregnancy prevention—that is, which are truly contraceptive. Which is to say, there are methods of preventing pregnancy that prevent conception rather than preventing implantation. There are methods of pregnancy prevention that do not have any abortifacient agency and do not kill children. Sadly, these methods do not include some of the most common methods of birth control used today.

IUDs, the Pill, and the Prevention of Implantation

Among the 61 percent of women in the United States between the ages of 15 and 49 using some method of pregnancy prevention in 2019, close to half (27 percent of the same demographic) employed methods with an abortifacient agency.[46] IUDs and all hormonal birth control methods include a significant agency of preventing a very young child from attaching himself to the wall of the uterus. For a few days the little one lives, but then he is denied the nurture and protection of his mother's womb, and this kills him.

The official and scientific sources confirming this are endless, and have been for generations. For this reason scientific and medical authorities changed the definition of conception in the 1960s, as documented above.

This subterfuge enabled them to declare that IUDs and hormonal birth control methods are *absolutely not* abortifacients. This subterfuge enabled our obstetricians and gynecologists also to redefine the beginning of life as implantation—not fertilization. Because of this deception, these forms of birth control have been embraced by an unknowing public for nearly sixty years now. And through these years, our obstetricians, gynecologists, and pharmacists, Christian and pagan alike, have been assuring us there's no danger of the products they prescribe killing our little ones.

The project is larger than denying these little ones are living human beings. This denial requires a prior denial that IUDs and hormonal methods of birth control have any agency at all of preventing implantation. Christians and pagans have thus become allies, joining together in opposing and obstructing woman's wonderful nature decreed by God as "the mother of the living" and "life-giver."[47]

---

46. "Contraceptive Use by Method 2019: Data Booklet," United Nations Department of Economic and Social Affairs (United Nations, 2019), 22, https://www.un.org/development/desa/pd/sites/www.un.org.development.desa.pd/files/files/documents/2020/Jan/un_2019_contraceptiveusebymethod_databooklet.pdf.

47. In Genesis 3:20, Adam names the woman Eve (Hebrew חַוָּה, ḥaûâ), which literally means

Some would claim it doesn't really matter if a woman's method of birth control prevents the little one from attaching himself to his mother's womb so long as the prevention of implantation is not the primary agency of the mother's choice of birth control. The risk is small and neither her doctor nor her pharmacist are selling her drugs with the intent to kill her babies. Their intent is simply to help their client interrupt her normal cycle; or, failing that, to help the woman's body to attack her husband's sperm so it is unable to fertilize any egg that happens to make it down her fallopian tubes. They go on to point out that all of life has risks, and this risk of killing the little one is reasonable given the large benefit of preventing the birth of another "unwanted child," or a child who would harm the chances of his siblings going to college.

Thus what Hannah Arendt referred to as the banality of evil[48] continues into the twenty-first century, although Jews and "useless eaters" are no longer the intended victims. Lately, the victims are our own sons and daughters. If, over the course of twenty or thirty years of fertility, killing a few of her children is the cost of one mother limiting her painful pregnancies and childbirth, and minimizing the burden of raising a child to adulthood—it's a small price to pay for such a significant relief.

Of course, it's neither the mother nor her husband paying any price, but rather their dead sons and daughters. It cost these little ones their lives. They didn't live a life of slavery. They were murdered in the womb before they saw the light of day or took a breath.

It would be preferable not to have to discuss the pragmatic and callous rationalizations Christians employ to justify their murder of their unborn children, but such rationalizations are common within the church. Men and women today style themselves sensitive to the suffering of others, but unborn children haven't made the cut. Christian men and women assure one another that compassion is their highest commitment, but let's look carefully at this fruit of our compassion.

We sympathize with sisters in Christ fearful of being overwhelmed by scads of children. We sympathize with Christian mothers of a certain age

---

"living," "living one," or "life-giver." The Holy Spirit tells us that Adam named her this "because she was the mother of all the living."

48. Thomas White, "What Did Hannah Arendt Really Mean by the Banality of Evil?" *Aeon*, April 23, 2018, https://aeon.co/ideas/what-did-hannah-arendt-really-mean-by-the-banality-of-evil.

fearful of giving birth to a child with a genetic defect. We sympathize with Christian mothers who are tired of being pregnant and want to "get on with life." We sympathize with Christian mothers who want to defer having their own biological children so they can adopt others' unwanted children. We sympathize with women who suffer debilitating pain from conditions, such as endometriosis, whose doctors prescribe the Pill to relieve that pain. We sympathize with Christian mothers who give all these reasons for using abortifacient methods of birth control.

Of course, all of us should have and express sympathy in such situations, but that sympathy must issue from a compassion that is true, not false. How do we recognize false sympathy and compassion?

False compassion has no patience for truth. It brushes it aside. Concerning conception and the life of the preborn, false compassion expresses sympathy to the mother who is visible while leaving the child who is not present alone in his vulnerability, invisibility, and silence.

Having compassion is godly, but only if that compassion is godly, which necessarily means only if that compassion is truthful. Yes, we are called by God to have compassion on women bearing these burdens and having such a desire, but that compassion must always be expressed to the mother for both her life and the lives of her babies. In our day of cheap sentiments spread through social media by emoticons, Christians should balk at the whole mess, understanding how costly true compassion is, and having the unerring ability to see where it needs to be defended.

Flannery O'Connor, that great southern author who had such an unerring instinct for the ways original sin twists our lives, compared the tenderness of past ages to the tenderness of our own age:

> . . . now, we govern by tenderness. It is a tenderness which, long since cut off from the person of Christ, is wrapped in theory. When tenderness is detached from the source of tenderness, its logical outcome is terror. It ends in forced-labor camps and in the fumes of the gas chamber.[49]

Our tender sympathies have borne the fruit of infant slaughter. We must face it.

---

49. Flannery O'Connor, *Mystery and Manners: Occasional Prose* (Farrar, Straus, and Giroux, 1969), 226–228.

Princeton ethicist Paul Ramsey pointed out that a deer hunter is guilty of manslaughter if he finds himself wondering what that movement is in the underbrush, but goes ahead and pulls the trigger, and kills a man. The law requires the hunter to wait to shoot until he's established his target is not a man. Man is the most precious of all God's creatures,[50] and thus it is a criminal act to take unnecessary risks of shedding his blood. He alone bears God's image and likeness. Even a minute or two old, he is known and precious in God's sight.

In light of this basic moral principle, we stop and consider the fact that hormonal methods of birth control have an agency of preventing the little one from availing himself of the nurture and protection of his mother's womb. This fact is scientifically incontrovertible. Over the years, there have been some Christians who have tried to deny it, but the testimony of secular scholars, physicians, and pharmaceutical firms is nearly unanimous: IUDs and hormonal methods of birth control have an undeniable abortifacient agency.[51]

Taking hormonal methods, specifically, the simplest search of the web returns page after page from pharmaceutical firms, non-profits working to limit world population, and healthcare information sites, all matter-of-factly stating their agency of preventing implantation. Such statements vary in terminology, but here are typical examples.

Here is an excerpt from an article on the website of the National Center for Biotechnology Information of the National Institutes of Health:

> The hormones in contraceptives don't only prevent ovulation. Some also prevent fertilized eggs from implanting into the womb.[52]

The American Society for Reproductive Medicine publishes Reproduc-

---

50. "Are not two sparrows sold for a cent? And yet not one of them will fall to the ground apart from your Father. But the very hairs of your head are all numbered. So do not fear; you are more valuable than many sparrows." Matthew 10:29–31.

51. Here is a helpful summary of some Christian physicians' efforts to deny hormonal birth control methods are abortifacient, followed by documentation of their errors: Randy Alcorn, *Does the Birth Control Pill Cause Abortions?*, 11th edition (Eternal Perspective Ministries, 2011), https://www.epm.org/static/uploads/downloads/bcpill.pdf.

52. Institute for Quality and Efficiency in Health Care, "Contraception: Hormonal Contraceptives," InformedHealth.org, updated June 29, 2017, https://www.ncbi.nlm.nih.gov/books/NBK441576/.

tiveFacts.org, where they ask the question, "How do hormonal contraceptives work?" Here is their answer:

> Hormonal contraceptives contain a progestin (progesterone medicine) with or without an estrogen. . . . These two hormones together, or the progestin alone, work in several ways to prevent a pregnancy:
> - They can prevent ovulation (the release of an egg).
> - They make the mucus around the cervix (mouth of the womb) thicker so that sperm cannot enter the uterus (womb).
> - They make the lining of the uterus (womb) thinner to prevent a fertilized egg from attaching itself.[53]

The following is from the University of Michigan Health website:[54]

Method	How it prevents pregnancy
Hormonal	• Prevents ovulation • Thickens mucus at the cervix so sperm cannot pass through • Changes the environment of the uterus and fallopian tubes to prevent fertilization and to prevent implantation if fertilization occurs

Intrauterine device (IUD)	• There are two types of IUDs (hormonal and copper). Both types may work by preventing:
	  ○ Fertilization of the egg.
	  ○ Implantation in the uterus.

Similar documentation is spread across the web. One prominent example is an online course in human embryology developed by the prestigious Swiss universities of Fribourg, Lausanne, and Bern. In their module 6.5, we read:

---

53. "Hormonal Contraception," English Fact Sheets & Info Booklets, ReproductiveFacts.org, American Society of Reproductive Medicine, accessed June 23, 2022, https://www.reproductivefacts.org/news-and-publications/patient-fact-sheets-and-booklets/documents/fact-sheets-and-info-booklets/hormonal-contraception/.
54. "How Birth Control Methods Prevent Pregnancy," University of Michigan Health, accessed June 23, 2022, https://www.umwomenshealth.org/health-library/tb1025.

Contraception can take place on three different levels: preventing oocytes from meeting sperm cells, hindering ovulation, [or] hindering fertilization or the implantation of the fertilized oocyte.[55]

The embryology course's supplementary link goes on to specify this concerning hormonal birth control:

They transform the uterine endometrium so it becomes pseudoatrophic, thereby making an implantation practically impossible, should an ovulation and fertilization take place.[56]

They describe the *primary* abortifacient agency of the IUD:

With an intra-uterine device (IUD) a double function is involved: firstly, implantation is hindered and, secondly, sperm cells are immobilized.

Some researchers are working to prove this abortifacient agency of the IUD is minor or absent, as shown by a recent (2020) study published in *Nature*'s *Scientific Reports*.[57] Relias Media cites one of the study's authors, Karen Smith-McCune:

We always assumed, from the 1980s on, that the IUD was preventing implantation, but that's never been proven.[58]

Consider carefully this long-held assumption. It was the cover for governmental, scientific, and medical authorities to promote, prescribe, sell, and insert IUDs for decades, all the while knowing their IUDs were abortifacients.

---

55. "Contraception Methods That Hinder Implantation," embryology.ch (Online course in embryology for medical students), Universities of Fribourg, Lausanne and Bern (Switzerland), accessed June 23, 2022, https://embryology.ch/en/embryogenese/implantation/contraception-methods/introduction.html. Note here, as everywhere in the literature, that "hindering . . . the implantation of the fertilized oocyte" is labeled "contraception."

56. https://embryology.ch/en/embryogenese/implantation/popup/contracep.html.

57. Karen Smith-McCune et al., "Differential Effects of the Hormonal and Copper Intrauterine Device on the Endometrial Transcriptome," *Scientific Reports* 10, art. no. 6888 (2020), https://doi.org/10.1038/s41598-020-63798-8.

58. "Study: Copper IUDs Do Not Appear to Prevent Implantation or Increase HIV Risk," Relias Media, July 1, 2020, https://www.reliasmedia.com/articles/146320-study-copper-iuds-do-not-appear-to-prevent-implantation-or-increase-hiv-risk.

Smith-McCune goes on to report her study found hormone-releasing IUDs indeed caused inflammation of the uterine wall, but copper-releasing IUDs did not. From this Smith-McCune concludes copper-releasing IUDs do not prevent implantation. Her conclusion, however, is logically wrong; copper-releasing IUDs might have other effects preventing implantation consistent with the traditional assumption. The authors indirectly admit the weakness of their conclusion, calling it a "suggestion." In a matter of life and death, why would serious researchers content themselves with suggestions? Smith-McCune seeks to answer that question:

> I think the results present a counterargument to resistance to the IUD. Policymakers who are resistant to IUD use can take our data as evidence that strongly suggests it is not preventing implantation.

Note in her statement the distinction between hormonal and copper-releasing IUDs has conveniently disappeared. Moreover, note this is not science. The study is catering to political interests intent on breaking down political resistance against the use of IUDs based on moral grounds.

Furthermore, Smith-McCune's suggestion cannot account for the fact that IUDs, whether copper or hormonal, are over 99 percent effective as "emergency contraception" for up to five days after intercourse, just like the morning-after pill.[59]

Now then, once more: What follower of Jesus Christ is satisfied with assurances that his chances of killing his child are small, with suggestions that some IUDs might work differently than others? Remember that all he and his wife must do to avoid killing their child is refuse to use the IUD and other hormonal forms of birth control.

It's understandable for worldlings to be dismissive of such violations of the Sixth Commandment, but Christians? Have we forgotten the warning of the Apostle John concerning "murderers," that they "will be in the lake that burns with fire and brimstone, which is the second death" (Rev. 21:8)? Is God's commandment, "Whoever sheds man's blood, by man his blood shall be shed" (Gen. 9:6), limited to babies we allow to be born? Babies we allow to attach themselves to their mother's womb?

---

59. "IUD," Planned Parenthood, accessed June 23, 2022, https://www.plannedparenthood.org/learn/birth-control/iud.

Those who hate God and His moral law are unconcerned about such matters, but are we not God's people? Have we not heard His warnings that He hates those who shed the blood of innocents? Are babies anyone's enemies? Do we not welcome and rejoice in His precious gift of life? Do we not join our forefathers in giving Him praise and thanks for opening the womb of our mothers and wives?

The Significance of Our Lord's Incarnation

One of the most beautiful things about recovering the personhood of the embryo created by God and only a couple days old is that we recover the beauty and wonder of the incarnation of our Lord Jesus. When we sing, "Lo, He abhors not the Virgin's womb,"[60] our thoughts naturally turn to a visible baby bump and Jesus residing there with blessed Mary resting her hands on her womb, radiating her love to the Son of God. Which is to say, who thinks of our Lord's incarnation when it was but a day or two old?

The King of Glory through whom the stars were formed, and the earth holds together yet today, dignified the embryonic life of each of us by living that life Himself. This is amazing and must surely instruct us concerning reverence due the embryonic life He still creates and places in woman, the life-giver. We may callously dismiss this life, but we do so forgetting the Son of Man was Himself a mere second old, and was that very second fully Man and fully God. Would we dare to deny His Personhood the millisecond after the Holy Spirit came upon Mary and she became pregnant with the Savior of the world? And if we would not deny His Personhood at that moment, why would we deny any baby's personhood whom Jesus Himself brothered by His own conception?

Theologian Thomas F. Torrance writes:

> The Son of God became a human being for us in the womb of the Virgin Mary, bone of our bone and flesh of our flesh. He became what we are. Think of the importance of the incarnation, then, for our understanding

---

60. God of God, Light of Light;
    Lo, He abhors not the Virgin's womb;
    Very God, begotten, not created...

    (John Francis Wade [attr.], "O Come All Ye Faithful" [1751], trans. Frederick Oakeley [1841])

of and regard for the unborn child. Every child in the womb has been brothered by the Lord Jesus. In becoming a human being for us, he also became an embryo for the sake of all embryos, and for our Christian understanding of the being, nature and status in God's eyes of the unborn child. So, to take no thought, or no proper thought, for the unborn child is to have no proper thought of Jesus himself as our Lord and Savior or to appreciate his relation as the incarnate Creator to every human being.[61]

Consider this account written by the physician Luke, found in the first chapter of his gospel. There we read that the angel Gabriel told the Virgin Mary:

> Do not be afraid, Mary; for you have found favor with God. And behold, you will conceive in your womb and bear a son, and you shall name Him Jesus.

The angel tells Mary, "you will conceive in your womb." She hasn't yet conceived, but at some point in the future, she "will."

Mary asked how this could be, since she was a virgin. The angel explained:

> The Holy Spirit will come upon you, and the power of the Most High will overshadow you; and for that reason the holy Child shall be called the Son of God.

At some point in the future, the Holy Spirit "will come upon" her, and "the power of the Most High will overshadow" her. Again, at some point in the future these things "will" be accomplished. It's as certain as every word of God, but its accomplishment is not yet. The holy Child "shall" be called.

Jesus will be fully man, but is not yet. The prophecy has been given, but it has not yet been fulfilled. His taking on manhood through His conception is still in the future.

---

61. Thomas F. Torrance, "The Being and Nature of the Unborn Child," address given at the Presbyterians Pro-Life General Assembly Luncheon, 212th General Assembly of the Presbyterian Church (USA), June 25, 2000 (Glen Lorien Books, 2000), 4–5, http://www.togetherforadoption.org/wp-content/media/Torrance-paper-on-the-Unborn.pdf.

Then Gabriel strengthens Mary's faith:

> And behold, even your relative Elizabeth has also conceived a son in her old age; and she who was called barren is now in her sixth month. For nothing will be impossible with God.

After this shocking announcement that her relative Elizabeth has miraculously conceived and is in her sixth month, we read Mary declaring her submission to God's will, after which the angel Gabriel leaves her.
Then what?

> Now at this time Mary arose and went in a hurry to the hill country, to a city of Judah, and entered the house of Zacharias and greeted Elizabeth.

We aren't told where Elizabeth and her husband Zacharias lived—only that it was a city of Judah in "the hill country." We're also told as soon as the angel left her, Mary arose and "went in a hurry" there. When did the Holy Spirit come upon her, and the power of the Most High overshadow her, so that the embryonic Savior indwelt her? Sometime between Gabriel's announcement that she would (future tense) become pregnant and her arrival and entry to Elizabeth's house there in the hill country. How do we know she was pregnant when she arrived?
Because of this account of her arrival, also by the beloved physician Luke:

> When Elizabeth heard Mary's greeting, the baby leaped in her womb; and Elizabeth was filled with the Holy Spirit. And she cried out with a loud voice and said, "Blessed are you among women, and blessed is the fruit of your womb! And how has it happened to me, that the mother of my Lord would come to me? For behold, when the sound of your greeting reached my ears, the baby leaped in my womb for joy."[62]

There it is: "blessed is the fruit of your womb!" Mary is now pregnant. She is now bearing fruit. She is now "the mother" of our Lord.

---

62. Luke 1:30ff.

How old is our Lord at this moment?

Our best guess is somewhere around a week of age. We're not sure Mary left to visit Elizabeth the same day she received the prophecy. She may have left a day or two later. What we do know is that as the angel Gabriel left her, it was "at this time" that she "arose" and "went in a hurry." Various guesses are made about the town Mary traveled to and its distance. If we accept church tradition, the village was Ein Karem, about eighty miles from Nazareth, so it took Mary about a week to get there.

If our Lord took up His embryonic residence in Mary's womb immediately upon Gabriel's departure, right as Mary began hurrying to Elizabeth's home, Jesus was likely somewhere between seven and ten days old. If Mary conceived our Lord halfway through her journey, Jesus was likely somewhere between three and seven days old.

Stop and consider that little ones normally take five or six days to implant themselves on the wall of their mother's uterus. It's possible then, and maybe even likely, that as His mother traveled, Jesus did also, moving towards the rest, safety, and nourishment of attachment to Mary's womb.

Jesus brothered us at conception. Not any time later. Not at implantation. Not at quickening. Not at birth. His conception, no less than His implantation, quickening, and birth, redeemed our own conception, no less than our own implantation, quickening, and birth.

There is no place for the follower of Jesus Christ to kill any human being at any stage of life which He, our Lord Jesus, blessed by living it with and for us. No Christian kills an embryo any more than he or she kills a newborn baby with Down syndrome or an elderly parent who's had a stroke.

We protect the weak and vulnerable. We do not kill them.

The Body Count

Coming face to face with the lies and bloodshed, we can't help seeking to quantify the slaughter around us. What is a truthful estimate of the number of little ones we have sacrificed through abortion since the 1950s and '60s?

As Christians and pro-lifers in general have tried to come to terms with the slaughter of the twentieth and twenty-first centuries, it's become commonplace to speak in terms of large figures that boggle the mind, but even the most informed pro-lifers today speak only of "millions" of babies lost. Anything larger seems needlessly inflammatory, and "billions"? Surely not . . .

Let's take a count of the victims of our bloodshed.

Surgical and Chemical Abortions

Back in 1999, Planned Parenthood's research arm, the Guttmacher Institute, published "The Incidence of Abortion Worldwide," in which they stated, "Worldwide, about one-fourth of the approximately 180 million pregnancies known to occur each year are resolved by abortion."[63] At the time, this would have been 0.75 percent of the world's population killed each year, but this was decades ago.

Acknowledging the growth of abortions worldwide across the past twenty years, a 2020 article in *The Lancet* estimated that between 2015 and 2019 the yearly average of abortion victims had increased to 73 million—0.98 percent of the world's population.[64] At this rate, it takes thirteen and a half years to reach a billion. Meanwhile, keep in mind that abortions have been common in Russia and Eastern Europe since the early fifties, and the United States since the seventies.

China is unique due to their longtime enforcement of population control. From 1980 through 2016, the Chinese government worked to reduce their nation's birth rate by limiting most married couples to one child.[65] They enforced this policy by forcibly aborting mothers' babies[66] so that, from the adoption of China's one-child policy in 1980 through the government's repeal of the policy on January 1, 2016,[67] China's Health Ministry

---

63. Stanley Henshaw, Susheela Singh and Taylor Haas, "The Incidence of Abortion Worldwide," *International Perspectives on Sexual and Reproductive Health* 25, January 1999, 30–38, https://www.guttmacher.org/journals/ipsrh/1999/01/incidence-abortion-worldwide.
64. Bearak et al.
65. China's policy applied to cities, but the countryside and some ethnic minorities were granted exceptions.
66. Ma Jian, "China's Barbaric One-Child Policy," *The Guardian*, May 6, 2013, https://www.theguardian.com/books/2013/may/06/chinas-barbaric-one-child-policy.
67. The policy allowed for a second child in more rural areas and among certain ethnic minorities if a couple's first child was female.

revealed it had done 336 million abortions.[68] During those years alone, China committed one-third of a billion abortions.

From statistics compiled over the years, the Guttmacher Institute now places the number of babies murdered at 1.6 billion (and no, they don't call it "murder"). Yet if we examine this abortion count more deeply, it becomes clear the Guttmacher Institute's numbers are still drastically underreported.

Accounting for Hormonal Birth Control and IUDs

Recall how prevalent hormonal birth control methods are across the world and that one of their agencies is preventing implantation. How many deaths of little ones due to this agency of hormonal methods have occurred in the world since 1950? Let us consider all hormonal methods including pills, injectables, implants, IUDs, and emergency contraceptive pills (ECPs).

To enforce its one-child policy, not only has China engaged in forced abortion, but government authorities have implanted IUDs in their nation's women so that, as the *New York Times* reports, "from 1980 to 2014, according to official statistics, 324 million Chinese women were fitted with IUDs."[69] Those 324 million IUDs prevented countless births by obstructing little ones from attaching themselves to their mother's womb. What was the death toll in China?

But beyond China and IUDs, recall how prevalent hormonal birth control methods are across the world. Can we estimate how many women lost their babies through these birth control methods since their normalization in the 1960s?

Because current and hard data is not available on these questions, we must take recourse to some estimates to get an idea of the order of magnitude we should think about. Let's start with the Pill. In 1999, Dr. William F. Colliton reported data from the Guttmacher Institute indicating that 10.4 million women were using the Pill in the US.[70] Based on 28-day cycles and

---

68. Tom Strode, "China: 40 Years; 336 Million Abortions," *The Baptist Messenger*, March 28, 2013, https://www.mydigitalpublication.com/display_article.php?id=1358181&view=152240.

69. Sui-Lee Wee, "After One-Child Policy, Outrage at China's Offer to Remove IUDs," *New York Times*, January 7, 2017, https://www.nytimes.com/2017/01/07/world/asia/after-one-child-policy-outrage-at-chinas-offer-to-remove-iuds.html.

70. William F. Colliton, "Birth Control Pill: Abortifacient and Contraceptive," *The Linacre Quarterly* 66, no. 4, art. 2, https://epublications.marquette.edu/lnq/vol66/iss4/2/.

a 14 percent chance of an ovulation occurring for women taking the Pill, this would imply 18.95 million exposures to pregnancy per year. Taking into account the likelihood of spontaneous abortions, Dr. Colliton estimated that the number of abortions induced by the Pill making the womb less hospitable for fertilized eggs to between 1.1 million and 1.9 million per year. He also reported a more cautious estimate based on a 20 percent fecundity rate that put the number of Pill-induced abortions to between 0.1 million and 1.6 million per year.

More recent CDC data indicate that currently about 10.2 million women in the US take the Pill.[71] Based on a pregnancy rate of 85 percent for women using no birth control and 9 percent for women using the Pill, 76 percent of these 10.2 million, or 7.7 million would have become pregnant in a given year had they not used the Pill nor any other birth control method.[72] Given that the Pill reduces the frequency of ovulation by 57.4 percent to 98.75 percent,[73] the loss of births due to the reduction of ovulation frequency would be between 4.4 million and 7.6 million. If the remaining losses of births are caused by the abortifacient effect of the Pill, the number of induced abortions would be between 0.97 million and 3.3 million. This corresponds to between 0.0095 and 0.33 Pill-induced abortions per woman taking the Pill every year. This means that a woman using the Pill runs the risk of unknowingly killing one of her children between once in three years and once in one hundred years.

According to United Nations data, 152.1 million women of childbearing age around the world were taking the Pill in 2018.[74] Applying the US estimate, the number of Pill-induced abortions would range between 1.4 million and 50.2 million annually. We emphasize again that these are rough estimates only. But they clearly show us that we are looking at a large phenomenon. Keep in mind that we are here talking only about the Pill. We

---

71. "Current Contraceptive Status Among Women Aged 15–49: United States, 2017–2019," NCHS Data Brief No. 388 (October 2020), https://www.cdc.gov/nchs/products/databriefs/db388.htm.

72. James Trussell, "Contraceptive Failure in the United States," *Contraception* 83, no. 5 (May 2011): 397–404, https://www.ncbi.nlm.nih.gov/pmc/articles/PMC3638209/. See also "How Effective Is Contraception at Preventing Pregnancy?" NHS, last reviewed April 17, 2020, https://www.nhs.uk/conditions/contraception/how-effective-contraception/.

73. Ian Milsom and Tjeerd Korver, "Ovulation Incidence with Oral Contraceptives: A Literature Review," *Journal of Family Planning and Reproductive Health Care* 34, no. 4 (October 2008): 237–246, https://doi.org/10.1783/147118908786000451.

74. UN, "Contraceptive Use by Method 2019: Data Booklet," 15.

have not included other hormone-based birth control methods such as injectables, implants, and IUDs which, in 2019, the UN estimated at 10 percent of the 60 percent of women of childbearing age employing "any method" of birth control. Nor does this estimate include ECPs (morning-after pills).[75]

Considering all IUDs (inert, copper, and hormonal), each has post-fertilization effects preventing pregnancies.[76] These work by preventing the fertilized egg access to the endometrium, prohibiting the little one's attachment there. Stanford and Micolajczyk estimate that the post-fertilization effects of inert IUDs inhibit implantation in 99.1 percent of all cases of fertilized eggs. For copper and hormonal IUDs their estimates vary between 99.1 percent to 99.5 percent and 99.8 percent to 99.95 percent, respectively. Thus the post-fertilization effects are very powerful, and they must be, given the relatively large rate of fertilizations per cycle (15.6 percent for inert IUDs, 4.1 percent to 8.1 percent for copper IUDs, and 14 percent for hormonal IUDs) on the one hand, and the low rate of pregnancies of women wearing IUDs on the other. The authors estimate that 0.72 to 1.97 fertilized eggs fail to implant per woman wearing inert IUDs per year. For copper and hormonal IUDs, the corresponding numbers are 0.19 to 1.04 and 0.19 to 1.82, respectively. That is, women wearing copper IUDs are likely to effectively abort a child between once a year and once every five years. Women wearing hormonal IUDs are likely to abort a child between every 6.6 months and every five years.

According to UN data released in 2019, 8.3 percent of the 74.7 million women of childbearing age in the US (6.2 million women) were using IUDs of some kind.[77] Taking the above numbers, the implied annual loss of fertilized eggs (little ones bearing the image of God) due to the post-fertilization effects of IUDs in the United States alone would be between 1.18 million (if all IUDs were copper and the low estimate prevails) and 12.2 million (if all IUDs were inert and the high estimate prevails).

---

75. Practice of birth control in Europe and North America among 246,000,000 women 15–49, by percentages: any method 58.2, female sterilization 6.3, male sterilization 2.5, pill 17.8, injectable 1.1, implant 1.1, IUD 7.9, male condom 14.6, rhythm 1.4, withdrawal 4.1, other methods 1.4. Ibid.
76. Joseph Stanford and Rafael Micolajczyk, "Mechanisms of Action of Intrauterine Devices: Update and Estimation of Postfertilization Effects," *American Journal of Obstetrics & Gynecology* 187, no. 6 (December 2002): 1699–1708.
77. UN, "Contraceptive Use by Method 2019: Data Booklet," 22.

Let us reiterate that these estimates are the number of lives lost in the US each year merely from the abortifacient agency of IUDs, and that no estimates of the death toll from prevention of implantation after conception are ever included in any organization's reports of numbers of abortions. Their statistics are only the number of babies killed after those babies have survived through implantation.

Accounting for In Vitro Fertilization

Now consider the death toll from IVF.[78] Here, the true cost of human life in this process is again hidden by definitions of conception and the use of medical jargon, but the Human Fertilisation & Embryology Authority (HFEA), an organization in the United Kingdom that is responsible for regulating the practice of IVF throughout the UK, reported to Parliament that from August 1, 1991, to December 31, 2011, 3,546,818 embryos were created. Of these, 1,714,570 were "discarded," i.e., thrown away like trash (whether because they died in the lab, or for reasons of quality, or for reasons of eugenics, the report does not say). Meanwhile, 5,876 embryos were frozen with the intent to give them to research (a sentence of death), while 841,396 were frozen for future use. Only 1,388,443 of the created embryos from this period were "transferred" to a womb, thus creating a pregnancy.[79] For a nearly coterminous period—1991 to June 30, 2010—the HFEA reported that 101,605 embryos were given for research—again, a sentence of death.[80] When we put the numbers together from these slightly diverging time periods of embryos discarded or given for research, the death toll for this twenty-year period comes to 1,816,175. But this death toll is not yet complete, as we will see.

According to the 2012 annual report of the HFEA, "In the UK, 224,196

---

78. See, among others, "1.5 Million Embryos Killed through IVF Since 1991 in Britain," *LifeSiteNews*, July 27, 2011, https://www.lifesitenews.com/news/15-million-embryos-killed-through-ivf-since-1991-in-britain/.

79. *Hansard*, HL Debates, vol. 742, January 8, 2013, cols. WA22–WA26, https://publications.parliament.uk/pa/ld201213/ldhansrd/text/130108w0001.htm#column_WA26.

80. *Hansard*, HL Debates, vol. 729, July 20, 2011, cols. WA305–WA308, https://publications.parliament.uk/pa/ld201011/ldhansrd/text/110720w0001.htm#column_WA305. It is not certain whether the HFEA refers to the entirety of 1991 in this report, or the period beginning August 1, 1991.

babies were born after IVF treatment between 1991 and 2011."[81] Subtracting the number of babies born from the number of embryos transferred to a woman's womb, we see that 1,164,247 embryos died during pregnancy.[82] This plus the previous death toll gives us 2,980,422 dead little ones. Simplifying this data, the numbers indicate that for every one baby born via IVF in the UK between 1991 and 2011, roughly sixteen embryos were created. Of these sixteen, nine were "discarded," five died during pregnancy, one was frozen, and one was born.

Getting an exact number of how many children have been sacrificed and placed in "concentration cans" worldwide through IVF is difficult. In 2018, the International Committee for Monitoring Assisted Reproductive Technology reported that more than 8 million IVF children had been born since IVF's introduction in 1978.[83] When we consider that the UK's practice of IVF is very well-regulated in comparison to, for instance, that of the United States,[84] it is hard to accept a ratio of one child born to sixteen children created, or a ratio of one child born to fourteen children dead, as a realistic ratio for the entire world—the actual ratio is likely to be significantly worse. But accepting it for the sake of an estimate, we find that 8 million IVF children born means that 128 million IVF children were created, 112 million were killed outright or died, and another 8 million were frozen to await one fate or another. That makes 120 million children conceived through IVF who were not born, from 1978 through 2018.

The Total

Based on the reporting of *The Lancet* that abortions worldwide have increased to 73 million (0.98 of current world population) per year, and assuming the accuracy of the Guttmacher Institute's statistics on world abortions presently totaling 1.6 billion, we conclude that, by 2027, the

---

81. "Fertility Treatment in 2012: Trends and Figures," HFEA, https://www.hfea.gov.uk/media/2080/hfea-fertility-trends-2012.pdf. Again, it is not certain whether the HFEA refers to the entirety of 1991, or the period beginning August 1, 1991.
82. This number does not account for embryos that became twins or triplets.
83. ESHRE, "More Than 8 Million Babies."
84. See, e.g., "The Fertility Center Regulation Crisis in the United States" Peiffer Wolf Carr and Kane (law firm), August 7, 2019, https://peifferwolf.com/wp-content/uploads/2020/01/PWCK_Fertility-Center-Regulation-Crisis-Issue-Briefer_FINAL.pdf.

little ones slaughtered after their survival of implantation will be greater than 2 billion.

Now stop and consider how many little ones aren't included in *The Lancet* and Guttmacher Institute totals. How many babies have been frozen or killed through in vitro fertilization? How many babies have been killed by IUDs preventing their implantation? How many babies have been killed by mothers using the 255 forms of hormonal birth control sold by pharmaceutical firms and reviewed on Drugs.com?[85]

Conclusion: Genocide

To summarize, the twentieth century has seen mankind keep descending down into the moral abyss of bloodshed which started with world wars, moved to world wars targeting civilians, then to governments targeting their own countrymen; and finally, to fathers and mothers waging war against their own sons and daughters. At each stage of these changes in the method and scale of the killing, the number of deaths multiplied so that, now, the death toll of our war on unborn babies dwarfs the combined death tolls of all these previous bloodsheds. Mankind today has turned inward against himself, devouring his own offspring.

How do we reckon with such unspeakable horrors? Are there words able to convey such savagery? Are there texts of Scripture revealing the Almighty's hatred of such wickedness and the certainty of His coming judgment of those who have committed such crimes?

Living in a day puffed up with the pride over its concern for what it speaks of as "basic" or "fundamental" human rights, we must puncture this pride with such firm conviction and will that those who hear us may never lie to themselves again concerning their pursuit of "social justice" or "compassion," nor of their being in any way righteous because of any stand they have taken against systemic evils. A good beginning to the destruction of this pride can be accomplished by applying a label to the slaughter of the unborn which has been avoided before this present time.

---

85. "Medications for Birth Control (Contraception)," Drugs.com, accessed June 23, 2022, https://www.drugs.com/condition/contraception.html.

From Greek *genos* ("birth, race, kind") and Latin *caedere* ("kill"), this word has long been used to refer to the slaughter of a group distinguished by ethnicity or nationality. Age, though, is a parallel category to race and ethnicity. Further, unborn children are, in fact, distinguished by specific physical characteristics, being housed and protected within their mothers' wombs. From here on out, we must make it a habit of speaking of the intentional destruction of unborn children as *genocide*.

Some might cavil that there is no widespread targeting of unborn children *in toto*, but rather only those children in specific circumstances. But even granting the premises of such a wicked counterargument does not nullify the argument we make here. Genocide does not require the intention to kill *all* members of the *genos*, but only the intentional targeting and killing of members of that class *as such*.[86] Note this resolution by the UN General Assembly back in 1946, whose concepts became cornerstones of international law regarding genocide:

> Genocide is a denial of the right of existence of entire human groups, as homicide is the denial of the right to live of individual human beings; such denial of the right of existence shocks the conscience of mankind, results in great losses to humanity in the form of cultural and other contributions represented by these human groups, and is contrary to moral law and the spirit and aims of the United Nations.[87]

The cornerstone of child murder today is a denial of unborn babies' right to existence. It "shocks the conscience" of those consciences not yet deadened to it. It causes unthinkable "losses to humanity" in the potential it snuffs out, and it is certainly contrary to the moral law of God.

This is genocide, and we, the people of God, must acknowledge our complicity and participation in it.

No doubt Asia's long history of the bloodshed of its children is a consequence of the East's commitment to false religion across thousands of years. But let us examine the West.

---

86. Stalin's plan was not to kill all Ukrainians worldwide, nor were the Turks intent on killing all Armenians across the world. Yet their crimes, as well as many other similar ones, have always been condemned as genocide.

87. UN General Assembly, Resolution 96(I), The Crime of Genocide, A/RES/96-I (December 11, 1946), https://documents-dds-ny.un.org/doc/RESOLUTION/GEN/NR0/033/47/img/NR003347.pdf?OpenElement.

Within the pagan idolatry of the ancient Roman Empire there was no question of the absolute authority of the father of the household over the life and death of his children. Called *patria potestas*, this power enabled fathers to throw their children on the hillsides, exposed there to die. This was the context of the New Testament church as it grew in its first few centuries, and in time the witness—the salt and light of the church—first caused these little ones who were the cast-offs from pagan idolatry to be rescued and adopted by Christians, then caused this horror to be outlawed as Christendom displaced the immoralities of paganism.

For most of the past two thousand years, Christendom has been identified by this same love and protection of the weak and defenseless—particularly children. Now though, we find the West hell-bent on flipping every godly commitment of Christendom upside down, starting with its former protection of those on the margins of society. Nor have we ever been as hell-bent on this reversal as in our return to the slaughter of children. The slaughter of children pervasive across our world today could not possibly be more of a rejection of the Christian faith.

What is the moral responsibility of the church in this?

Christians know the truth that life begins with conception. God blesses a husband and his wife with the fruit of the womb and that fruit bears His own image and likeness from the moment of conception. From that point forward, all the little one needs is his mother's womb. Christians know (or have no excuse for not knowing) that we kill that little one when we obstruct his implantation. (And those who claim ignorance are helped by this present document, which is part of its purpose.) Christians must never lie about murder. Christians must never dissimulate about bloodshed. Christians must move heaven and earth to avoid placing a stumbling block in the path of just one of our Lord's little ones.

So now, how do God's people stand in the presence of God and worship Him given a death toll for abortions this past century that is surely in the billions? Given that our ground is saturated by blood?

> Do not defile yourselves with any of these things; for by all these the nations are defiled, which I am casting out before you. For the land is defiled; therefore I visit the punishment of its iniquity upon it, and the land vomits out its inhabitants. (Lev. 18:24–25)

> So you shall not pollute the land where you are; for blood defiles the land, and no atonement can be made for the land, for the blood that is shed on it, except by the blood of him who shed it. Therefore do not defile the land which you inhabit, in the midst of which I dwell; for I the Lord dwell among the children of Israel. (Num. 35:33–34)

As we live and God's patience remains, we may repent; and repent we must. It is our prayer that, through this paper, all of us who belong to God will turn and rend our garments and throw ashes on our heads in repentance.

In this section we have opened up our bloodlust. Now, we must hear again the decrees of God against it, found both in His Word and in nature as created by the Word Himself. As churchmen, as magistrates, and as men, what must we do to repent of this wickedness so that God may see fit to renew our minds and hearts, restoring to us and our children His law, His perfections, and His love for little ones?

> May God, who alone hath the power, inscribe these teachings on the hearts of those who hold sway over the Christian world. May He grant to them a mind possessing knowledge of divine and human law, and having ever before it the reflection that it hath been chosen as a servant for the rule of man, the living thing most dear to God.[88]

---

88. Hugo Grotius, *De Jure Belli ac Pacis Libri Tres* (1646), trans. Francis W. Kelsey, Carnegie Classics of International Law, ed. James Brown Scott, vol. 2 (Oxford: Clarendon Press, 1925), 862 (3.25.8).

CHAPTER 2

Abortion's Assault upon God's Character and Law

Our purpose here is not to provide an exhaustive treatment of the moral issues surrounding abortion. Such a work would fill volumes. Yet in the spirit of saying *something* so that we be not silent,[1] we provide here some limited accounting of the moral harm caused by abortion. Any of these examples of abortion's moral harm is sufficient to demonstrate to tender Christian consciences the wickedness of abortion. Taken together, these examples expose the monstrosity of this sin.

Moral Arguments

From birth to death, every man knows that to kill another man is a crime against man and God. Scripture and history provide irrefutable evidence that God has written this law on every man's heart. This testimony of man's conscience is ineffaceable. Indeed, even the national, state, and local battles fought over abortion during the twentieth and twenty-first centuries bear witness to the testimony of the Spirit of God against this form of murder. Despite the corruption of man's fallen nature, the horrors of this crime against the little ones cry out against us.

---

1. Augustine, *On the Trinity* 7.6.11.

Overthrowing Our Creator's Command against Murder

To murder has always been a great wickedness. From Creation, all races, nations, and societies have recognized that, if any crimes exist, murder is the most fundamental. Abortion is no exception.

Denial of the Right to Life

Abortion denies the most fundamental right God has given man, which is the right to live. For centuries, arguments have raged over the nature and extent of man's right to live, and in what judicial cases man forfeits that right. What has been undeniable under the rule of law of the Western world is that no individual may decide whether another lives or dies. That prerogative is one owned solely by God and those institutions to whom He delegates the sword in the exercise of justice.

Yet in 1973—and quite suddenly—the Supreme Court of the United States declared the laws against murder by abortion null and void—laws which were, at the time, written on the books of almost every state of the Union. Planned Parenthood records the change enforced by *Roe v. Wade* this way:

> *Roe* has come to be known as the case that legalized abortion nationwide. At the time the decision was handed down, nearly all states outlawed abortion except to save a woman's life or for limited reasons such as preserving the woman's health, or instances of rape, incest, or fetal anomaly. *Roe* rendered these laws unconstitutional.[2]

This federal reversal of states' laws was unprecedented and led to an embarrassing dilemma among physicians. Sadly, like most Americans of the time, the medical establishment raised no outcry over the newly invented right of mothers to kill their babies. Now that this right had been created, the question remained: Who would carry out these murders?

At that time, the nation's physicians had been initiated into the practice of medicine by taking the Hippocratic Oath, part of which read:

---

2. "*Roe v. Wade*: Its History and Impact," Planned Parenthood Federation of America, 2014, https://www.plannedparenthood.org/files/3013/9611/5870/Abortion_Roe_History.pdf.

I shall never give a deadly drug (*pharmakon*) to anyone if asked, nor shall I recommend such counsel; and likewise I shall not give a woman a pessary for an abortion.

    With purity and in accordance with divine law I will keep my life and my art.[3]

The Hippocratic Oath originated two and a half millennia ago, and it represented the most basic commitments of physicians in their practice of the healing arts. So, when *Roe v. Wade*'s new mandate came down, it raised the question whether physicians would continue to honor their oath. Or, would they begin to accept money in payment for "causing an abortion"?

    There was never any significant debate. Doctors across our nation began to break their oath and take money from mothers seeking doctors' assistance in killing their little ones. To clean up the mess, the Hippocratic Oath was sometimes edited and sometimes removed from physicians' initiation rites.

The Removal of Woman's Moral Agency

Abortion also required the diminishment of woman's moral agency. At the heart of personhood is individual responsibility for one's own deeds. The rule of law flows from this individual moral agency. Whether in the workplace, government, church, or family, the rule of law holds every man and woman accountable for his actions. The roofer is accountable to put on a roof that doesn't leak. The lawyer is accountable to provide his client truthful counsel. The judge is accountable to issue just judgments that do not abandon the meek and lowly to oppression by the sleek, rich, and educated. The pastor is accountable to keep his sheep's blood off his hands by speaking to them precisely what God commands.

    Concerning moral agency, feminism had long argued that male authority diminished female responsibility. Feminists declared it would only be when male authority was brought to an end that women would possess full personhood equal to men, and thus bear the full weight of the

---

3. οὐ δώσω δὲ οὐδὲ φάρμακον οὐδενὶ αἰτηθεὶς θανάσιμον, οὐδὲ ὑφηγήσομαι συμβουλίην τοιήνδε: ὁμοίως δὲ οὐδὲ γυναικὶ πεσσὸν φθόριον δώσω. ἁγνῶς δὲ καὶ ὁσίως διατηρήσω βίον τὸν ἐμὸν καὶ τέχνην τὴν ἐμήν.

consequences of their actions. They must be granted self-determination and freedom to choose. Only when this equality was established could women be said to have the same moral agency as men. These themes are constant across feminist and pro-abortion literature of the past fifty years.

When feminists promoted abortion, though, they set this claim aside. No mother was to be judged for procuring the murder of her child.

Today, the male authority that God established when He created Adam first, then Eve, has been repudiated, and yet it is notable that mothers who pay doctors to murder their little ones are viewed as the victims of their boyfriends, husbands, fathers, or a patriarchal society. If there is any moral judgment involved in any abortion, it is the condemnation of bad men who force good women to kill their children. Society is condemned for robbing women of power and self-determination, forcing them to commit bloodshed in order to establish their power and self-determination. Personhood begins with freedom of choice, and what freedom of choice do women have if they are unable to rid their own bodies of these parasites clinging to their wombs? In fact, the ability to choose abortion is said to be central to women's self-determination. Women cannot truly be free and equal until they are granted this fundamental freedom of choice. Feminists demand that their sex's life-givingness[4] must be subject to the mother's choice whether or not to allow this life God has placed in her to continue. This is necessary to establish women's equality and personhood.

This is the grotesque reasoning feminists have used to reduce mothers to the very status they had previously condemned. In order to gain moral agency on a par with men, feminists demanded women be granted the right to kill their children. And yet, if women exercised this right, they were to bear no guilt for it. Rather, they must be judged to have killed their children under compulsion. They are free of any responsibility for the murder of their little ones they paid to have killed.

But when guilt is denied, repentance is also denied. What is purportedly done from respect for women results in barring women from confessing their sin to the holy God and receiving forgiveness through the mercy and love of God in Jesus Christ. If women commit no crime subject to man's

---

4. Adam named his wife Eve, which means "living one" or "life-giver," "because she was the mother of all the living." Genesis 3:20.

law when they kill their babies, the only logical conclusion is that women who kill their babies commit no sin subject to God's law either.

Women must not seek God's forgiveness for shedding the blood of the children God gave them as His blessing, and the civil authorities must enact no laws testifying to their maternal bloodguilt. The woman has, in effect, become what the feminists feared: a non-agent, functioning only as the victim of male figures in her life, denied any responsibility for her own actions.[5]

Yet why should this be so? After all, the man who beats his wife or children is responsible for the harm and suffering he causes the members of his household. Equally so the woman who beats her husband or children: she too is responsible for the harm and suffering she causes her intimate family members. If a father rapes or murders one of his children, no prosecutor, court, judge, or jury will hesitate to punish him for his crimes. Equally so the mother who rapes or murders one of her children: any just society will demand her trial and punishment, and the judicial system will carry out this difficult work.

Why, then, have eighty-three pro-life leaders of national and state organizations issued a press release opposing any laws to "punish" mothers who kill their preborn children? Their press release was issued in the weeks following *Politico*'s leak of Justice Alito's draft opinion in *Dobbs v. Jackson Women's Health Organization*, and it was drafted and signed by the leaders of organizations including the Ethics and Religious Liberty Commission of the Southern Baptist Convention, the US Conference of Catholic Bishops, Americans United for Life, the Faith & Freedom Coalition, Life Issues Institute, the National Association of Pro-Life Nurses, and the National Right to Life. The letter reads:

> **Women are victims of abortion and require our compassion and support . . .**

---

5. The reactions of many women on social media to the threatened overturning of *Roe v. Wade* illustrate this reality. For example, Twitter user @Darlyn215 said on May 3, 2022, "You know what's so interesting? Women can't get themselves pregnant. It's men who cause abortions," accessed May 5, 2022, https://twitter.com/Darlyn215/status/1521595279077744641. Twitter user @photogjoy said on May 4, 2022, "Let's force vasectomies on men who get women pregnant so the MAN has to pay the price as well," accessed May 5, 2022, https://twitter.com/photogjoy/status/1521822320628748288, emphasis original.

> As national and state pro-life organizations, representing tens of millions of pro-life men, women, and children across the country, let us be clear: We state unequivocally that we do not support any measure seeking to criminalize or punish women and we stand firmly opposed to include such penalties in legislation. . . .
>
> We understand better than anyone else the desire to punish the purveyors of abortion who act callously and without regard to the dignity of human life. But turning women who have abortions into criminals **is not the way.**[6]

While it is true women and men other than the baby's mother usually share the bloodguilt of the murder of the preborn, it remains hard to fathom this denial of the moral agency of the women who most often are the ones who actually pay for the drugs or surgery to kill their baby. Wise Solomon recognized the mother who wanted the baby dead to be the evil moral agent in the dispute, and penalized her for it.[7] Was Solomon wrong?

How have we come to think so lightly of the minds, consciences, and souls of women, that we issue statements absolving them of any responsibility for their murder of their own children? Do these pro-life leaders claim to speak for God in their dispensing this public absolution to mothers who have aborted their preborn children?

No murder is hidden from God. Every one of us will soon give an accounting for our bloodguilt on that Final Day of Judgment, when the secrets of all men will be revealed before the Great Judge Eternal. It is of the essence of the gospel message preached by John the Baptist, Jesus Christ, the Apostles, and every gospel witness down through two millennia of church history to "flee the wrath to come." How then can those professing faith in Jesus issue public statements that women who have murdered their preborn children are merely "victims of abortion" who "require our compassion and support," and that they are adamantly opposed to any law which would declare these women "criminals"?

To be sure, these post-*Roe* days will require wisdom in the writing and

---

6. "An Open Letter to State Lawmakers from America's Leading Pro-Life Organizations," May 12, 2022, https://www.nrlc.org/uploads/communications/051222coalitionlettertostates.pdf. Emphases original.

7. 1 Kings 3:16–28.

debate over states' abortion legislation. No two states are alike, and civil authorities of each state will bear the responsibility of decisions concerning who should be held accountable for the shedding of these little ones' blood, as well as how, when, and in what way. Given a particular state's demography, it may be wise not to use the force of law against mothers who buy the murder of their preborn children. Nevertheless, no follower of Jesus Christ should ever declare moral or criminal absolution concerning such mothers. God will judge us, and it is no kindness for any leader to declare that those bearing bloodguilt are only "victims" of this abortion they have purchased, and that no one should "punish" them.

On the other hand, assuming such pro-life leaders are successful in their attempts to stave off any criminalization or punishment of mothers who abort their little ones, the truth always held precious by the church of Jesus Christ remains with us today—to proclaim repentance for the forgiveness of this sin too, as also every other form of wickedness:

> [Jesus] said to them, "Thus it is written, that the Christ would suffer and rise again from the dead the third day, and that repentance for forgiveness of sins would be proclaimed in His name to all the nations. (Luke 24:46–47)

The path forward from the bloodguilt of abortion is not claiming victimhood and denying one's moral agency, but acknowledging our guilt and fleeing to the cross of Jesus Christ for His forgiveness. Those of us who love Jesus have done the same (and continue to do so daily) and will welcome you into the household of faith, the church of the Living God.

The Death of the Conscience

Mother Teresa of Calcutta used to say there are two deaths in every abortion:

> The mother herself kills, destroys, murders her own child. Created by God Himself for greater things: to love and to be loved. Created in the image of God. Created to be His presence in the world today. I mean destroying. And in killing that living reality of the tenderness of God's love, the mother

kills two: the child and her (own) conscience. For life she will know she has murdered her own child with her own decision.[8]

God's moral law is written on each man's heart so that our conscience testifies to each of us what ought and ought not to be done. When women and men act against their conscience, particularly on an issue of such gravity, they sear their conscience and leave it on life support.

Despite all the supposed evidence denying the suffering of mothers who choose abortion, the murderess bears her guilt and shame for the rest of her life. Grievous (and often, repeated) sin of this nature can so harm the conscience that it ceases to function. Such a woman has lost not only her child, but God's gift of knowing what sin she has committed. For herself, her family, and her society, this grave evil gives birth to grave consequences among all those who know and love her. They may not know the cause of her moral disease, but they suffer it along with her. As one example, the children she chooses to give birth to end up being her *wanted* children, and they too suffer guilt and shame, sometimes called "post-abortion survivor syndrome."[9]

We must not allow our bloodlust to fool us:

> Be not deceived; God is not mocked: for whatsoever a man soweth, that shall he also reap. For he that soweth to his flesh shall of the flesh reap corruption; but he that soweth to the Spirit shall of the Spirit reap life everlasting. (Gal. 6:7–8, KJV)

Natural Law Arguments

All creation declares abortion's ingratitude and rebellion against our Creator. But men make science their god and mock God's truths, so we are

---

8. Mother Teresa, "Address to Commissioners of 200th General Assembly of the Presbyterian Church (USA), St. Louis, Missouri; June 7, 1988."
9. Philip Ney, Claudia Sheils, and Marek Gajowy, "Post-Abortion Survivor Syndrome: Signs and Symptoms," *Southern Medical Journal* 99, no. 12 (December 2006): 1405–1406, https://doi.org/10.1097/01.smj.0000251372.56344.bf.

tempted to retreat within the walls of special revelation, consigning the natural world and its scientific investigation as a pagan domain. This is a grave mistake. Natural revelation is a key part of knowing and understanding God. God's book of nature helps us to know *what* He has done and *how* He works among us. Indeed, Scripture itself teaches us to ask, "Does not even nature itself teach you?" (1 Cor. 11:14).

Those truths proclaimed by nature must not be abandoned in favor of those truths revealed by Scripture.[10] Nature is a handmaid to Scripture. It too reveals the character of God, at times in areas Scripture does not. Sacred Scripture is infallible, yet not all texts of Scripture are spoken with equal clarity; where Scripture is unclear, the book of nature helps us evaluate what interpretations of God's Word are most sound.[11] Some of our fallible understandings of Scripture need refinement by nature.[12] Properly understood, natural revelation cannot contradict special revelation.[13] Any conflict between natural and special revelation, then, is due to some error in our interpretation of either (or both).

Conversely, when both of God's spheres of revelation address a matter, we do well to take special heed. Thus we here state that our condemnation

---

10. "When they are able, from reliable evidence, to prove some fact of physical science, we shall show that it is not contrary to our Scripture. But when they produce from any of their books a theory contrary to Scripture, and therefore contrary to the catholic faith, either we shall have some ability to demonstrate that it is absolutely false, or at least we ourselves will hold it so without any shadow of a doubt. And so we will cling to our Mediator, 'in whom are hidden all the treasures of wisdom and knowledge,' that we will not be led astray by the glib talk of false philosophy or frightened by the superstition of false religion." Augustine, *Literal Commentary on Genesis* 1.21.41, trans. J. H. Taylor.

11. Thus Augustine, on the question of the physical disposition of heaven: "But someone may ask: 'Is not Scripture opposed to those who hold that heaven is spherical, when it says "who stretches out heaven like a skin"?' Let it be opposed indeed if their statement is false. The truth is rather in what God reveals than in what groping men surmise. But if they are able to establish their doctrine with proofs that cannot be denied, we must show that this statement of Scripture about the skin is not opposed to the truth of their conclusions. . . . But if it is necessary, as it surely is, to interpret these two passages so that they are shown not to be contradictory but to be reconcilable, it is also necessary that both of these passages should not contradict the stories that may be supported by true evidence, by which heaven is said to be curved on all sides in the shape of a sphere, provide only that this is proved." *Literal Commentary on Genesis* 2.9.

12. "It is admitted that theologians are not infallible, in the interpretation of Scripture. It may, therefore, happen in the future, as it has in the past, that interpretations of the Bible, long confidently received, must be modified or abandoned, to bring revelation into harmony with what God teaches in his works. This change of view as to the true meaning of the Bible may be a painful trial to the Church, but it does not in the least impair the authority of the Scriptures. They remain infallible; we are merely convicted of having mistaken their meaning." Charles Hodge, *Systematic Theology*, 3 vols. (1872–73; Eerdmans, 1982), 1:59.

13. Indeed, because God is infallible in *all* His works and cannot err in His revelation of Himself, both natural and special revelation may be said to be infallible, but not any *interpretation* of those revelations.

of abortion is not only based on God's written moral law, but also God's book of nature. Together they bear unanimous testimony against the monstrosity of this crime.

Man as Unique Creation

Scientific research shows that, from the moment of conception, the unborn child possesses all the genetic information that distinguishes him from any other created species or being. The unborn child conceived in his mother is not a tree, monkey, or tumor.[14] He is a human being bearing the image of God with forty-six chromosomes and the DNA that sets him apart from the rest of creation. He is demonstrably different from either his father or mother, with DNA drawn from both of them. He is a unique human being.

As detailed earlier, physicians have tried to change the definition of *conception* from fertilization to successful implantation in the mother's womb. But this change makes a mockery of science and reason. The safe attachment of the child to his mother's womb does not change him in any way. There is no scientific or rational reason why implantation should define the beginning of life or qualify that life for protection. It is true that, from implantation, the little one's reliance on his mother for nourishment increases, but this increase does not bear on his right of protection. Indeed, such an argument contradicts one typical argument for abortion "rights"—namely, that one person dependent on another is *less* deserving of protections and rights. What a callous response to the interrelatedness of life, and specifically the charity God commands between us in light of His charity toward us!

Personhood from the Beginning

If, for the sake of argument, we grant that the personhood of the human embryo is not yet proven to exist at fertilization, arguments based on this irrational supposition still fall flat. For, in order to justify the moral rectitude of abortion at any point, one would need to establish that there

14. "Well, after all, it's living, isn't it? And if it's living, what is it if it's not a human being? A mouse? A dog? A monkey?" Richard John Neuhaus in an unpublished paper given at the Consultation on the Church and Abortion, sponsored by Presbyterians Pro-Life, Princeton Theological Seminary, February 28–29, 1992.

is no possibility of the abortion killing a person. Yet it is impossible to demonstrate the newly conceived embryo lacks personhood. Indeed, all the evidence is to the contrary.

Again, if for the sake of argument we were to accept this irrational premise, it would immediately leave us asking at what stage of later embryonic development personhood is acquired? At what stage does what is not man somehow become man?

The irrationality of this project is clear to everyone who has not allowed himself to become a bloody ideologue. This little one is a living human being when he emerges from his mother's womb because he is a living being at the moment when his life *qua* human begins—always and forevermore at conception.

Yes, we can muddy the waters by raising abstract, speculative questions on ensoulment, personhood, or quickening, desperately working to deny that conception is the beginning of life. But why such intensity in our efforts to deny protection to these little ones? The truth is, throughout history, men (often with better intentions than our own) have discussed the mystery of how and when our heavenly Father "ensouls" an infant. Many of the church fathers wrote extensively on the matter, yet their opinions were never settled matters of dogma, in large part because Scripture does not directly address the topic.[15] Nor did these theories cause the slightest hesitation in their condemning abortion as a grave sin from the moment of conception. In *Evangelium Vitae,* John Paul II puts it directly:

> Some people try to justify abortion by claiming that the result of conception, at least up to a certain number of days, cannot yet be considered a personal human life. But in fact, "from the time that the ovum is fertilized, a life is begun which is neither that of the father nor the mother; it is rather the life of a new human being with his own growth. It would never be made human if it were not human already...."
>
> Furthermore, what is at stake is so important that, from the standpoint of moral obligation, the mere probability that a human person is involved

---

15. See Job 10:8–12: "Your hands fashioned and made me altogether, and would You destroy me? Remember now, that You have made me as clay; and would You turn me into dust again? Did You not pour me out like milk and curdle me like cheese; clothe me with skin and flesh, and knit me together with bones and sinews? You have granted me life and lovingkindness; and Your care has preserved my spirit."

ABORTION'S ASSAULT UPON GOD'S CHARACTER AND LAW

would suffice to justify an absolutely clear prohibition of any intervention aimed at killing a human embryo. Precisely for this reason, over and above all scientific debates . . . , the Church has always taught and continues to teach that the result of human procreation, from the first moment of its existence, must be guaranteed that unconditional respect which is morally due to the human being in his or her totality and unity as body and spirit.[16]

The church has always taught and continues to teach that abortion is the direct assault upon the providence and authority of God, our Creator.

SLED Arguments

Many of the arguments employed by advocates of abortion can be divided into four categories referred to by the acronym SLED, referring to the Size, Level of development, Environment, and Degree of dependency of the preborn child.[17]

1. *Size:* Some argue abortion is justified because these little ones are beyond our view. It is permissible to kill the little one because he is too small to see hidden inside his mother's womb.
   Yet God's creation is full of small organisms and many of them have the protection of law and the sympathy of society, such as the world's smallest primate and smallest marine mammal. Shall we justify the killing of these organisms because of their size? On the contrary, it is much more grievous to destroy these little ones because of how tiny and defenseless they are. Only a monster would argue that the smaller and weaker the baby, the less claim that baby has on our protection.
2. *Level of development:* Some argue the limitations of the child during his early development make it permissible to kill him. The unborn

---

16. John Paul II, *Evangelium Vitae*, March 25, 1995, §§ 60–61, https://www.vatican.va/content/john-paul-ii/en/encyclicals/documents/hf_jp-ii_enc_25031995_evangelium-vitae.html, quoting Sacred Congregation for the Doctrine of the Faith, *Declaration on Procured Abortion*, November 18, 1974, §§ 12–13, https://www.vatican.va/roman_curia/congregations/cfaith/documents/rc_con_cfaith_doc_19741118_declaration-abortion_en.html.

17. The SLED acronym was developed by the Roman Catholic philosopher Stephen Schwarz in his 1990 book *The Moral Question of Abortion* (Loyola University Press).

child can't feel pain, can't think, isn't self-aware, and is not yet sentient, so we may kill him.

Yet science is proving the little one's sensitivity to his environment at younger and younger stages of his life in the womb.[18] The limitations of development are irrelevant. One's right to life is not dependent on one's capacities to enjoy life or assert his personhood. Children or adults who suffer sickness, wounds, or genetic anomalies which leave them with limited capacities have as much claim to society's protection as those with no such limitations, both outside and inside the womb.

3. *Environment:* Some argue the environment in which the unborn child exists invalidates his right to be considered human. Since the unborn child doesn't, for example, breathe air, he is sufficiently "other" so that he deserves no protection.

Of course, the same argument would never be made concerning residents of the South Pole or the International Space Station. Neither of those locations can sustain life naturally without the provision of extraordinarily complicated and costly artificial supports. The same can be said concerning victims of polio who have, for decades, continued to live only by the support of an iron lung.[19]

4. *Degree of dependence:* Some argue the unborn child's dependence upon his mother undermines his right to the protection of his life.

This argument is especially pernicious, for it strikes at the heart

---

18. Re: sight, eye movements and reactions occur as early as 12 weeks. See Tryphena Humphrey, "Some Correlations between the Appearance of Human Fetal Reflexes and the Development of the Nervous System," in *Progress in Brain Research*, vol. 4, *Growth and Maturation of the Brain*, ed. Dominick P. Purpura and J. P. Schadé (Elsevier, 1964), 93–135, https://doi.org/10.1016/S0079-6123(08)61273-X.

Re: hearing, see Christine Moon, Hugo Lagerkrantz, and Patricia Kuhl, "Language Experienced In Utero Affects Vowel Perception after Birth: A Two-Country Study," *Acta Paediatrica* 102, no. 2 (February 2013): 156–160, https://doi.org/10.1111/apa.12098; also Eino Partanen et al., "Learning-Induced Neural Plasticity of Speech Processing before Birth," in *Psychological and Cognitive Sciences* 110, no. 37 (August 26, 2013): 15145–15150, https://www.ncbi.nlm.nih.gov/pmc/articles/PMC3773755/.

Re: pain, recent research has continually pushed back the developmental threshold at which the unborn are known to be able to feel pain. See, e.g., Stuart Derbyshire and John Bockmann, "Reconsidering Fetal Pain," *Journal of Medical Ethics* 46, no. 1 (2020): 3–6, http://dx.doi.org/10.1136/medethics-2019-105701. For other aspects of early fetal development, see Katrina Furth, *15 Facts at 15 Weeks*, On Science 3 (Arlington: Charlotte Lozier Institute, 2021), https://lozierinstitute.org/15-facts-at-15-weeks/.

19. Linda Rodriguez McRobbie, "The Man in the Iron Lung," *The Guardian*, May 26, 2020, https://www.theguardian.com/society/2020/may/26/last-iron-lung-paul-alexander-polio-coronavirus.

of one of the principal blessings God has ordained in human society, which is our interdependence. God has woven interdependence across His creation: the tree and soil, the citizen and ruler, the husband and wife, teacher and student, doctor and patient; and most preciously, mother and child.

No man is an island.[20] No man is independent. By arguing that dependence diminishes value, this argument also targets the handicapped, the elderly, the sick, the infirm, and anyone who depends on another for nourishment and care. This is the trajectory of the pro-abortion argument. This world of callous disregard for the weak and defenseless must be rejected.

Societal Arguments

Man as Social Being

God has ordained men to live, not to themselves, but in bonds of fellowship one with another, so that when one suffers, all suffer. This has been seen more clearly in recent days as the negative effects of isolation because of Covid have continued to make themselves known. As Calvin put it:

> The human race has been joined together by a sacred link of community. . . . They are all next to [or, neighbors to] one another. To be our next [neighbor], it is enough for someone to exist as a human being, for we do not have the right to destroy our common nature.[21]

Not coincidentally, the account of the first assault on God's gift of life committed by Cain, who murdered his brother Abel, records Cain's justification: "Am I my brother's keeper?" Cain was denying his obligation to love his neighbor. The answer implied by Cain given his question is, "No, I am not my brother's keeper." This is the heartless answer implicit in every violation of the second table of God's moral law: we are not our neighbor's keeper. No violation of neighbor-keeping, of loving our neighbor as we

---

20. John Donne, *Devotions upon Emergent Occasions* (1624), ch. 17.
21. Comments on Luke 10:30, trans. Jürgen von Hagen.

love ourselves, is more fundamental than robbing our neighbor of his very life.

God's condemnation of the manslayer Cain demonstrates the wickedness of Cain's self-justification. We are in fact our neighbor's keeper, and this sacred duty declared by God has governed all subsequent human society. By God's design, society is a fellowship of His image-bearers. Men are bound together in this mutuality. We have a large degree of freedom, yet that freedom is defined by the moral law requiring that we love and defend our neighbor.

Notwithstanding the corruption of man by Adam's Fall, human societies throughout history and across the world have enacted statutes against murder. From the Code of Hammurabi to the law codes of Draco and Solon to the Roman Twelve Tables to the laws of the Zhou Dynasty and the three constitutional principles of the Han Dynasty, man's societies have recognized that murder destroys the foundation of the consent under which men live together bound by law; and that, left unchecked, murder leads to disarray, anarchy, and ruin:

> Protecting the life of the unborn child has been a major concern of the earliest laws known to us. It has continued to be an object of law-making in every subsequent civilization which has contributed to our own because it springs from a universal feeling which in the past has ceased to move men only when a nation was in decay.[22]

When anyone kills another man (even himself) with whom we are bound in union, it is not a "personal decision," or a "reproductive choice," but an offense against all. And so it is with the unborn:

> A choice cannot be private which affects another's life. The child in the womb has blood and brains, a respiratory system, a circulatory system, a urinary system that are not those of his or her mother. The child in the

---

22. Eugene Quay, "Justifiable Abortion," *The Georgetown Law Journal*, Winter 1960, 178. Quay, the founding editor of *The Georgetown Law Journal*, was a member of the American Law Institute whose work recommending legislative changes toward judicial reform were, at the time, being corrupted by a movement promoting the liberalization of state laws concerning abortion. "Justifiable Abortion" was his witness against this movement.

womb is not the property of his or her parent. The body of the child in the womb is not that of his or her parent. Sexuality may be private, reproduction may be private, but the taking of the life of the unborn cannot be private. It is a social act. Multiplied by 1 million times a year, it is a social act amounting to atrocity.[23]

The Loss of Potential

Much has been made in recent years of man's squandering of the earth's natural resources. But the resource with the most potential for the betterment and sustainability of human society is neither geological nor ecological, but anthropological. Man is the ultimate resource created by God, called by Him to "subdue" the rest of His creation.

God commanded us to subdue creation, and man's obedience to this command has been responsible for every advancement in law, medicine, politics, and art. Even conservation comes through man managing creation towards the betterment of mankind and the prosperity of the rest of creation.

Abortion, birth control, and contraception attack man's potential to bless all creation in this and other ways. To refuse God's blessings of children is to steal from future generations the benefits He has ordained we bequeath them. The loss of each child by that murder of abortion is the loss of immeasurable blessings which otherwise would rain down from heaven on our descendants. Perhaps that child would have been the next Jonas Salk, curing not polio, but cancer. Perhaps that child would have been the next Bach. The next Da Vinci? The next Martin Luther? The next George Washington Carver? The next Edison? Or even the next Fred Rogers?

Each of these men blessed multiple generations through those gifts God gave them. Are we not grateful their parents did not kill them? Are we not grateful they were conceived and born during a time when their societies still forbade mothers killing their unborn children?

23. John T. Noonan, "Restoring the Protection of Life to the Constitution," prepared statement in *Constitutional Amendments Relating to Abortion: Hearings Before the Subcommittee on the Constitution of the Committee on the Judiciary, United States Senate, Ninety-seventh Congress, First Session, on S.J. Res. 17, S.J. Res. 18, S.J. Res. 19, and S.J. Res. 110* (1983), 46.

Economic Considerations

In their 2005 book *Freakonomics*,[24] Steven D. Levitt and Stephen J. Dubner argued that the liberalization of abortion led to a significant reduction in the crime rate. Empirically, their argument was based on the observation that the crime rate in states that allowed abortion fell some fifteen years after the new legislation came into effect. Specifically, Levitt and Dubner argue that *Roe v. Wade* was the cause of the drop in crime rates in the early 1990s. The argument is simple and cynical: *Roe v. Wade* made abortions cheaper so that abortions became affordable to low-income women. Unwanted children of low-income mothers are more likely to be criminals later in life.[25] Hence the benefit of *Roe v. Wade* is fewer criminals, fewer prison inmates, and thus a fiscal gain to society.

Apart from the fact that any correlation spanning over fifteen years is necessarily tenuous because there are a multitude of intervening factors that need to be controlled for, it is also completely inappropriate for the issue at hand. Levitt and Dubner say that "one study has shown that the typical child who went unborn in the early years of legalized abortion would have been 50 percent more likely to live in poverty" and in a single parent home.[26] They do not indicate where that study was published. They go on, citing "another study [that] has shown that low maternal education is the single most powerful factor leading to criminality [of the child]."[27] They don't bother telling the reader where this study was published and by whom. Did Levitt and Dubner make it up? Maybe. We don't know. In any case, two "studies" with no references and no explanation of data or methodology cannot be used to justify the deaths of some 750,000 human beings in the first year after *Roe v. Wade*.[28] Far from being serious economists, Levitt and Dubner wrote a book to amuse their readers and themselves with absurd statements and they amused themselves with the deaths of millions of children.

Levitt and Dubner's argument is also flawed because abortion occurs not only among low-income classes. They would have had to show that

---

24. Steven D. Levitt and Stephen J. Dubner, *Freakonomics* (William Morrow, 2005).
25. Ibid., 137.
26. Ibid., 138.
27. Ibid., 139.
28. Ibid., 138.

after *Roe v. Wade*, abortions occurred *primarily* in low-income families. Yet we know that they occur in all income groups. We also know that abortions often cause mental harm—the treatment of which must be counted against what Levitt and Dubner seem to perceive as a fiscal benefit to US society.

How then should we look at the economic implications of abortion? For every economy today, it remains true that human beings contribute the most to economic well-being. In the US, the labor share (i.e., the percentage of annual value added that accrues to workers and proprietors as compensation for their work) is around 60 percent.[29] It is slightly higher on average in the twenty most important economies of the world (the G20).[30] This implies that every aborted child inflicts an economic damage on the US economy in the form of lost income.

Can we estimate that damage?

We begin by noting that the average productivity of an American is annual GDP per employed person, which was $131,812[31] in 2019.[32] (We use data for 2019, since these are not affected by the Covid pandemic.) Next we calculate his or her average years in the workforce by multiplying Americans' years of age by their age-specific participation rates, i.e., the percentage of Americans in that age group being in the workforce.[33] Then we multiply their years in the workforce by their age-dependent productivity, assuming that Americans' relative productivity over the life-cycle is reflected by relative weekly earnings over the life-cycle.[34] Finally, we take the present value over their lifetimes; that is, we sum up their average productivity over the ages of their lifetime and discount the values after their first entry into the workforce. We assume an annual real (i.e., inflation-adjusted) interest rate of 4 percent, which is realistic for the US economy. This yields an estimate

29. Michael Giandrea and Shawn Sprague, "Estimating the U.S. Labor Share," *Monthly Labor Review*, U.S. Bureau of Labor Statistics, February 2017, https://doi.org/10.21916/mlr.2017.7.
30. See "Labour Share of GDP, Comprising Wages and Social Protection Transfers," Sustainable Development Goals, United Nations Economic Commission for Europe, https://w3.unece.org/SDG/en/Indicator?id=30.
31. All values are in US dollars.
32. "Level of GDP Per Capita and Productivity," Organisation for Economic Co-operation and Development, https://stats.oecd.org/index.aspx?DataSetCode=PDB_LV.
33. "Employment Status of the Civilian Noninstitutional Population by Age, Sex, and Race," Labor Force Statistics from the Current Population Survey, U.S. Bureau of Labor Statistics, https://www.bls.gov/cps/aa2019/cpsaat03.htm.
34. Table 3 under "Access to Historical Data for the Tables of the Usual Weekly Earnings of Wage and Salary Workers," U.S. Bureau of Labor Statistics, https://www.bls.gov/webapps/legacy/cpswktab3.htm.

of average lifetime productivity and, therefore, an estimate of the economic loss to the US economy from aborting a child.

This number is 14.5 times the annual GDP per employed person, or $1.91 million. This is the loss of economic wealth the US economy incurs due to an abortion in 2019. Take this times the number of aborted per year, which was 629,898 in 2019 according to CDC data,[35] and you have the estimated economic cost of abortion. The result is a loss of wealth due to abortions in 2019 of $1.2 trillion, roughly 1.1 percent of total household wealth in the US in 2019,[36] or 5.6 percent of annual economic output in 2019. Clearly, abortion inflicts a serious economic damage on the US economy.

The discount factor obviously plays a large role in these calculations. In the above calculations, we assumed that there is no productivity growth over the lifetime of a person born today. This is clearly unrealistic in light of past evidence. Productivity growth effectively reduces the annual discount rate. If productivity grows at an average rate of 1 percent over the lifetime of the individual (conservative estimate), the relevant real interest rate falls to 3 percent and his lifetime production is 17.9 times annual production. The discounted value of an individual's lifetime production would be $2.36 million.

Some people object to this, arguing that abortion is necessary to keep overpopulation in check. For example, Mumford and Kessel argued in 1986 that developed countries needed to maintain an abortion rate of 201 to 500 per 1,000 live births to keep their population growth rates close to 1 percent or less.[37] Max Kummerow claims that opposition to abortion is today's equivalent of the Roman Catholic Church forcing Galileo to recant his claim that the earth revolves around the sun (which, incidentally, never happened).[38] Kummerow argues that abortion should be regarded as a valid instrument of keeping population growth in check, which, he proposes, is necessary to assure that mankind does not deplete Earth's resources.

---

35. Katherine Kortsmit et al., "Abortion Surveillance—United States, 2019," *Surveillance Summaries* 70, no. 9 (November 26, 2021): 1–29, CDC, https://www.cdc.gov/mmwr/volumes/70/ss/ss7009a1.htm.

36. Credit Suisse Research Institute, *Global Wealth Report 2019*, 44.

37. S. D. Mumford and E. Kessel, "Role of Abortion in Control of Global Population Growth," *Clinical Obstetrics and Gynecology* 13, no. 1 (March 1986): 19–31.

38. Max Kummerow, "Reproductive Biology of Abortion," The Overpopulation Project, January 13, 2019, https://overpopulation-project.com/reproductive-biology-of-abortion/.

Such arguments seem plausible, but lack economic substance. Kummerow refers to the (in)famous "Meadows Report," published as *The Limits to Growth* by the think tank Club of Rome in 1972, as well as its update published in 2004.[39] Both reports argue that unless mankind manages to reduce population growth by all means, the current economic system will collapse. The original report predicted that collapse would occur around 2010. It also predicted that the world would run out of crude oil by that time. Neither one has happened.

Why not? Because the authors of these and similar reports are engineers who do not understand economics. The economics of resource depletion is that when resources become scarce, their prices increase and this creates incentives in a variety of directions: economizing on the use of these resources, increasing the use of recycled materials, investing in new technologies to detect and exploit resource deposits. Today, the estimated time to deplete currently known crude oil deposits at current extraction rates is about forty to fifty years from now, very similar to what the 1972 report foresaw. In the developed world, the oil intensity of economic production, measured in terms of barrels of crude oil per $1,000 of GDP, has declined by 56 percent since 1973.[40] Because of the "green revolution," the development of more productive rice plants and other grains, there is no food scarcity in principle on earth today. The world's food supply in terms of calories per day per capita has increased by 34 percent between 1947 and 2018. Today's level of 2,928 calories well exceeds the daily need per person of 1,800 calories calculated by the Food and Agricultural Organization (FAO), a branch of the United Nations. Still, the FAO estimates that some 690 million people globally, or 8.9 percent of the world's population suffer from chronic hunger today.[41] But they do so because they lack *access* to food, not because food itself is lacking. Human greed and hatred toward other human beings are the causes of hunger. This goes right to the heart of the Christian faith: 690 million people starve from a lack of brotherly love.

---

39. Donella Meadows et al., *The Limits to Growth* (Universe Books, 1972), http://www.donellameadows.org/wp-content/userfiles/Limits-to-Growth-digital-scan-version.pdf.

40. Christof Rühl and Titus Erker, executive summary in "Oil Intensity: The Curiously Steady Decline of Oil in GDP," Center on Global Energy Policy at Columbia University SIPA, September 9, 2021, https://www.energypolicy.columbia.edu/research/report/oil-intensity-curiously-steady-decline-oil-gdp.

41. FAO, IFAD, UNICEF, WFP and WHO, *The State of Food Security and Nutrition in the World 2020* (Rome: FAO, 2020), ch. 1, https://www.fao.org/3/ca9692en/online/ca9692en.html#chapter-1_1.

Overpopulation is not the problem. In fact, given today's state of agricultural productivity, the world could sustain a population larger by 62 percent. Even the wildest population forecasts do not foresee such an increase. Population growth rates have long been falling. To the best of our knowledge, the world's population will reach 10 billion by 2050 and then first stagnate and finally decline.

Obviously, then, abortion is not required to keep population growth in check and prevent a global hunger crisis. Ultimately, killing a baby is the most explicit expression of denying him access to food and all other parts of the comforts of life. Call it greed and hatred, if you wish. An economic rationale for abortion simply does not exist.

Devaluing One Devalues All

In modern society, the rights of the underprivileged are top government priorities. Every good citizen will champion the unique gifts that these groups bring to society as a whole. Why does this not hold true for those being murdered in their mother's wombs? Why does society not hear their voices too? To speak bluntly about the hypocrisy, the very voices that vociferously condemn any slightest insensitivity toward the underprivileged are the same voices that aggressively promote the continuance of our slaughter of the unborn. The same voices known for denouncing the slightest indifference toward the plight of other underrepresented ethnic, racial, or socioeconomic minorities show not the slightest concern for that most underrepresented of all minorities, the unborn.

Keep in mind that devaluing the rights of others is a slippery slope. Those protections found in the United States Constitution are predicated on God's creation of men equal in His sight. Abortion denies this truth that is fundamental to the rule of law. Abortion disenfranchises an entire category of unrepresented across our society, consigning them to death. Our nation's fathers in past generations declared their slaves to be worth only three-fifths of other men in representation.[42] As unjust as our past laws were, though, today we have decayed to such a morally degraded state that we say the unborn are worth nothing at all. Early twentieth-century laws

---

42. To this point, embryos (i.e., embryos created via IVF) are transferred from one person to another under property law in the United States, denying them personhood.

were enacted to prevent "deficient" people from "breeding."[43] Today, we have enacted laws denying the unborn birth itself.

How can any society that denies the rights of its unborn claim to value the rights of any other class of vulnerable persons? What madness is it that drives a society to protect a host of special people groups while decreeing the wholesale slaughter of its own children? Any society that refuses to defend its innocent and defenseless babies highlights the high hypocrisy of every other social justice it preens itself over. If unborn children are devalued, every other group is as well, and so are we all. Mother Teresa speaks truly:

> America needs no words from me to see how your decision in *Roe v. Wade* has deformed a great nation. The so-called right to abortion has pitted mothers against their children and women against men. It has sown violence and discord at the heart of the most intimate human relationships. It has aggravated the derogation of the father's role in an increasingly fatherless society. It has portrayed the greatest of gifts—a child—as a competitor, an intrusion, and an inconvenience. It has nominally accorded mothers unfettered dominion over the independent lives of their physically dependent sons and daughters. And, in granting this unconscionable power, it has exposed many women to unjust and selfish demands from their husbands or other sexual partners. Human rights are not a privilege conferred by government. They are every human being's entitlement by virtue of his humanity. The right to life does not depend, and must not be declared to be, contingent on the pleasure of anyone else, not even a parent or a sovereign.[44]

The History and Destruction of the Unborn's "Right to Life" in the West

Today, any discussion of man's interaction with his fellow man in society introduces the notion of rights. This is true above all on the matter of laws, mores, and customs protecting unborn babies from being killed. For several

---

43. Daniel Kevles, "Eugenics and Human Rights," *The BMJ* 319 (August 14, 1999): 435–438, https://www.ncbi.nlm.nih.gov/pmc/articles/PMC1127045/.
44. Mother Teresa, "Notable and Quotable," *Wall Street Journal*, February 25, 1994, A14.

hundred years now, Christian philosophers and theorists have recognized that God, as Creator and the Source of all political equity and liberty, has given man as the crown of His creation certain rights that flow from his identity as the crown of God's creation and possessor of the *imago Dei*. Chief among these is a right to life.[45]

Yet a Christian must tread carefully here. In the last two hundred years here in the West, and with amazing speed in the late twentieth and early twenty-first centuries, rights have proliferated. Almost everything is declared a right: healthcare, housing, food security, education, euthanasia—even access to the internet. Perhaps compensating for the lack of substance to such claims, people declare almost anything desired a fundamental human right. With such a plethora of rights, the meaning of human rights has depreciated socially and morally.

Thirty years ago, an American legal dictionary defined "right" fairly accurately as follows:

> As a noun, and taken in the *concrete* sense, a power, privilege, faculty, or demand, inherent in one person and incident upon another. Rights are defined generally as "powers of free action." And the primal rights pertaining to men are enjoyed by human beings purely as such, being grounded in personality, and existing antecedently to their recognition in positive law. But leaving the abstract moral sphere, and giving to the term juristic content, a "right" is well defined as "a capacity residing in one man of controlling, with the assent and assistance of the state, the actions of others."[46]

This is a useful rendering of the meaning in several respects. First, one

---

45. Cf. John Locke, *Second Treatise of Government* 2.6: "The state of nature has a law of nature to govern it, which obliges every one: and reason, which is that law, teaches all mankind, who will but consult it, that being all equal and independent, no one ought to harm another in his life, health, liberty, or possessions: for men being all the workmanship of one omnipotent, and infinitely wise maker; all the servants of one sovereign master, sent into the world by his order, and about his business; they are his property, whose workmanship they are, made to last during his, not one another's pleasure: and being furnished with like faculties, sharing all in one community of nature, there cannot be supposed any such subordination among us, that may authorize us to destroy one another, as if we were made for one another's uses, as the inferior ranks of creatures are for our's. Every one, as he is bound to preserve himself, and not to quit his station wilfully, so by the like reason, when his own preservation comes not in competition, ought he, as much as he can, to preserve the rest of mankind, and may not, unless it be to do justice on an offender, take away, or impair the life, or what tends to the preservation of the life, the liberty, health, limb, or goods of another."

46. *Black's Law Dictionary* 1324 (6th ed. 1990). Emphasis in original.

man's right always implies another man's corresponding duty. Second, not all rights are of equal importance. Third, natural rights (referred to in the definition as "primal") exist independently of and prior to recognition in man's law. In other words, man's law does not create or grant such rights; man's law can only discern and enforce them. Fourth, a man may invoke the state to vindicate his right against another man.

This meaning applies perfectly to the right to life. First, a man is obligated to avoid taking the life of another man unless justified by self-defense, just war, or the exercise of capital punishment. Second, the right to life is of paramount importance. Without life, it is impossible to exercise any other right. Third, God gives a man life, and thus a right to life that civil authorities must recognize and faithfully secure. In other words, civil authorities do not grant and cannot withdraw (unless justified) a man's right to life. Fourth, a man can invoke the power of the state to secure his life against harm from another man.

In the formulation of the American Declaration of Independence, government is instituted to secure a man's basic rights, including his right to life: "all men are created equal, that they are endowed by their Creator with certain unalienable Rights, that among these are Life, Liberty and the pursuit of Happiness. That to secure these rights, Governments are instituted among Men . . ."

We must recognize that a government itself violates the right to life when, having the ability to do so, it refuses to secure any man's life from dangers. When civil authorities neglect their duty to protect life on a mass scale over a long period, they nearly forfeit their reason for existence. Government, because of its obligation to defend the oppressed from the predator, shares culpability when it refuses to protect the unborn. It is not simply a matter of one private individual committing harm against another private individual. Some civil authorities themselves will be judged by God for their active sin of commission in legitimating abortion as lawful; other civil authorities will be judged for their sins of omission in failing to protect vulnerable unborn lives.

The Fifth Amendment to the US Constitution (ratified in 1791) protects the right to life: "No person shall be . . . deprived of life, liberty, or property, without due process of law." The Fourteenth Amendment (ratified in 1868) similarly protects the right to life from deprivation by the

State: "nor shall any State deprive any person of life, liberty, or property, without due process of law."

British common law recognized an unborn child's right to life at quickening:

> I. The right of personal security consists in a person's legal and uninterrupted enjoyment of his life, his limbs, his body, his health, and his reputation.
> 1. Life is the immediate gift of God, a right inherent by nature in every individual; and it begins in contemplation of law as soon as an infant is able to stir in the mother's womb. For if a woman is quick with child, and by a potion or otherwise, killeth it in her womb; or if any one beat her, whereby the child dieth in her body, and she is delivered of a dead child; this, though not murder, was by the ancient law homicide or manslaughter. But the modern law doth not look upon this offence in quite so atrocious a light, but merely as a heinous misdemeanor.[47]

Medical science and knowledge advanced in the 1800s, making it impossible to cavil that life begins at any time other than at conception. These advancements also included the introduction of anesthesia and instruments to make childbirth safer and less agonizing. The American Medical Association led the effort to strengthen legal protections of the preborn through state statutes codified in the mid- to late-1800s. These protections expanded the civil authority's criminalization of abortion to include the killing of the preborn before quickening—at any time after the moment of conception. These laws also punished the advertising and use of abortifacient drugs, which to that point had been advertised in many newspapers and kept for sale by local druggists in a wink-wink, under-the-counter manner. This progress in protection of preborn life was in keeping with the general acknowledgment that the common law had defects which needed correction.

Bouvier's Law Dictionary, a then-respected law dictionary published in its third revision in 1914, indicates that the legal profession had modernized (in the best sense of the word) its formerly antiquated and ignorant understanding of the beginning of a preborn infant's life. In other words, the legal profession had rejected that life began at "quickening":

---

47. 1 William Blackstone, *Commentaries* 129–130.

It was formerly supposed that either the child was not alive until the time of quickening, or that it had acquired some new kind of existence that it did not possess before: hence the presumption of law that dates the life of the child from that time [i.e., quickening].

The child is, in truth, alive from the first moment of conception, and, according to its age and state of development, has different modes of manifesting its life, and, during a portion of the period of gestation, by its motion. By the growth of the embryo, the womb is enlarged until it becomes of too great a size to be contained in the pelvis, it then rises to the abdomen, when the motion of the foetus is for the first time felt.

Quickening as indicating a distinct point in the existence of the foetus has no foundation in physiology: for it arises merely from the relation which the organs of gestation bear to the parts that surround them; it may take place early or late, according to the condition of these different parts, but not from any inherent vitality for the first time manifested by the foetus.[48]

In the latter third of the twentieth century, *Griswold v. Connecticut*, *Roe v. Wade*, and *Doe v. Bolton* abolished these legal protections through what one Supreme Court Justice White (dissenting in *Roe v. Wade*) called a "raw exercise of judicial power." Thus judicial fiat established the mother as sole arbiter of her preborn child's life. Ignoring over a hundred years of scientific knowledge and medical advancements, the Supreme Court's abortion opinions were a retrograde movement back to a more primitive and barbaric (if not sophistical and self-interested) belief about the beginning of life.

Now, in 2022, in God's kind providence the unexpected has come to pass, as a majority of the Supreme Court in *Dobbs v. Jackson Women's Health Organization* has finally recognized what has been patently obvious to all: the penumbras of *Roe* were a legal fiction designed to grant the murder of children the protection of law, and such judicial inventions should not be allowed to stand as precedent. Without question, the overturning of *Roe* is a victory to those who have fought for years to remove this stench of legal manipulation from the books. Writing for the majority, Justice Alito speaks truly:

---

48. "Quickening," *Bouvier's Law Dictionary*, vol. 3, 3rd ed. (West Publishing, 1914), 2784–2785.

We hold that *Roe* and *Casey* must be overruled. The Constitution makes no reference to abortion, and no such right is implicitly protected by any constitutional provision. . . .

. . . *Roe*'s defenders characterize the abortion right as similar to the rights recognized in past decisions involving matters such as intimate sexual relations, contraception, and marriage, but abortion is fundamentally different, as both *Roe* and *Casey* acknowledged, because it destroys what those decisions called "fetal life" and what the law now before us describes as an "unborn human being."

. . . *Roe* was egregiously wrong from the start. Its reasoning was exceptionally weak, and the decision has had damaging consequences.[49]

That *Roe* has been overturned is a victory. Yet this victory must not blind Christians to what is glaringly absent in the majority opinion of *Dobbs*: the recognition of the personhood of the unborn child. Omission of this was perhaps understandable in previous ages, but as has been detailed here, the last two hundred years of scientific progress and discovery has rendered this failure inexcusable. *Dobbs* may result in repealing some of the barbarism on blatant display for the last fifty years, but it leaves us still inferior to even our recent forefathers in recognizing the personhood bestowed by God on every human being made in His image.

This failure of the *Dobbs* majority is compounded by their refusal to admit the abortifacient agency of much "contraception" today. In a section of their final *Dobbs* opinion added since the Alito draft was leaked, the majority defend themselves against attacks of the dissenters who would accuse them of abandoning *stare decisis*:[50]

> [T]he dissent suggests that our decision calls into question *Griswold, Eisenstadt, Lawrence,* and *Obergefell*. But we have stated unequivocally that "[n]othing in this opinion should be understood to cast doubt on

---

49. *Dobbs v. Jackson Women's Health Organization*, No. 19-1392, 2022 WL 2276808, at *7 (US June 24, 2022). This quote is from pp. 5–6 of Justice Alito's opinion published in the slip opinion in the morning on June 24, 2022, accessed June 24, 2022, https://www.supremecourt.gov/opinions/21pdf/19-1392_6j37.pdf.

50. *Stare decisis*: "a doctrine or policy of following rules or principles laid down in previous judicial decisions unless they contravene the ordinary principles of justice." *Merriam-Webster.com Dictionary*, Merriam-Webster, https://www.merriam-webster.com/dictionary/stare%20decisis.

precedents that do not concern abortion." We have also explained why that is so: rights regarding contraception and same-sex relationships are inherently different from the right to abortion because the latter (as we have stressed) uniquely involves what *Roe* and *Casey* termed "potential life."[51]

This statement begs the questions, "What is abortion?" and "What is contraception?" Their use of these terms is equivocal. They claim *Griswold* has nothing to do with "abortion," but only "contraception," yet much that is commonly called "contraception" today has an abortifacient agency. In the 1972 *Eisenstadt* decision, the Supreme Court declared an unmarried person had as much right to contraception as a married person. In support of this then newly-discovered penumbra, the majority reasoned:

> If the right of privacy means anything, it is the right of the *individual*, married or single, to be free from unwarranted governmental intrusion into matters so fundamentally affecting a person as the decision whether to bear or beget a child.[52]

The muddle of this reasoning (the fundamental right to decide whether to become pregnant with a child or whether, once pregnant, to continue carrying that child) has ascended to the *Dobbs* pantheon of untouchable precedent. Surely the *Dobbs* majority know—armed as they are with the best Ivy League pedigrees, the best law clerks, the best libraries, and briefs by the most skilled litigators—that certain contraceptive methods have abortifacient properties. *Roe* is gone, but chemical abortifacients will continue to do their deadly work under the faded banner of the Court's contraception precedents.

Earlier in the opinion, Justice Alito writes:

> The most striking feature of the dissent is the absence of any serious discussion of the legitimacy of the States' interest in protecting fetal life. This is evident in the analogy that the dissent draws between the abortion right and the rights recognized in *Griswold* (contraception). . . . [T]he dissent's analogy is objectionable for . . . what it reveals about the dissent's views on the protection of what *Roe* called "potential life." The exercise of the

---

51. *Dobbs*, 2022 WL 2276808, at *39 (slip op. at 71).
52. *Eisenstadt v. Baird*, 405 US 438, 453 (1972). Emphasis original.

rights at issue in *Griswold* . . . does not destroy a "potential life," but an abortion has that effect.

Here the majority point out that "the dissent evinces no similar regard for a State's interest in protecting prenatal life," adding "the viability line" upon which *Roe v. Wade* was based "makes no sense. It was not adequately justified in *Roe*, and the dissent does not even try to defend it today. Nor does it identify any other point in a pregnancy after which a State is permitted to prohibit the destruction of a fetus."

Finally, we read this stunning declaration:

> Our opinion is not based on any view about if and when prenatal life is entitled to any of the rights enjoyed after birth. The dissent, by contrast, would impose on the people a particular theory about when the rights of personhood begin. According to the dissent, the Constitution *requires* the States to regard a fetus as lacking even the most basic human right—to live—at least until an arbitrary point in a pregnancy has passed.[53]

Our justices bear the sword and thus hold the power, after the exercise of due process, to deprive a man of his life. Yet, these same justices feign to be impotent or ignorant in recognizing when a man's life begins. Our Court, instead, should have built their opinion on the rock of personhood beginning at the moment of conception. A man enjoys a right to life from the moment of conception. It's no theory or philosophy. It's a simple truth that not even the Beltway and all its pomps can efface. The Court should have done its duty and recognized an unborn child's right to life from the moment of conception.

The Witness of Church History

As Protestants, we hold that only the testimony of Scripture is infallible. Yet not all areas of Scripture are equally clear, so there has been significant

---

53. *Dobbs*, 2022 WL 2276808, at *23 (slip op. at 37–38). Emphasis original.

variation in many areas of doctrine across the history of the church. But on the matter of abortion, this has not been so. For over two thousand years, there has been unanimity in declaring abortion a grave evil and crime.

Long before God became flesh and dwelt among us, God's people abominated abortion.[54] Among the Jews, it was offensive, and indeed the Jews were famous for their hostility to both exposure[55] and abortion.[56] As was true with the later church fathers, there was debate and discussion on matters related to ensoulment and quickening, but deliberate abortion was considered a violation of the law of God, and an affront to the sanctity of life.[57] Former chief justice of the Supreme Rabbinical Court of America, Rabbi Marvin S. Antelman, offers this summary:

> All major religions have their parochial and their universal aspects, and the problem of abortion is *not* a parochial one. It is of universal morality, and it is neither a Catholic problem, nor a Jewish problem, nor a Protestant problem. It involves the killing of a human being, an act forbidden by *universal* commandment.[58]

Similarly, Chief Rabbi Dr. Immanuel Jakobovits of the United Kingdom explains Jewish thinking on the value of human life:

> Jewish law sees every human life as having the sanctity of intrinsic and infinite worth. One life has as much value as one hundred or one thousand; you cannot multiply infinity and you cannot divide it. So every human being has an identical worth and is identically worth saving.[59]

---

54. For one of the best summaries of historical Jewish teaching on abortion, see J. David Bleich, "Abortion and Jewish Law," *New Perspectives on Human Abortion*, ed. Thomas Hilgers, Dennis Horan, and David Mall (Aletheia Books, 1981), 405–419.

55. As noted earlier, it was a common practice for Roman fathers to abandon their infant children to die of exposure.

56. Tacitus, *Histories* 5.5: "Yet they [the Jews] take care that their multitude grows; for indeed to kill any of their children is unspeakable, and they hold that the souls of those killed in battle or by penalty of death are immortal: hence their love of reproducing and their disregard for dying. They bury rather than burn their dead."

57. Thus Josephus, *Against Appion* 2.202: "[The Law] mandates that they raise all the children, and forbids women either from aborting the seed or from destroying it; but if any [woman] should appear [to have done this], she would be a child murderer, having destroyed a soul and diminished the race."

58. "Why Jews Oppose Abortion," *The Review of the News*, May 1, 1974, 1–6. Emphasis in the original.

59. As quoted in Bill Moloney, "Jewish View," *National Right to Life News*, June 1979, 6.

This care for the life of the unborn is precisely what we witness in the Jewish world recorded by the gospels. We see the affirmation of the agency of John the Baptist in the womb of Elizabeth, and her reaction thereto testifying to her son's personhood (Luke 1:41–45). We see the great care taken by Joseph and Mary for our Lord, which perfectly accords with a culture that affirmed the preciousness of life. We see the revulsion of the Apostle Matthew who, through the Holy Spirit, exposes Herod's murder of the innocents with no hint that it could ever be excusable (Matt. 2:16–18). And we see in our Lord's words the care for the unborn and the recognition of their personhood (John 16:21).[60]

With the development of the New Testament church, some of the defining features that had marked God's people began to change. With the abrogation of Old Testament ceremonial law and the expansion of faith and the covenant people to the Gentiles, many of the old distinguishing marks between God's chosen people and the rest of the world became obsolete. In such an environment, one might anticipate the stringency of earlier Judaic condemnations of abortion would be softened, or fall by the wayside.

What happened was just the opposite. Christian condemnations of abortion intensified beyond earlier Jewish ones. The Jews had focused on abortion as a crime against man, but Christians came to speak of abortion as a crime against God. Where Jewish rabbis had refrained from according status to the unborn, even carving out exceptions where abortion might be permitted,[61] Christians were adamant, speaking in absolute terms concerning its evil.

Opposition to abortion had previously been a feature of close-knit Jewish communities, but with the new Christian church crossing national boundaries, the rejection of abortion no longer remained an ethnic distinctive. It was now a fundamental moral commitment of the new, burgeoning, multiethnic Christian church. Jewish opprobrium towards abortion and the exposure of infants was common across the Roman Empire, but this opprobrium focused on their own communities. It was not so with the Christians. It was no longer enough for God's people to condemn abortion

---

60. Jesus speaks of "joy that a human being has been born into the world," indicating that the human being exists prior to birth. For more on the biblical teaching of personhood prior to birth, see the next section of this paper, "The Testimony of Scripture."

61. For more on this, see Daniel Schiff, "Evaluating Life," in *Abortion in Judaism* (Cambridge University Press, 2002), 27–57.

and exposure as unworthy of the covenant community, but now the Christian church opposed these murders even among the pagans—in rhetoric, in policy, and eventually in law. Most importantly, Christians rescued these little ones exposed by their pagan parents, taking them from the hillsides into their homes and adopting them as their own children. This act of Christian compassion was well-known across the Empire. It was a defining mark of these first Christians.

It is not surprising, then, that during the Apostolic Age and immediately thereafter, we find clear prohibitions of abortion in the writings of church fathers:

> You shalt not murder a child by abortion, nor kill that which is begotten.
> (*Didache* 2.2, AD 50–100)

> You shall not murder a child by abortion, nor in turn shall you kill him after it is born. (*Letter of Barnabas* 19, AD 80–130)

> All of life could proceed according to nature for us if we exert power over our desires from the beginning and do not by evil devices and schemes kill the human offspring, designed by divine forethought and intention. For those women who, to cover their immorality, use abortifacient drugs [*phthoriois pharmakois*] that expel the matter entirely dead, abort along with the embryo their own affection for mankind.
> (Clement, *The Tutor* 2.10.96.1, c. AD 198)

> But for us [Christians], since homicide has once for all been forbidden, it is not permitted to pull apart even what has been conceived in the womb. . . . Prevention of birth is hastened homicide; nor does it matter whether one tears away a life that has been born or pulls apart one in the midst of birth. He who will be a man is a man already: for indeed the entire fruit exists already in the seed.
> (Tertullian, *Defense of the Christians Against the Heathen* 9, c. AD 197)

> Therefore the fetus is a human being in the womb from the time that its form is complete. For also the law of Moses judges abortion worthy of penalties, given there exist already the rudiments of a man, since to him is

already allotted the condition of life and death when he is assigned to his fate—even though, by still living within the mother, he shares his fate for the most part with her. (Tertullian, *A Treatise on the Soul* 37, AD 208–212)

When a woman has with intentionality destroyed (*phtheirasa*) a fetus, she is held to be guilty of murder. No fastidious distinction (*akribologia*) between "completely formed" and "unformed" exists with us. For in this case not only the child about to be born will be vindicated, but also the woman herself who plotted against herself: inasmuch in most cases women perish from such attempts. And there is added to this also a second murder, the destruction (*phthora*) of the embryo—at least as far as the purpose of those who dare these things.

(Basil, *Letter to Amphilocus on the Canons* 188.2, fourth century AD)

Also, the rich themselves, lest their inheritance be divided among many, kill their own offspring in the womb, and by parricidal liquids they snuff out the children of the womb in the genital organs themselves—and life is taken away before it be imparted. Who except man has taught us how to renounce our own sons? (Ambrose, *Hexameron* 5.18.58, AD 386–390)[62]

You shall not use magic. You shall not use potions; for He says, You shall not permit witches [*lit.*, potionists] to live. You shall not slay your child by abortion, nor kill that which is begotten; for everything that has been formed and has received a soul from God shall be avenged if slain, as unjustly destroyed. (*Apostolic Constitutions* 7.1.3, AD 375–380)

Some, when they know they have conceived through wickedness, turn to abortive drugs; often, when they too have themselves perished, they are brought to the lower world guilty of three crimes: suicide, adultery against Christ, and parricide of their unborn child. (Jerome, *Letters* 22.13, c. AD 384)

Indeed, sometimes this lustful cruelty or cruel lust [*libidinosa crudelitas vel libido crudelis*] extends so far that it obtains poisons of sterility [*sterilitatis*

---

62. "Ipsae quoque divites, ne per plures suum patrimonium dividatur, in utero proprios necant fetus, et parricidalibus succis in ipso genitali alvo pignora sui ventris exstinguunt, priusque aufertur vita quam tradatur. Quis docuit nisi homo filios abdicari?"

venena]; and, if nothing else works, [it] snuffs out and breaks up by some means the offspring conceived in the womb, preferring its own offspring to perish before it lives [*prius interire quam vivere*]; or, if it was already living in the womb, to be killed before being born [*occidi antequam nasci*].
(Augustine, *On Marriage and Concupiscence* 1.17 [15], AD 419–420)[63]

Over a millennium later, the Protestant reformers repeated this condemnation of abortion—always a distinctive mark of Christian morality and charity:

How great, therefore, the wickedness of human nature is! How many girls there are who prevent conception and kill and expel tender fetuses, although procreation is the work of God! Indeed, some spouses who marry and live together in a respectable manner have various ends in mind, but rarely children. The God who declares that we are to be fruitful and multiply regards it as a great evil when human beings destroy their offspring.
(Martin Luther, comments on Gen. 25:1–4)[64]

The foetus, though enclosed in the womb of its mother, is already a human being, and it is almost a monstrous crime to rob it of the life which it has not yet begun to enjoy. If it seems more horrible to kill a man in his own house than in a field, because a man's house is his place of most secure refuge, it ought surely to be deemed more atrocious to destroy a foetus in the womb before it has come to light. (John Calvin, comments on Exod. 21:22ff.)[65]

From ancient times down to the present day, the position of the church across all its branches—Roman Catholic, Orthodox, and Protestant—has been adamant and unchanging: abortion in all its manifestations is a grave, unspeakable evil:

---

63. "Aliquando eo usque pervenit haec libidinosa crudelitas vel libido crudelis, ut etiam sterilitatis venena procuret et si nihil valuerit, conceptos fetus aliquo modo intra viscera exstinguat ac fundat, volendo suam prolem prius interire quam vivere, aut si in utero iam vivebat, occidi ante quam nasci. Prorsus si ambo tales sunt, coniuges non sunt; et si ab initio tales fuerunt, non sibi per connubium, sed per stuprum potius convenerunt."

64. *Lectures on Genesis Chapters 21–25*, ed. Jaroslav Pelikan, vol. 4 in *Luther's Works* (St. Louis: Concordia, 1955–1986), 304.

65. Trans. Charles William Bingham (1852), in *Harmony of the Law*, vol. 3, The Ages Digital Library Commentary (Books for the Ages, 1998), 32.

Throughout Christianity's two thousand year history, this same doctrine of condemning all direct abortions has been constantly taught by the Fathers of the Church and by her Pastors and Doctors. Even scientific and philosophical discussions about the precise moment of the infusion of the spiritual soul have never given rise to any hesitation about the moral condemnation of abortion.[66]

The Testimony of Scripture

Leaving all other arguments to the side, Scripture's authority is absolute. Scripture is not the word of man, but the Word of God. We must submit our judgments concerning abortion to Scripture, where the duty of God's people to uphold His image placed in mankind is everywhere revealed, both implicitly and explicitly.

Imago Dei

We begin with the doctrine from which flows the clearest condemnation of abortion. God created man in His own image:

> Then God said, "Let Us make man in Our image, according to Our likeness; and let them rule over the fish of the sea and over the birds of the sky and over the cattle and over all the earth, and over every creeping thing that creeps on the earth." God created man in His own image, in the image of God He created him; male and female He created them. God blessed them; and God said to them, "Be fruitful and multiply, and fill the earth, and subdue it; and rule over the fish of the sea and over the birds of the sky and over every living thing that moves on the earth."
> (Gen. 1:26–28)

While all creation proclaims God's glory, the singularity of man is clearly

---

66. John Paul II, *Evangelium Vitae*, § 61.

stated to be that he alone—both male and female—bears the *imago Dei*. None of the rest of God's creatures bear His image and likeness, and although we may argue concerning the precise meaning of "image" and "likeness," God doesn't leave us guessing as to its central significance in life-and-death matters.

We find this significance stated in connection with Scripture's second mention of man bearing God's image and likeness in Genesis 9:

> And God blessed Noah and his sons and said to them, "Be fruitful and multiply, and fill the earth. The fear of you and the terror of you will be on every beast of the earth and on every bird of the sky; with everything that creeps on the ground, and all the fish of the sea, into your hand they are given. Every moving thing that is alive shall be food for you; I give all to you, as I gave the green plant. Only you shall not eat flesh with its life, that is, its blood. Surely I will require your lifeblood; from every beast I will require it. And from every man, from every man's brother I will require the life of man.
>
> > "Whoever sheds man's blood,
> > By man his blood shall be shed,
> > For in the image of God
> > He made man.
> > "As for you, be fruitful and multiply;
> > Populate the earth abundantly and multiply in it."
>
> (Gen. 9:1–7)

Today, intellectuals, philosophers, and scientists (as well as some pastors and theologians) join together in assuring man that God is not his Maker, and he need not fear returning to God for judgment following his death. They contradict Scripture's declaration, "It is He who hath made us, and not we ourselves" (Ps. 100:3). From their fervid religious commitment to evolution, they declare the opposite: "It is not He who hath made us, but we ourselves."

Abortion is the godless pagans' most terrible violation of nature, but this violation didn't start with abortion. It began with their denial that God created all things, and that man as male and female is the crown of

His creation. Consider the ways the text above from Genesis 9 teaches this truth and could not be more contrary to the spirit of our age.

First, through Noah, God commands the race He named "man" (Hebrew *'ādām*) to "be fruitful, and multiply, and fill the earth." Not just "be fruitful," but "multiply." Not just "multiply," but "fill the earth." This series of commands is then repeated at the end of the passage.

Man is God's priority on His earth, and He goes on to make man's primacy more clear by declaring, as a blessing, that man will strike "fear" and be a "terror" to all other creatures. This is God's doing, and therefore it is good. Then He makes it even more clear by stating to man concerning all other creatures of His creation, "into your hand they are given."

He adds that, just like plants, animals are His gift to man for food, and that man is free to kill the creatures, whereas the creatures are forbidden to kill man: "Surely I will require your lifeblood; from every beast I will require it."

Then, not only animals are forbidden to kill man, but man himself is forbidden to kill man. Why? Because man is God's image-bearer:

> Whoever sheds man's blood,
> By man his blood shall be shed,
> For in the image of God
> He made man.

Flip this upside down and we have the spirit of our age. Man's population must decline. Man must discipline his fecundity so that his numbers on the earth stop expanding and begin to contract. Rather than subduing the earth and its creatures, man must subdue his multiplication because his multiplication is unsustainable. Man must not rule creation. Such anthropocentric thinking is not creation-keeping, but creation-destroying.

Contradicting God, the spirit of our age declares nature must not serve man, but man must serve nature. It declares there is no distinction in principle between man and animal, and thus the high priest of paganism, Princeton ethicist Peter Singer, writes:

> My suggestion, then, is that we accord the fetus no higher moral status than we give to a nonhuman animal at a similar level of rationality,

self-consciousness, awareness, capacity to feel and so on. Because no fetus is a person, no fetus has the same claim to life as a person. Until a fetus has some capacity for conscious experience, an abortion terminates an existence that is—considered as it is and not in terms of its potential—more like that of a plant than of a sentient animal like a dog or a cow.[67]

We see how deeply this rebellion against God has infiltrated the church in any number of ways, but note particularly how many believers choose dogs and cats over children. Also note how many Christians today decline to eat the very animals God gave us to eat when He declared, they "shall be food for you." Of course, Christians who are vegans and vegetarians are eager to reassure other believers this is only their preference—not their principle. But note how meatlessness grows in the church even as Singer promotes his ethical anarchy—and then the entire world prattles on about cruelty to animals and free-range chickens. Five centuries ago, Calvin made this observation which is still true:

> It is usual with hypocrites to reckon it a greater crime to kill a flea than to kill a man.[68]

Given this flipping of God's order of creation, it should surprise no one that we've also flipped capital punishment upside down. God commands that murderers be executed because murder destroys an image-bearer. Today, though, man outlaws the execution of murderers. Today, it's murderers who awaken the compassion of men and women. Murderers are protected from execution while innocent babies are abandoned.

The various Green advocates of sustainability have repudiated God as the Creator of the universe, and have thus inevitably denied man's dignity as the crown of God's creation. These pagans have replaced the truths of God with the worship of creation, ushering back into Christendom the very idolatries and sexual perversions condemned by the Apostle Paul in the first chapter of his letter to the church in Rome. Refusing to honor and give thanks to their Creator, pagans are turned over by God to the same

---

67. Peter Singer, *Practical Ethics* (Cambridge University Press, 1993), 136.
68. Calvin, comments on John 18:28, *Commentary on the Gospel According to John*, vol. 2 trans. William Pringle (Wipf & Stock, 2021), 205.

unimaginable horrors that led God to command the sons of Israel to wipe out the Canaanites of the Promised Land.

The image of God marks man's whole being, body and soul. Thus to kill a man is to destroy God's image in that man, and thus openly defy the God who placed it there. To kill a man or woman, boy or girl, is wrong not only because of the harm done to the individual, but also because of the assault upon God. When one man murders another, it is an act of war against God. God declares the shedding of innocent blood pollutes the land and must be avenged by the execution of the manslayer:

> So you shall not pollute the land in which you are; for blood pollutes the land and no expiation can be made for the land for the blood that is shed on it, except by the blood of him who shed it. You shall not defile the land in which you live. (Num. 35:33–34)

"Your Hands Formed Me"

God is Creator, and every child conceived reveals the purposeful and formative hand of God in His design.[69] Scientific advancement has done much to open up the astonishing nature of conception, yet this ought not cause us to be materialists in our understanding, supposing that new life can be explained simply in terms of sperm, egg, DNA, mitosis, and so on. To be sure, our Lord shows us His glory through these means, but He also fashions each child in invisible, spiritual, and unfathomable ways:

> Just as you do not know the path of the wind and how bones are formed in the womb of the pregnant woman, so you do not know the activity of God who makes all things. (Eccles. 11:5)

Abortion is an assault on this secret and divine creation. It takes the greatest mystery in our lives, the creation of life, and destroys it. It takes one of God's greatest mercies to sinful man and mocks it. It is an extolling of death, and thus a denial of God. God creates life. Satan hates and destroys life.

---

69. Psalms 119:73; 139:13.

Woman as Life-Giver

The gift of procreation was only given to man when God created woman. As companion to Adam, she was to be a help meet (fitting or suitable) for him, and central to that suitability for man is woman's gift of bringing life into the world. When Adam named her "Eve" ("living one," or "life-giver"), this was not merely descriptive, but prescriptive:

> Now the man called his wife's name Eve, because she was the mother of all the living. (Gen. 3:20)

> Now the man had relations with his wife Eve, and she conceived and gave birth to Cain, and she said, "I have gotten a manchild with the help of the LORD." (Gen. 4:1)

> God created man in His own image, in the image of God He created him; male and female He created them. God blessed them; and God said to them, "Be fruitful and multiply, and fill the earth, and subdue it." (Gen. 1:27–28)

Life-giving is fundamental to the mission of woman. God is pleased to bring life into this world through her:

> For as the woman originates from the man, so also the man has his birth through the woman; and all things originate from God. (1 Cor. 11:12)

Life-giving is woman's highest calling and most noble purpose. This is not to say woman's only value is her ability to give life. Many women are single. Many married women have not had their wombs opened by God. Nevertheless, to declare that God created woman's physiology, nature, and being as life-giver is no abuse of women who are childless. It is simply to state what is the doctrine of Scripture and has been obvious to all men everywhere across the ages. Moreover, this blessing of God will continue to be obvious both in Scripture and nature until our Lord returns. We may strive against it and seek to twist and deform our sisters, daughters, and wives until their lives are a visible effort to deny this truth, but nature and nature's God will have the victory.

It is this life-giving nature of woman that abortion attacks. Turning God's creation and distinctions upside down once more, the modern worshiper of Molech tells woman that God's greatest gift is only a gift if she herself desires it. He repeats the serpent's lies, assuring woman that by denying God's command she may be like God.

Thus, Satan promises the very thing we lose if we believe his lies: fertility. Human and child sacrifice have been connected with fertility cults down through history. "Molech" may be a separate deity that we know little about, but the name may also simply be an epithet for Baal,[70] the Canaanite god of fertility.

Why would a woman sacrifice her child?

Dr. Josephine Quinn of Oxford University's Faculty of Classics suggests that Carthaginians did it because they believed "the good the sacrifice could bring the family or community as a whole outweighed the life of the child."[71] Likewise, in 2013 an author in *Salon* acknowledged the same motivation for abortion, saying, "She understands that [abortion] saves lives not just in the most medically literal way, but in the roads that women who have choice then get to go down, in the possibilities for them and for their families. And I would put the life of a mother over the life of a fetus every single time—even if I still need to acknowledge my conviction that the fetus is indeed a life. A life worth sacrificing."[72]

Similarly, in 2010, the "Urban Shaman and ritual expert" Mama Donna Henes wrote an article in *HuffPost* titled "Harvest Rites: The Connection Between Fertility and Sacrifice." She begins her explanation of the fertility benefits of human sacrifice as follows:

> At the harvest, one can easily imagine that the Earth Goddess has offered up Her life in the form of the fruits of the land, and that in doing so, She

---

70. One biblical argument for this position is that "the pagan altars in the valley of Ben-Hinnom where children were sacrificed are also described as altars to Ba'al by the prophet Jeremiah." Caleb Strom, "Was Moloch Really Ba'al, the Ancient God Who Demanded Child Sacrifice?" Ancient Origins, February 10, 2019, https://www.ancient-origins.net/myths-legends-asia/identity-moloch-0011457. For more information, see the sources referenced Strom, as well as the references in the article on "Moloch" on Wikipedia, https://en.wikipedia.org/wiki/Moloch#References.

71. "Ancient Carthaginians Really Did Sacrifice Their Children," News & Events, University of Oxford, January 23, 2014, https://www.ox.ac.uk/news/2014-01-23-ancient-carthaginians-really-did-sacrifice-their-children.

72. Mary Elizabeth Williams, "So What If Abortion Ends Life?" *Salon*, January 23, 2013, https://www.salon.com/2013/01/23/so_what_if_abortion_ends_life/.

commits the supreme sacrifice. She expends all of Her generative energy. It is as if Mother Nature in autumn is in the midst of Her menopause, Her sacred seed spent. In grateful response, people fed Her fresh blood to replenish Her powers of procreation.[73]

She then proceeds to recount unapologetically the cruel, barbaric practices from civilizations around the world that have given themselves to human sacrifice in a quest for fertility. Starting with "the Kandhs of Bengal" who "sacrificed a person for the Earth Goddess, Tari Pennu, in order to ensure healthy crops," then moving to "the Uraons of Chota Nagpur [who] offered human sacrifices to Anna Kuari, who blesses the harvest. And the Lhota Naga of Brahmapootra severed the heads, hands and feet of their victims and planted them in the fields for fertilizer." She then describes the Aztecs: "At the celebration of the broom harvest of the Earth Mother, first an older woman, and then a young girl were beheaded and their blood spread on fruit, seeds and grain to guarantee abundance." After numerous other examples, she concludes with a defense of the practices:

> With the martyred death of the sacrificial victim, the fertile blood seed, like the grain, brings life anew to the world. And, thus, the circle is complete. The death of the old grain, the old sun, the old season, feeds the continuing life of the people. The death of a representative person is then offered in obeisance as repayment of the ultimate debt of life. Death feeds life feeds death, the enduring saga of the eternal cycle of survival.

So it is today as women seek control over their own fertility, sacrificing some children in order to have others through IVF, or choosing the sacrifice of abortion, supposedly for the sake of the financial benefits that will accrue to her and the greater community as a result. This is nothing less than blood sacrifice to the goddess of fertility.

Thus this beautiful creature, woman, whom God has made life-giver, enticed by the serpent and his willing helpers, turns her womb into a grave. She is convinced her individual destiny, the integrity of her personhood, and the well-being of the community require her to destroy the life God gave her as a blessing to husband, family, and God's green earth.

73. October 4, 2010, https://www.huffpost.com/entry/harvest-rites-blood-for-b_b_746169.

God as Sanctifier of Birth

God sanctifies and calls us from the womb. Not only does He form and fashion our substance, but from the womb He also establishes our course and sets our feet on His path. Note His words to the prophet Jeremiah:

> Before I formed you in the womb I knew you,
> And before you were born I consecrated you;
> I have appointed you a prophet to the nations.
> (Jer. 1:5)

Through his movements inside his mother, the yet-to-be-born prophet John the Baptist testified to the presence and glory of our yet-to-be-born Savior Jesus Christ, who was then inside the womb of His mother, Mary:

> When Elizabeth heard Mary's greeting, the baby leaped in her womb; and Elizabeth was filled with the Holy Spirit. And she cried out with a loud voice and said, "Blessed are you among women, and blessed is the fruit of your womb! And how has it happened to me, that the mother of my Lord would come to me? For behold, when the sound of your greeting reached my ears, the baby leaped in my womb for joy." (Luke 1:41–44)

To the ancient world, the true scandal of Christianity was not so much the divinity of our Lord, but His manhood. It was unthinkable the divine Word would enter into physical creation, take on human flesh, and experience the suffering, indignity, and weakness of our mortal frame. Yet conceived by the Holy Spirit and born of a woman, our Lord sanctified what was considered the indignity of man and woman's corporeal existence:

> "For thou," says He in the Psalms, "art He that took Me out of the womb." Mark that carefully, He that took Me out of the womb, signifying that He was begotten without man, being taken from a virgin's womb and flesh. For the manner is different with those who are begotten according to the course of marriage.
>
> And from such members He is not ashamed to assume flesh, who is the framer of those very members. But then who tells us this? The Lord says

ABORTION'S ASSAULT UPON GOD'S CHARACTER AND LAW

unto Jeremiah: "Before I formed you in the belly, I knew you: and before you came forth out of the womb, I sanctified you." ... It is God who even now creates the children in the womb, as it is written in Job, "Have you not poured me out as milk, and curdled me like cheese? You have clothed me with skin and flesh, and hast knit me together with bones and sinews." There is nothing polluted in the human frame except a man defile this with fornication and adultery. He who formed Adam formed Eve also, and male and female were formed by God's hands. None of the members of the body as formed from the beginning is polluted. Let the mouths of all heretics be stopped who slander their bodies, or rather Him who formed them.[74]

That the ineffable God should become the weakest of all creatures, an embryo seeking to attach himself to his mother's womb, opposed all the wisdom of the world. Yet our Lord flew in the face of that wisdom, putting on eternal display the glory of the womb by His divine presence and occupancy there for nine months at the very inception of His incarnation. Conceived by the Holy Spirit there, He was nourished in the body of the Virgin Mary, dignifying for all time the glorious motherhood of conception, gestation, and birth. Thus every woman who presents her womb to God in obedience to His will of fruitfulness follows blessed Mary in her own submission of her life-givingness to her Creator.

Children as Gift from the Lord

Children are a gift from the Lord. This is the categorical and unequivocal declaration of God:

> Behold, children are a gift of the LORD,
> The fruit of the womb is a reward.
> Like arrows in the hand of a warrior,
> So are the children of one's youth.
> How blessed is the man whose quiver is full of them;
> They will not be ashamed
> When they speak with their enemies in the gate.
> (Ps. 127:3–5)

---

74. Cyril of Alexandria, *Catechetical Lectures* 12.25–26, trans. Edwin Hamilton Gifford.

Throughout Scripture, then, a barren womb is the occasion of grief. Elkanah's wife Hannah is typical in Scripture, which records that it was God who "closed her womb" and caused her heartache:

> When the day came that Elkanah sacrificed, he would give portions to Peninnah his wife and to all her sons and her daughters; but to Hannah he would give a double portion, for he loved Hannah, but the Lord had closed her womb. Her rival, however, would provoke her bitterly to irritate her, because the Lord had closed her womb. It happened year after year, as often as she went up to the house of the Lord, she would provoke her; so she wept and would not eat.
>
> Then Elkanah her husband said to her, "Hannah, why do you weep and why do you not eat and why is your heart sad? Am I not better to you than ten sons?" (1 Sam. 1:4–8)

Throughout the sacred text of Scripture, fruitfulness is declared one of God's greatest blessings. The endless statements that fruitfulness is God's blessing never vary. We may say without hesitation that children are still as much a blessing today as they were when God presented Eve to Adam, then Cain and Abel to Eve and Adam. Even the children of evil, pagan rulers are given by God's blessing and creative power (Gen. 20:18).

Murder Incompatible with God's Character

God's decrees flow from His character, and are the final standard for all ethics and law. His law from Genesis onward, revealed most directly in the Ten Commandments, explicitly forbids murder (Exod. 20:13). Who could ever conceive of this not including the murder of the unborn child? Is he not also our neighbor?

And what is the penalty for murder? Scripture declares murderers will not inherit the kingdom of God (1 John 3:15).

Man Accountable to God for the Shedding of Blood

Deuteronomy 21:1–9 teaches that God holds whole communities accountable for the shedding of innocent blood:

If a slain person is found lying in the open country in the land which the LORD your God gives you to possess, and it is not known who has struck him, then your elders and your judges shall go out and measure the distance to the cities which are around the slain one. It shall be that the city which is nearest to the slain man, that is, the elders of that city, shall take a heifer of the herd, which has not been worked and which has not pulled in a yoke; and the elders of that city shall bring the heifer down to a valley with running water, which has not been plowed or sown, and shall break the heifer's neck there in the valley. Then the priests, the sons of Levi, shall come near, for the LORD your God has chosen them to serve Him and to bless in the name of the LORD; and every dispute and every assault shall be settled by them. All the elders of that city which is nearest to the slain man shall wash their hands over the heifer whose neck was broken in the valley; and they shall answer and say, "Our hands did not shed this blood, nor did our eyes see it. Forgive Your people Israel whom You have redeemed, O LORD, and do not place the guilt of innocent blood in the midst of Your people Israel." And the bloodguiltiness shall be forgiven them. So you shall remove the guilt of innocent blood from your midst, when you do what is right in the eyes of the LORD.

Notice that even if the people are not guilty of slaying the man, nor of standing idly by when the crime was committed, they still bear responsibility before God for the innocent man's blood. They must investigate the death, ensure that justice is done as far as possible, make a sacrifice to atone for the blood, and, essentially, recommit themselves to protecting the innocent. Until they do all these things, God holds them responsible for bloodguilt.

God's Hatred for the Shedding of Blood

Alongside God's command not to murder our neighbor and our obligation to deal with the shedding of innocent blood is God's promise of justice to all whose blood is shed. He will vindicate those robbed by the murderer of their lives. His retributive justice will fall on the murderer (Gen. 4:10; 9:5; Deut. 19:10). This promise of God's retributive justice against the manslayer is repeated throughout Scripture—from His condemnation of Cain for his fratricide (Gen. 4:10), to His overthrowing of the Canaanites whose bloodshed and child murder caused the land to vomit them out (Lev. 18:25), to the denunciation of King Manasseh for filling Jerusalem with blood (2 Kings 21:16), to the final judgment when God our Maker will judge and condemn the nations "drunk with the blood of the saints, and with the blood of the witnesses of Jesus" (Rev. 17:6).

God's retribution against those who shed blood is clear and severe. He has promised He will not hear the prayers of those whose hands are covered in blood (Isa. 1:15). He has promised to bring retribution on those who practice this evil, but also those who give bloodshed their hearty approval (Rom. 1:32). And specifically, He has promised He will set His face against, and cut off from His people, those who act as if they don't see or know about the shedding of the blood of innocent babies:

> Then the LORD spoke to Moses, saying, "You shall also say to the sons of Israel:
> 'Any man from the sons of Israel or from the aliens sojourning in Israel who gives any of his offspring to Molech, shall surely be put to death; the people of the land shall stone him with stones. I will also set My face against that man and will cut him off from among his people, because he has given some of his offspring to Molech, so as to defile My sanctuary and to profane My holy name. If the people of the land, however, should ever disregard that man when he gives any of his offspring to Molech, so as not to put him to death, then I Myself will set My face against that man and against his family, and I will cut off from among their people both him and all those who play the harlot after him, by playing the harlot after Molech. (Lev. 20:1–5)

Not one drop of blood will be forgotten. When Cain killed his brother Abel, God said to Cain, "What have you done? The voice of your brother's blood is crying to Me from the ground" (Gen. 4:10). He has promised retribution against those who kill his prophets; that He will exact all their blood from Abel down to this present generation (Matt. 23:35). Finally, note particularly God's condemnation of the sons of Ammon for their heinous sin:

> Thus says the LORD,
> "For three transgressions of the sons of Ammon and for four

I will not revoke its punishment,
Because they ripped open the pregnant women of Gilead
In order to enlarge their borders."

(Amos 1:13)

God's Particular Hatred for the Shedding of the Blood of Children

Consider the eye-for-eye passage found in Exodus 21:22–25.[75] Elsewhere in the law, punishment was only demanded when actual physical harm was brought upon one of the parties, but here restitution is required for the harm caused to the child (and thereby to the mother, father, and family). Whether "life for life" refers to mother or child, God opposes even the accidental bloodshed of the unborn.

The condemnation of child sacrifice is ubiquitous across the Old Testament, and what's horrible to read is that these condemnations are pronounced alike against the Canaanites and the sons of Israel.[76] The people

---

75. "And when men strive, and have smitten a pregnant woman, and her children have come out, and there is no mischief, he is certainly fined, as the husband of the woman doth lay upon him, and he hath given through the judges; and if there is mischief, then thou hast given life for life, eye for eye, tooth for tooth, hand for hand, foot for foot, burning for burning, wound for wound, stripe for stripe" (Young's Literal Translation).

There has been much debate over the interpretation of this text. Perhaps the biggest question is how to understand the Hebrew here translated "mischief." Some modern scholars have even tried to make the case that the text supports elective abortion. Evangelical scholars have responded by arguing "mischief" (Hebrew *'āsôn*, אסון) does not refer to miscarriage, but premature birth. Cf. U. Cassuto, *Commentary on the Book of Exodus* (Jerusalem Magnes, 1967), 275; H. W. House, "Miscarriage or Premature Birth: Additional Thoughts on Exodus 21:22–25," *Westminster Theological Journal* 41 (Fall 1978): 108–123; W. C. Kaiser, *Toward Old Testament Ethics* (Zondervan, 1983), 102–104, 168–172; also J. Calvin, *Commentary on the Four Last Books of Moses* (Baker, 1979); C. F. Keil and F. Delitzsch, *Exodus* (Eerdmans, n.d.). See also John Makujina, "The Semantics of אסון in Exodus 21:22: Reassessing the Variables That Determine Meaning," *Bulletin for Biblical Research* 23, no. 3 (2013): 305–321.

The interpretation held more broadly across history is "miscarriage." See Russell Fuller, "Exodus 21:22–23: The Miscarriage Interpretation and the Personhood of the Fetus," *Journal of the Evangelical Theological Society* 37, no. 2 (June 1994): 169–184; also Makujina.

A second, related matter involves the LXX reading of this passage, which, instead of understanding the issue as one of "mischief" or "no mischief," distinguishes between a "formed" and "unformed" fetus. This distinction depends upon ancient opinions about ensoulment, and represents the interpretation of most of the church fathers. A majority of modern exegetes prefer the Hebrew Masoretic reading here, yet arguments in favor of the LXX's reading are substantial, and should not be dismissed out of hand in reference to the "formed" and "unformed" child. Cf. Stanley Isser, "Two Traditions: The Law of Exodus 21:22–23 Revisited," *The Catholic Biblical Quarterly* 52, no. 1: 30–45.

Regardless of one's conclusions concerning the text's meanings and interpretations, Exodus 21:22–23 provides no support for elective abortion.

76. See, e.g., Deuteronomy 12:31; 18:10; 2 Kings 16:3; 17:17; 17:31; 21:6; 2 Chronicles 28:3; 33:6; Jeremiah 7:31; 19:5; and Ezekiel 16:21; 20:26, 31; 23:37.

of Israel were surrounded by Canaanite religion and its demon gods worshiped through the sacrifice of the Canaanites' little ones. Molech worship required that a child be placed in the mouth of the god as a burnt offering. This is a sin so heinous to God that it is the only evil said never to have entered His mind (Jer. 32:35).

This ancient child sacrifice reached its nadir in Carthage where the burial ground Tophet, containing infants in their urns, was excavated, first in 1925, then again in 1970. It proved to be "the largest cemetery of sacrifice of humans ever discovered," containing infants' remains who were sacrificed over the course of six centuries. Archeologists have estimated that between 400 and 200 BC, as many as twenty thousand urns containing the remains of little children were buried there.[77]

What was the nature of these child sacrifices? Here is a paraphrase of a description from an ancient Greek writer, Kleitarchos, during the third century BC:

> Out of reverence for Kronos [the Greek equivalent of Ba'al Hammon], the Phoenicians, and especially the Carthaginians, whenever they seek to obtain some great favor, vow one of their children, burning it as a sacrifice to the deity, if they are especially eager to gain success. There stands in their midst a bronze statue of Kronos, its hands extended over a bronze brazier, the flames of which engulf the child. When the flames fall upon the body, the limbs contract and the open mouth seems almost to be laughing, until the contracted [body] slips quietly into the brazier. Thus it is that the "grin" is known as "sardonic[78] laughter," since they die laughing.[79]

Tertullian, the church father of the late second and early third century AD, lived in Carthage and wrote:

---

77. Lawrence Stager and Samuel Wolff, "Child Sacrifice at Carthage—Religious Rite or Population Control?" *Biblical Archeology Review*, January/February 1984: 32–51. For a time scholars attempted to deny that child sacrifices to the gods really happened as reported, but new research published in the journal *Antiquity* leaves it beyond question, even suggesting that it might be one of the reasons the city was founded in the first place.

78. The word comes, through French and Latin, from Greek *sardonios*, itself an alteration of Greek *sardinia*, associated with a plant from Sardinia. The ancients believed that eating this plant caused facial convulsions and led to death. See Stager and Wolff, 33.

79. Translation by P. G. Mosca, *Child Sacrifice in Canaanite and Israelite Religion: A Study in Mulk and Molech*, PhD dissertation, Harvard University, 1975, 22, as quoted in Stager and Wolff, 33.

In Africa infants used to be sacrificed to Saturn, and quite openly, down to the proconsulate of Tiberius, who took the priests themselves and on the very trees of their temple, under whose shadow their crimes had been committed, hung them alive like votive offerings on crosses; and the soldiers of my own country are witnesses to it, who served that proconsul in that very task. Yes, and to this day that holy crime persists in secret. . . . Saturn did not spare his own children; so, where other people's [children] were concerned, he naturally persisted in not sparing them, and their own parents offered them to him, were glad to respond, and fondled their children that they might not be sacrificed in tears. And between murder and sacrifice by parents—oh! the difference is great![80]

Now then, we read with some understanding this most awful judgment by God against His people spoken by His prophet Jeremiah:

Thus says the LORD, "Go and buy a potter's earthenware jar, and take some of the elders of the people and some of the senior priests. Then go out to the valley of Ben-hinnom, which is by the entrance of the potsherd gate, and proclaim there the words that I tell you, and say, 'Hear the word of the LORD, O kings of Judah and inhabitants of Jerusalem: thus says the LORD of hosts, the God of Israel, "Behold I am about to bring a calamity upon this place, at which the ears of everyone that hears of it will tingle. Because they have forsaken Me and have made this an alien place and have burned sacrifices in it to other gods, that neither they nor their forefathers nor the kings of Judah had ever known, and because they have filled this place with the blood of the innocent and have built the high places of Baal to burn their sons in the fire as burnt offerings to Baal, a thing which I never commanded or spoke of, nor did it ever enter My mind; therefore, behold, days are coming," declares the LORD, "when this place will no longer be called Topheth or the valley of Ben-hinnom, but rather the valley of Slaughter. I will make void the counsel of Judah and Jerusalem in this place, and I will cause them to fall by the sword before their enemies and by the hand of those who seek their life; and I will give over their carcasses as food for

---

80. *Apology* 9.24, from *Apology and De Spectaculis*, trans. T. R. Glover (Loeb Classical Library, 1931).

the birds of the sky and the beasts of the earth. I will also make this city a desolation and an object of hissing; everyone who passes by it will be astonished and hiss because of all its disasters. I will make them eat the flesh of their sons and the flesh of their daughters, and they will eat one another's flesh in the siege and in the distress with which their enemies and those who seek their life will distress them." ' " (Jer. 19:1–9)

We too must tremble at the wrath of God against our own filling of our place with the blood of our own innocents.

The New Testament's Condemnation of *Pharmakeia*

Advocates of permissive abortion laws commonly argue that Scripture never addresses abortion. Aside from disregarding the texts of Scripture enumerated above, they also take no account of New Testament passages which condemn *pharmakeia* (Greek φαρμακεία) and those who pay for these services.

Words with this root occur five times in the New Testament. While the basic meaning of *pharmak-* is "drug," its derivatives have a broad semantic range encompassing "poison," medicinal and psychotropic "drugs," "potions," etc. These words often carry nuances of magic or the occult.

Most significant for our purposes, though, throughout the ancient world these words referred to drugs, potions, and spells that were associated with abortions.[81] John Riddle, a pro-abortion Harvard scholar whose work has overturned prior assumptions about birth control in the ancient world, writes:

> Some statements by the Christians indicate that they did not approve of drugs employed for birth control. . . . In Galatians 5:20 Paul provides us with a list of sins of the flesh, and among them is the sin of *pharmakeia*,

---

81. Thus, for φαρμακεία, the Liddell, Scott, Jones Ancient Greek Lexicon gives "of abortifacients" as one definition, citing Soranus (1.59; fl. 1st/2nd century AD). By contrast, BDAG does not include this specific gloss for either *pharmakeia* or *pharmakon* despite Soranus having written within the New Testament time period and BDAG's inclusion of citations from several less significant medicinal writers. One might anticipate a correction of this oversight in future editions. See also Hippocrates, *Oath* 18–20: "Neither will I administer a poison [*pharmakon*] to anybody when asked to do so, nor will I suggest such a course. Similarly, I will not give to a woman a pessary to cause abortion."

often translated into English as "sorcery" or "magic." . . . This is the same word that Socrates through Plato had used in reference to birth control: "drugs [*pharmakia*] and incantations." . . . There is likely a direct connection between the *pharmakia* [*sic*] of the New Testament and the "root poisons" of Hebrew literature.[82]

English Bible translations have had difficulty expressing the range of *pharmakeia*'s nuances. It was not this way when Jerome produced his fourth-century Vulgate. He translated this word into Latin as *veneficium*, and here, the Latin closely matches the Greek, admirably preserving the choices possible among *pharmakeia*'s variable meanings. In English, though, we have nothing close to these Greek and Latin words, so translations have overly emphasized the occult element, translating *pharmakeia* as "witchcraft" (KJV) or "sorcery" (more recent translations).

Why have scholars translated *pharmakeia* as "sorcery"?

In the ancient world, many of the categories we think of as distinct were blurred. This is particularly evident reading the medical authorities of the time. Like us (especially if they were what we might refer to as middle or upper class), they would consult a doctor about their illness. But unlike us, they might also hire a conjurer—someone with spiritual power who used incantations in conjunction with chemicals we today refer to as "drugs." In other words, the line between medicine and magic was blurred in a way it isn't for us today.

Moderns are tempted to sever the body from the soul, thinking medicine has only to do with the body. We congratulate ourselves on having arrived at a time when medicine is an entirely empirical science.[83]

Not so in the ancient world where the spiritual and physical were inseparable. Commitment to specific deities of Greco-Roman polytheism varied over time, but overall, men were acutely aware of the spiritual. The Apostle Paul made this simple observation:

> For our struggle is not against flesh and blood, but against the rulers, against

---

82. Riddle, *Eve's Herbs: A History of Contraception and Abortion in the West* (Harvard University Press, 1997).
83. For an extended discussion of medicine as "art," and not simply "science," as well as a stunning essay on abortion, see Richard Selzer, *Mortal Lessons: Notes on the Art of Surgery* (Harcourt Brace & Co., 1974). Selzer was a second-generation physician and denied the existence of God.

the powers, against the world forces of this darkness, against the spiritual forces of wickedness in the heavenly places. (Eph. 6:12)

Concerning conception and childbirth, the intermingling of flesh and blood and the spiritual forces of wickedness was not yet subjected to any post-Enlightenment hermeneutic.

The ancient world lived for children in a way our world finds incomprehensible. They had higher rates of fertility, and mother and child faced much higher rates of death during childbirth.[84] Childbirth was far more dangerous for them than for us today.

But whereas a woman today would rest her confidence in all kinds of "specialists," including her gynecologist, obstetrician, and midwife, in the ancient world a single figure often performed these roles. For the upper (and perhaps middle) class, that might have been a doctor; for the lower classes, more often it was a midwife (even a family member).

Thus when we consider the practice of *pharmakeia*, we must not think in modern medical terms—say, for instance, physicians and pharmacists. *Pharmakeia* did not include FDA-approved drugs whose agency and side effects were researched, graphed, and charted. It is more accurate to think of a shaman or medicine man, someone who is as connected to the occult as he (or she) is to medicine. In other words, the biblical prohibition of *pharmakeia* was closely connected to the prohibition of the occult.

In Greek, the terminology used to designate these figures is often ambiguous. A number of terms are used, including *mageos, pharmakeus,* and *pharmakos*.[85] Their semantic range is broad and overlaps. Such figures sold both drugs and incantations. They were as mindful of the spiritual as they were of the physical, for potions and incantations both accessed and manipulated the spirit world.

---

84. Precise data is absent, but a ballpark figure for the maternal mortality rate is between 0.5 and 2 percent.

85. These and other terms were broad, overlapping, and often used interchangeably; see, e.g., Matthew Dickie, *Magic and Magicians in the Greco-Roman World* (Routledge, 2001), 34; but on the other hand, Richard Greenfield, "Magic and the Occult Sciences" in *The Cambridge Intellectual History of Byzantium* (Cambridge University Press, 2017), 220.

Even a single term's meaning was often context dependent; cf. *magos* in the New Testament, which is used with reference to the *magi* of Matthew 2 as well as Simon the Magician in Acts 8. On balance, it is best to consider *magos, pharmakos,* etc., as related terms that sometimes retain their nuances—and indeed the standard lexica generally hold to this practice.

For this reason, Scripture forbids *pharmakeia* to the people of God. God's people are to have nothing to do with magic, mediums, incantations, amulets, and potions. The members of Christ's church are not to make the slightest effort to access or control the "secret things" of God (Deut. 29:29). Manipulation of this unseen world is a crime among God's covenant people of the Old Testament, and the New Testament condemns these practices also.[86]

The book of Acts records the interface of such occult practices and practitioners with the church of the Apostles in its record of the conversion and subsequent sin of Simon Magus:

> Now there was a man named Simon, who formerly was practicing magic [*mageuōn*] in the city and astonishing the people of Samaria, claiming to be someone great; and they all, from smallest to greatest, were giving attention to him, saying, "This man is what is called the Great Power of God." And they were giving him attention because he had for a long time astonished them with his magic arts [*mageiais*]. But when they believed Philip preaching the good news about the kingdom of God and the name of Jesus Christ, they were being baptized, men and women alike. Even Simon himself believed; and after being baptized, he continued on with Philip, and as he observed signs and great miracles taking place, he was constantly amazed.
>
> Now when the apostles in Jerusalem heard that Samaria had received the word of God, they sent them Peter and John, who came down and prayed for them that they might receive the Holy Spirit. For He had not yet fallen upon any of them; they had simply been baptized in the name of the Lord Jesus. Then they began laying their hands on them, and they were receiving the Holy Spirit. Now when Simon saw that the Spirit was bestowed through the laying on of the apostles' hands, he offered them money, saying, "Give this authority to me as well, so that everyone on whom I lay my hands may receive the Holy Spirit." But Peter said to him, "May your silver perish with you, because you thought you could obtain the gift of God with money! You have no part or portion in this matter, for your heart is not right before God. Therefore repent of this wickedness of

---

86. Cf. Revelation 18:23.

yours, and pray the Lord that, if possible, the intention of your heart may be forgiven you. For I see that you are in the gall of bitterness and in the bondage of iniquity." But Simon answered and said, "Pray to the Lord for me yourselves, so that nothing of what you have said may come upon me."

(Acts 8:9–24)

Scripture does not explicitly designate Simon Magus as one who practiced *pharmakeia*, yet he well may have. It is not easy for us to be done with our lucrative past, so naturally Simon's temptation to continue profiting from manipulating the spiritual realm of secret things manifested itself immediately following his conversion. This temptation was also present in the church at large. Simon Magus was not a one-off, but representative of a larger danger among the people of God, and thus Scripture's New Testament condemnations of sorcery, whether the manipulation of the unseen world was referred to as *mageia* or *pharmakeia*.

Thus far, we have unpacked the nature of *pharmakeia* in the ancient world, focusing on its usage by *mageoi* and other occult figures. What remains, then, is to consider the specific instances of *pharmak-* words in Scripture and related documents, opening up the fact that "witchcraft" and "sorcery" don't give moderns a full enough picture of the sins being condemned.

Most of us have never known a sorcerer. Such figures remain within the realm of fairy tales or Disney movies. We think of the old man or woman with a hat, maybe with a magic wand, maybe standing over a cauldron, but of course we're sure such figures perished with the medieval world. Though the ancient *mageos* or *pharmakeus* did use spells and lurked in the shadows, they were far more common than we might think, with wide swaths of society employing their services. More to the point, *pharmakeia* included things we today do not think of as sorcery.

Given the universal importance of the fruitful womb in the life of man, few things were more subject to the desires to employ magic or occult control through *pharmakeia* than sex, marriage, conception, and childbirth—and this desire for control was both positive and negative. Women desired to possess a man as their husband or lover,[87] women desired to

---

87. Cf. Alciphron, *Epistolae* 4.10.3; also Basil, *Letters* 188.8.

conceive a child,[88] women desired their child to be born safely; but women also desired a lover other than their husband,[89] as well as the prevention of their own conception and birth of the children they were carrying in their womb. Further, evil women employed magic's potions and incantations for the purpose of destroying other women's marriages, conceptions, and safe childbirths.[90] Thus *pharmakeia* was bound up with love, sex, and childbirth. In a world where the processes of life and death were recognized as obscure and under the gods' control, those who could manipulate the levers of such divine powers also dispensed the *pharmaka*.

These men and women, then, had a specialized, and often occult, trade. They were marginal figures bearing some resemblance to yesterday's medicine men or snake oil salesmen, or today's theosophists, practitioners of mindfulness and yoga, naturopathic and holistic doctors, and faith healers.

In the ancient world, those intent on preventing pregnancy or aborting their children purchased their potions from similar marginal figures. Statistics on this are unavailable, but sources indicate the number of people making use of these *pharmaka* was significant. We also know that, even in the church, converts to the Christian faith included mothers (and fathers) who had aborted their children.[91] Luke records the conversion of Simon Magus, showing that the New Testament church did not just include former fornicators, idolaters, adulterers, effeminate, homosexuals, thieves, covetous, drunkards, revilers, and swindlers,[92] but also *mageoi*. As there were *mageoi*, so the church also included those who formerly had employed the *mageoi*, and thus were tempted to continue to employ their services.

We have the historical record of Simon's temptation to continue his practice of magic, but we also have a New Testament record of the ongoing temptation of Christians to pay for those services, including *pharmaka* used to murder their children.

---

88. Cf., among many others, Theophrastus, Περὶ φυτῶν ἱστορία 9.18.5.
89. Cf. Euripides, *Hippolytus* 509–516.
90. See, e.g., Apuleius, *Metamorphoses* 1.9ff. For more on reproductive spells, see also Jean-Jacques Aubert, "Threatened Wombs: Aspects of Ancient Uterine Magic," *Greek, Roman, and Byzantine Studies* 30, no. 3 (1989): 421–449.
91. See Jerome, *Ad Eustochium* (*Letters* 22.13).
92. 1 Corinthians 6:9–11.

This explains Scripture's warnings not being limited to the practice of magic, generally, but also *pharmakeia*, specifically. New Christians had paid the so-called *pharmakoi*, but also doctors and midwives, all of whom commonly dispensed *pharmaka* for the purpose of killing preborn children. Following the practice of the pagans who were their neighbors, Christians made use of *pharmakeia*, and thus had to be warned against it by the Apostle.

But if with *pharmakeia* we only think of a wizard in a pointy hat and miss the fact that abortion is the reality that often underlies the use of *pharmakeia*, we do not fully grasp the weight of Scripture's condemnations. Consider Galatians 5:19–21:

> Now the deeds of the flesh are evident, which are: immorality [*porneia*], impurity [*akatharsia*], sensuality [*aselgeia*], idolatry [*eidōlolatria*], sorcery [*pharmakeia*], enmities, strife, jealousy, outbursts of anger, disputes, dissensions, factions, envying, drunkenness, carousing, and things like these, of which I forewarn you, just as I have forewarned you, that those who practice such things will not inherit the kingdom of God.

Here, the first three terms pertain to sexual immorality of various sorts. The next term, idolatry, also has here a likely sexual component, given that pagan temple worship was often associated with sexual immorality. Next is *pharmakeia*, followed by seven terms that do not pertain to sexual immorality, but rather to "relational" sins.

Note the clear pattern and order of these terms. Where does *pharmakeia* fit in? It doesn't fit with the "relational" sins mentioned, such as jealousy, wrath, and ambition. But keeping in mind *pharmakeia* was employed for contraceptive and abortifacient purposes, its presence next to sexual sins is natural, for then the Apostle here condemns, first, the general category of impurity (*porneia*), then the specific manifestations of that impurity (adultery and lasciviousness), then idolatry (almost always at the core of sexual sin); and finally, the use of contraceptive/abortifacient potions to destroy the evidence of these sins.

All the above opens up the nature of *pharmakeia*, and we now have some understanding why it is translated into English as "sorcery." Killing the little one bearing the image of God safely nestled in his mother's womb prevents the normal course of nature, and thus defies our Creator who Himself gives life, the womb, and safe delivery to His little ones.

Consider also Revelation 9:21:

> And they did not repent of their murders or their sorceries [*pharmakeia*] or their sexual immorality or their thefts.

Here again, note *pharmakeia* is placed immediately between "murders" and "sexual immorality." Compare Revelation 21:8 where again the *pharmakoi* are listed alongside "murderers," the "sexually immoral," and "idolaters."[93]

Perhaps most revealing of the contraceptive and abortifacient nature of *pharmakeia* is evidence from the contemporaneous (AD 50–100) *Didache*. In its second chapter, this most ancient of the non-canonical documents of the church forbids a number of "grave sins":

> You shall not commit murder, you shall not commit adultery, you shall not commit pederasty, you shall not commit fornication [*porneuseis*], you shall not steal, you shall not practice magic [*mageuseis*], you shall not use potions [*pharmakeuseis*], you shall not murder a child by abortion [*phoneuseis teknon en phthora*], nor kill it after it is born [*gennēthen apokteneis*].[94]

This passage is especially helpful because the terms we've been discussing are placed in close proximity, yet also distinguished. *Mageuseis*, "practice magic," refers to a broad array of occult practices. *Phoneuseis teknon en phthora* and *gennēthen apokteneis* in the last two clauses forbid, respectively, abortion and infanticide. But then, right between *mageuseis* and the mention of abortion and infanticide is *pharmakeuseis*. What does this mean?

It could be another condemnation of "sorcery" (i.e., restating *mageuseis*), yet no other sin is repeated in this list. There's little reason to take *pharmakeuseis* as synonymous with *mageuseis*, nor with the condemnations of abortion and infanticide that follow.

---

93. "But the cowardly, unbelieving, abominable, murderers, sexually immoral, sorcerers, idolaters, and all liars shall have their part in the lake which burns with fire and brimstone, which is the second death." Revelation 21:8.

94. οὐ φονεύσεις, οὐ μοιχεύσεις, οὐ παιδοφθορήσεις, οὐ πορνεύσεις, οὐ κλέψεις, οὐ μαγεύσεις, οὐ φαρμακεύσεις, οὐ φονεύσεις τκνον ἐν φθορᾷ, οὐδὲ γεννηθὲν ἀποκτενεῖς. *Didache* 2.2.

The better choice exegetically is to understand this reference to *pharmakeuseis* to be the condemnation of any dispensing or use of the agents of a *pharmakos* (denounced likewise in Revelation) for contraceptive/abortifacient purposes. Such agents would generally have been in an occult context, though *pharmakeuseis* here condemns *all* uses, whether occult or not. Here, we've translated it "use potions," and this is a good, broad translation. What it condemns would then include (1) chemical contraceptives, (2) abortion (whether chemical or surgical), and (3) incantations or other tools of an occult *pharmakos*.

This understanding gives insight into the *Didache*'s thought progression. Knowing that "practice magic" (*mageuseis*) could encompass giving of potions (or poisons), abortion, and infanticide, what follows *mageuseis* could express a progression of time: *pharmakeuseis* indicating the first attempt to destroy the child, *phoneuseis teknon en phthora* the abortifacient recourse when the *pharmaka* failed, and *gennēthen apokteneis* being the final solution. Or, the continuum could express the ancients' awareness of the little one's development: the broad, mysterious *pharmakeuseis* representing the uncertainty of conception and how *pharmakeia* functioned; *phoneuseis teknon en phthora* making it clear that what was at issue was flesh and blood, a *child* (*teknon*), and he was being *murdered*; and finally, *gennēthen apokteneis* showing the sin in all its nakedness, for the child had been *born*. As our awareness of our sin's severity grows, so does the iniquity if we follow through. The *Didache*'s progression, from magic to potions to abortion to infanticide, recognizes this.

Given how close the *Didache* is in date, vocabulary, and style to the New Testament, we should assume that the NT uses *pharmakeia* and related terms in a way similar to that found in the *Didache*. Thus when Scripture condemns the use of *pharmakeia*, it is not simply sorcery as we understand it that's being condemned, but the related use of contraceptive/abortifacient potions.

Dealing with Common Justifications for Abortion

Rape and Incest

Readers who consider themselves strongly "pro-life" may yet be uncomfortable with the complete repeal of legalized abortion because of concern for the well-being of women who are pregnant as a result of rape and incest.[95] Should abortion be legal in these cases?

Even the discussion of these exceptional cases is dangerous. Pro-lifers have many scars they can show from times they've been foolish enough to condemn the killing of babies conceived in rape and incest. If they refused to modulate their position, the attack was vicious and left them tarred and feathered as an extremist, a monster.[96] Questions fly: "Why should a woman have to bear the consequences of her violation? Isn't this validating the sin of the rapist? How can anyone countenance requiring a woman to gaze, day after day, at this child who is a living reminder of the wicked man who violated her?"

The objections are weighty, but let's bring them into the light of day and examine them.

First, the proportion of abortions due to rape or incest is miniscule. For example, in Germany, the percentage of abortions related to rape or incest is around 0.02 percent annually.[97] In the United States, to the extent that such statistics are available,[98] the numbers are similar: less than 0.5

---

95. Although the crimes of rape and incest are distinct, the latter often involves the former, so we will mainly address rape.
96. For instance, during a debate, Richard Mourdock, the 2012 US Senate candidate for Indiana, uttered the words, "I just struggled with it myself for a long time but I came to realize: Life is that gift from God that I think even if life begins in that horrible situation of rape, that it is something that God intended to happen." His confession of faith in God's sovereignty brought an abrupt end to his previously successful candidacy. See Kevin Robillard, "Buchanan: Mitt Romney Rejects 'Rape' Remark," *Politico*, October 24, 2012, http://www.politico.com/news/stories/1012/82808.html.
97. See this report from the Gesundheitsberichterstattung des Bundes (Federal Health Monitoring System): https://www.gbe-bund.de:443/gbe/pkg_olap_tables.prc_archiv?p_indnr=240&p_archiv_id=1081842&p_sprache=E. Note as well that abortions related to the health of the mother make up less than 4 percent of the total, and this where health is defined broadly as physical and mental health, and a doctor must certify the threat in writing.
98. In the United States, government agencies almost never require the keeping of data on abortions after rape or incest, or due to health concerns related to the mother. See Kortsmit et al., "Abortion Surveillance."

percent are related to a prior rape.[99] We remember the legal maxim that hard or exceptional cases make bad law when we realize how exceedingly rare abortions due to rape and incest actually are, comprising much less than 1 percent of abortions. Such hard cases should not be allowed to form our nation's laws on abortion.

But leaving the question of law to the side, are there good reasons not to kill the little one conceived by rape and incest?

First, a word of caution. Since this question is fraught with emotion issuing from some of the most painful circumstances of life, it's difficult to discuss without surrounding that discussion with pastoral care that is sensitive and ministers to readers the compassion of our Lord for the oppressed and those who suffer. We do work to demonstrate His compassion and tenderness, but we know our efforts will fail to satisfy the needs of readers—needs that are wholly legitimate.

Two things, then: First, please understand that this document is completely taken up with consideration of parts of life and death which have caused many readers great anguish. In many cases such persons are inconsolable separate from the comfort of the Holy Spirit. "In the midst of life, we live in death," as the *Book of Common Prayer* states in the committal service at graveside. Rape, incest, and abortion are each part of that death. So yes, like abortion itself, rape and incest cause their victims awful suffering, and we write in full awareness that reading this discussion of these things will add to the suffering of those harmed by these crimes. Given it is true those who have suffered rape or incest are innocent of the crime while those who have committed abortion are guilty of the crime, discussion of these crimes will for many be torment. Yet discuss we must—because all these things are a matter of truth and falsehood, righteousness and

---

99. According to a 2004 anonymous survey conducted by the Guttmacher Institute among 1,209 women who had aborted their children, less than 0.5 percent were related to rape, and 4 percent to the mother's health. See Lawrence Finer et al., "Reasons U.S. Women Have Abortions: Quantitative and Qualitative Perspectives," *Perspectives on Sexual and Reproductive Health* 37 (2005), no. 3: 110–118. Florida is exceptional among the states, providing an annual report on abortions which includes a statement of reasons given for the abortion. In 2020, 0.16 percent of abortions were related to rape and incest, 1.68 percent to the mother's physical health, and 1.88 percent to the mother's psychological health. See "Reported Induced Terminations of Pregnancy (ITOP) by Reason, by Trimester," 2020, https://ahca.myflorida.com/MCHQ/Central_Services/Training_Support/docs/TrimesterByReason_2020.pdf.

wickedness, life and death. It is not possible to proceed with any discussion of the wickedness of abortion, rape, and incest without faith that truth is glorious and needs no justification, whether its discovery and recognition lead to joy or pain. God has fashioned truth in such a way that it is indispensable to the healing of sin and the pain it causes, whether that sin is others' or our own.

Second, the church is our household of faith and we need her ministry and instruction particularly while considering the subject of this document. The world will be of little help to us, but the church of Jesus Christ will teach and clean and exhort and rebuke and encourage and comfort us as she has every generation since her birth at Pentecost. Considering and repenting of abortion is a work to be done in community.

We have no illusion our arguments here can both convince and console. Nevertheless, these arguments *must* be marshaled and presented to the church if her members are to repent and give themselves to the protection of mothers and their children. Making those arguments requires raising these painful matters of rape and incest because, over the past half century, no justification of the murder of little ones in their mother's womb has been more constant and effective than the supposed necessity of the deaths of babies conceived by rape and incest. So now, we turn to it, asking our readers' understanding for the necessity of our discussion being less than exhaustive.

To begin, then, note that the arguments against abortion made throughout this chapter also apply to abortion in cases of rape and incest. Any murder attacks the image of God He has placed in each child, regardless of the circumstances of that child's conception. Abortion is a crime against society, destroying the bonds of mutual obligation and fellowship we share, regardless of the circumstances of our conception. Any abortion destroys a human being—the greatest natural resource God has placed on His green earth. Any and every abortion has been universally condemned by church fathers through two millennia and is a heinous crime against nature, man, and God.

Beyond the above, to use the circumstances of the conception of a child as justification for the murder of that child is a denial of a fundamental principle of justice, that we are to protect the innocent and punish the guilty. Who is more guilty than the rapist, and who is more innocent than the unborn child?[100] To kill an unborn child conceived in rape punishes that little one and her mother—not the rapist. Far from being a just and merciful alleviation of suffering, it multiplies the violence already surrounding this violent crime.

Many Christians are sympathetic to arguments in favor of aborting little ones conceived through rape and incest, but why? What is the nature of our vulnerability to this tactic of the abortionists?

There are several explanations for this vulnerability:

(1) As Christians, we feel intense pressure to state repeatedly that we share our culture's commitment to viewing rape as the highest, most horrible crime of violence against woman. It's as if we have to prove Christians are, in fact, concerned and respectful toward women, and never mind that all prior generations of Christians condemned rape as a heinous crime and subjected those committing it to the most severe penalties.[101]

Never mind that all past generations of Christian fathers, husbands, and sons loved, cared for, and defended their mothers, wives, and daughters. Never mind the records across Christendom of their grief over the terrible, lifelong suffering of women who had been raped. Why is this not enough for us today? Christians feel the need to prove their respect for women by

---

100. We are not declaring the unborn child's absolute innocence here. In Psalm 51, David confesses he was "conceived in sin." Saying this, David was not referring to any sin of his father and mother in the circumstances of his conception, but to his own sin. David's confession of his own original sin from the moment of his conception is equally true of all men and women. In terms of relative innocence, though, the unborn child is the most innocent of all men.

Still, in connection with the entirety of this paper, Calvin's comments on David's confession of guilt from his conception in the womb are instructive:

> Interpreters have very properly rendered [the Hebrew] "hath conceived me." The expression intimates that we are cherished in sin from the first moment that we are in the womb. David, then, is here brought, by reflecting on one particular transgression, to cast a retrospective glance upon his whole past life, and to discover nothing but sin in it.... [David] refers to original sin with the view of aggravating his guilt, acknowledging that he had not contracted this or that sin for the first time lately, but had been born into the world with the seed of every iniquity.
>
> The passage affords a striking testimony in proof of original sin entailed by Adam upon the whole human family. It not only teaches the doctrine, but may assist us in forming a correct idea of it.... The Bible, both in this and other places, clearly asserts that we are born in sin, and that it exists within us as a disease fixed in our nature. David does not charge it upon his parents, nor trace his crime to them, but... before the Divine tribunal, confesses that he was formed in sin, and that he was a transgressor ere he saw the light of this world. (Comments on Psalm 51:5, *Commentary on the Book of Psalms*, vol. 2, trans. James Anderson [Calvin Translation Society, 1846], 290)

101. Under the Mosaic Law, rape of a married woman was punishable by death (Deut. 22:22–23), and Western law has consistently punished rape with harsh penal sanctions.

joining the mob's attack on the innocent child, executing that child for the crimes of her father. Have we forgotten God's words to Ezekiel?

> The person who sins will die. The son will not bear the punishment for the father's iniquity, nor will the father bear the punishment for the son's iniquity; the righteousness of the righteous will be upon himself, and the wickedness of the wicked will be upon himself. (Ezek. 18:20)

We have not progressed in our moral discernment and compassion above our fathers and mothers in the faith before us. Rather, showing ourselves attentive and concerned for the violence of rape inflicted on the mother by condoning the killing of her child conceived through that act is proof our moral discernment and compassion have decayed. Even if our concern were limited solely to the mother, and not the child, do we not recognize this child shares her mother's DNA—that in every sense of the word, she is her mother's child? The execution of the mother's child for the sins of the child's father is a more violent attack on womanhood than rape.

In his *City of God*, Saint Augustine speaks of the comfort women who are the victims of the violence of rape may take in their undefiled chastity. He continues:

> A woman who has been violated by the sin of another, and without any consent of her own, has no cause to put herself to death . . . for in that case she commits certain homicide [for] a crime which is . . . not her own.[102]

If it is homicide for a mother to kill herself for the crime of another, it is also homicide for that mother to kill her baby for the crime of another. Certainly it seems harsh to warn a victim of rape against committing homicide, but this warning is needed. The temptations to utter despair and the crimes attendant upon such despair in the life of man and woman must

---

102. *City of God* 1.18: "Far be it from us to so misapply words. Let us rather draw this conclusion, that while the sanctity of the soul remains even when the body is violated, the sanctity of the body is not lost; and that, in like manner, the sanctity of the body is lost when the sanctity of the soul is violated, though the body itself remains intact. And therefore a woman who has been violated by the sin of another, and without any consent of her own, has no cause to put herself to death; much less has she cause to commit suicide in order to avoid such violation, for in that case she commits certain homicide to prevent a crime which is uncertain as yet, and not her own."

be anticipated and warned against. These warnings are the fruit of our understanding, love, and compassion.

In our pastoral care, we must not have one eye on our reputation among worldlings and pagans, and another on God. Keep in mind what may be our Lord's most sober warning:

> Do not fear those who kill the body but are unable to kill the soul; but rather fear Him who is able to destroy both soul and body in hell. (Matt. 10:28)

Rape does terrible violence to the body and soul of the woman, but there is no crime more awful than murder, which Scripture demonstrates by revealing the place "murderers" will be cast on the Day of Judgment:

> But for the cowardly and unbelieving and abominable and murderers and immoral persons and sorcerers and idolaters and all liars, their part will be in the lake that burns with fire and brimstone, which is the second death.
> (Rev. 21:8)

The point is not that abortion is such an awful crime against man and God that it is beyond the mercy of God in Jesus Christ. No and never! The blood of Jesus doesn't cleanse us from little sins or some sins, but "all" sins. Right here, given the tendency we have to minimize the sin of murder by maximizing the sin of rape, let us hear the word of God concerning our tendency to deny our own sin and refuse to confess the evil we ourselves have done, and also our tendency to consign some sins and sinners to being beyond any forgiveness:

> If we say that we have fellowship with Him and yet walk in the darkness, we lie and do not practice the truth; but if we walk in the Light as He Himself is in the Light, we have fellowship with one another, and the blood of Jesus His Son cleanses us from all sin. If we say that we have no sin, we are deceiving ourselves and the truth is not in us. If we confess our sins, He is faithful and righteous to forgive us our sins and to cleanse us from all unrighteousness. (1 John 1:6–9)

(2) Another explanation for our vulnerability to arguments in defense

of liberalized laws on abortion is that we can identify with the woman's suffering, but not the baby's. It is likely each of us knows a woman who has suffered this outrage. Our wife, our daughter, our mother. Those of us who are women can place ourselves in that situation; those of us who are men can sympathize to some extent because of our love for these women. Still, none of us can place ourselves in the womb with the unborn child. It is a hidden world unknown to us, and the child that lives in it for nine months is someone who cannot speak as her own advocate. So when the Deceiver comes to us and insinuates that the suffering of the woman takes precedence over the right of the unborn child to life, we're suckers. Our heart is bound up with the woman there in front of our eyes—not with the child who remains unseen and unheard. Thus we become guilty of the superficial judgment our Lord warns us about: "Do not judge according to the appearance, but judge with righteous judgment" (John 7:24).

(3) Another explanation for our vulnerability is our belief that it is unjust for us to suffer consequences for the sins of others. Increasingly, it is true that many of us think *grace* means freedom from consequences of any sin by anyone. But if going there is a bridge too far, we'll concede that Scripture teaches that *our own* sins have consequences. Samson and his libido. David and Bathsheba. Ananias and Sapphira. But bearing the consequences of *others'* sins? No way. The just God would never require that of anyone.

Yet He is just and He does require it. Scripture is full of such examples, from national and societal judgments (the Flood, the Canaanites, Israel, etc.) to sins whose punishment God visits upon families. This continues in our own day. When we are made late to work because of the traffic caused by a careless accident or a speeder. When the used car we bought turns out to have a dying engine because the seller never changed the oil. Sometimes it's more serious: When our father's coldness leaves us longing for affection. When we lose our home because of arson. Or even when we're injured because of a drunk driver. All through our lives, we suffer because of the sins of others. We may protest, arguing this is unjust; we may complain against God; but in the end, it's to no avail. No matter how big the consequence we think we've suffered, there's one that's far greater that every man has already suffered, and by God's decree: the imposition of God's curse upon each of us for our father Adam's sin. In light of this imputation of Adam's sin upon every woman and man, all our complaints of the injustice of the thing fall short.

So yes, the violation of a woman's soul and body at the hands of rape is a tragedy. It's a vile evil. It's a crime deserving of the harshest condemnation which ought to provoke our most tender compassion for its victim. But we may not conclude from this that we have a right to a life free from the consequences of others' sins. God disposes as He sees fit, and His arrangement of even the sins against us is done in His perfect will. He sees the end from the beginning. He also knows what each of us is able to endure the trials He sends our way (1 Cor. 10:13).

(4) Finally, we are vulnerable to arguments in favor of abortion in cases of rape and incest because we think large thoughts of our own justice, but small thoughts of God's ability to bring fruit out of suffering, not to mention His everlasting promise to bring every deed into the light at that great Day of Judgment.

Our thoughts and conceptions of justice are small and limited, but God's are perfect. He specializes in bringing light from darkness, life from death, and fruit from desolation. This is the testimony found across Scripture. We see it in the Garden where Adam's sin and condemnation bring with them the hope of future redemption through the seed of the woman. We see it in Joseph and his brothers, where the wickedness of his brothers leads to the sparing of God's people, but also the protection of the nation of Egypt from famine. As Joseph testifies, "God meant it for good" (Gen. 50:20).

Consider what is perhaps the most relevant case in Scripture which is one of the most sordid incidents in Scripture—the incest between Lot and his two daughters. Even in comparison to other sins in Scripture, this one stands out for its horror. It seems to us a filthy climax to Lot's descent, the final defilement of his body, name, and posterity, mating and producing children by lying with his own flesh and blood.

Yet that is not all of the story, for the account ends, not with Lot's nor his daughters' sin, but the fruit that resulted from that sin—in this case, the peoples of the Moabites and Ammonites that sprang from Lot's incestuous unions. Despite Lot's sin, despite his daughters' wickedness, God (as He does throughout Scripture) still grants them children who go on to become two great peoples.

"Some privilege!" the attentive reader of Scripture might say, for the

Moabites and Ammonites were not God's chosen people, but Israel's enemies. But once again, this too is *not* the end of God's story. For out of the vile Moabites God was pleased to bring godly Ruth, as well as her great-grandson who was a man after God's own heart. His name was David, and from David's line our Lord Jesus Christ descended. We may think it undignified to have the bloodline of our Lord extend back through Lot's daughters and their incest, yet here we have another example of God confounding the wisdom of the wise. Faithless men view Lot's sin with despair. But in God's economy, nothing is wasted. He is the steward of suffering and habitually produces fruit from that suffering.

Back in 1971, countercultural icon and author of *One Flew Over the Cuckoo's Nest*, Ken Kesey, gave an interview to Paul Krassner, publisher and editor of the national alternative journal *The Realist*. During the interview, the subject of abortion was raised—specifically abortion in the case of rape:

> Q. And yet, since you're against abortion, doesn't that put you in the position of saying that a girl or a woman must bear an unwanted child as punishment for ignorance or carelessness?
>
> A. In as I feel abortions to be probably the worst worm in the revolutionary philosophy, a worm bound in time to suck the righteousness and the life from the work we are engaged in, I want to take this slowly and carefully....
>
> . . .
>
> Punishment of unwed mothers? Bullshit! Care of neither the old nor the young can be considered to be punishment for the able, not even the care of the un-dead old or the un-born young. These beings, regardless not only of race, creed and color but as well of size, situation or ability, must be treated as equals and their rights to life not only recognized but *defended*! Can they defend themselves?
>
> You are you from conception, and that never changes no matter what physical changes your body takes. And the virile sport in the Mustang driving to work with his muscular forearm tanned and ready for a day's labor has *not one microgram more* right to his inalienable rights of life, liberty and the pursuit of happiness than has the three month's foetus riding in a sack of water or the vegetable rotting for twenty years in a gurney bed. Who's to know the value or extent of another's trip? How can we assume

that the world through the windshield of that Mustang is any more rich or holy or even sane than the world before those pale blue eyes? How can abortion be anything but fascism again, back as a fad in a new intellectual garb with a new, and more helpless, victim?

I swear to you, Paul, that abortions are a terrible karmic bummer, and to support them—except in cases where it is a bona fide toss-up between the child and the mother's life—is to harbor a worm of discrepancy.

Q. Well, that's really eloquent and mistypoo, but suppose Faye [Kesey's wife] were raped and became pregnant in the process?

A. Nothing is changed. You don't plow under the corn because the seed was planted with a neighbor's shovel.[103]

As moderns, we recoil at Kesey's terrible insensitivity, as we see it. Hearing him speak of the fruit of the rapist's sin horrifies us. How dare he speak of his wife's potential rape in such gross agricultural terms! How dare he attribute any blessing or fruit to rape!

As we ask our questions, it may become clear to us that our concern is not so much with life as it is with shame. The woman who suffers rape becomes covered with shame. She can't help herself. Her shame makes her want to die. Such shame requires something heavy. Something on the order of the sacrifice of her child. This shame cannot be healed or removed by talk of some hypothetical goodness or fruit proceeding from the rapist's violent and filthy ruination of her.

But shall we stop our train of thought long enough to consider that God's thoughts are not ours? That all of His attributes exist in perfect harmony, and thus there is no tension between the justice due the rapist and the justice due the mother and innocent child:

> The Lord has prepared everything for His purpose—
> even the wicked for the day of disaster.
>
> (Prov. 16:4, HCSB)

The rapist has his coming day of reckoning, if not by the state performing its duty, then by God carrying out His prerogative. Meanwhile, both the

---

103. "An Impolite Interview with Ken Kesey," *The Realist*, no. 90 (May/June 1971): 46–47, http://www.ep.tc/realist/90/46.html. Emphases original.

rapist's crime and God's punishment of him will conform to *God's* purposes, and not our own.

This is hard for us to fathom. We comfort ourselves with the lie that such terrible evils are outside God's appointments. Actually, though, this is no comfort at all, for then we are left with unchecked evil and a powerless or compassionless God.

In the end, we must face the God Who Is—not the idol we make of Him in our own mind. This *true* God is never the author of sin,[104] but neither is He a passive observer watching sin wreak its havoc. In His economy, the woman who suffers rape is not simply doomed to an interminable shame and victimhood from that moment onward. The God who forgives sin also heals shame, calling His redeemed ones to find their honor and glory in His adoption of them as His sons and daughters. He restores the years the locusts have eaten—and often that restoration comes in the form of new grain, new fruit, and new life brought about through others' sins against us.

This is a message of true compassion. It is not the compassion of the world, which postures itself as love for others while refusing to declare the truth. Rather, this is the true charity that mourns the indignity and outrage of rape and grieves with women and children, while also refusing to let their lives be consumed by it.

The true love that fully recognizes the terrible violation of woman such evil does will not be overcome by attacks upon God or the unborn little one, but only by the sustaining mercy of Christ. This true compassion will lead the sufferers to Christ. For Jesus knows what it is to be attacked, what it is to be innocent and violently abused, and what it is to commit His soul to the keeping of the One who is righteous. "With men this is impossible; but with God all things are possible" (Matt. 19:26).

Health of the Mother

After all the other arguments above, the final accusation abortionists throw at pro-lifers often sounds something like this:

> You men are so fixated on women giving you as many babies as possible

---

104. Westminster Confession of Faith, 3.1, https://evangelpresbytery.com/westminster-confession-of-faith/#III.

that you couldn't care less about their difficulties in pregnancy and childbirth! All you care about is babies and more babies. Even if her baby is killing her, you tell the mother she has to stay pregnant. She can't have an abortion even if it saves her life. She has to die so the baby can live. That's how insane you are!

Now maybe the many decades of our combined years in the anti-abortion movement aren't typical, but through those years we do not remember hearing any pro-lifer saying (or writing) that a mother must be told to die herself if a doctor tells her it's between her and her baby. Pro-lifers are quite reasonable and loving, and their love for babies is not greater than their love for mothers.

Anyhow, it's never going to be constructive during polemics with abortionists—speaking from the malice of their bloodguilt—for the Christian to try to have a rational discussion of various threats to a pregnant woman's health and the connection those threats may or may not have to the continuation of her pregnancy. For abortionists, this accusation is only a ploy. It's never a real argument.

Another thing to keep in mind is the tendency of abortionists to blur any distinction between mental and physical health and life. When they speak of "health of the mother," abortionists usually are referring to both the physical and emotional health of the mother. To them, both physical health concerns and mental health concerns are sufficient justification for killing the little ones.

Recall that this was the state of affairs prior to *Roe v. Wade*. At the time, abortion was largely legal for the purpose of protecting the emotional health of the mother—not just her physical health. One year prior to *Roe v. Wade*, back in 1972, abortion's death toll was already 586,760. What this shows is the limited protection our little neighbors have from death if the mother declares her emotional well-being is at stake.

If abortion were outlawed for reasons other than protection of the life of the mother, it's likely "life of the mother" would, in practice, be viewed expansively in its application in order to include threats to the mother's life due to mental health vulnerabilities, and many abortions would then be performed under these rubrics.

This is particularly so given the fact long known among medical professionals that no preborn child's death is necessary to save the life of his mother. Physicians both pro-life and pro-abortion have testified to this simple truth for decades now, and it has only become more true as those decades passed. Here's C. Everett Koop:

> Protection of the life of the mother as an excuse for an abortion is a smoke screen. In my 36 years in pediatric surgery I have never known of one instance where the child had to be aborted to save the mother's life.
>
> When a woman is pregnant, her obstetrician takes on the care of two patients—the mother-to-be and the unborn baby. If, toward the end of the pregnancy complications arise that threaten the mother's health, he will take the child by inducing labor or performing a Caesarian section.
>
> His intention is still to save the life of both the mother and the baby.... Because [the baby] has suddenly been taken out of the protective womb, it may encounter threats to its survival. The baby is never willfully destroyed because the mother's life is in danger.[105]

On the pro-abortion side, father of Planned Parenthood Alan F. Guttmacher corroborates this understanding:

> Today it is possible for almost any patient to be brought through pregnancy alive, unless she suffers from a fatal illness such as cancer or leukemia, and, if so, abortion would be unlikely to prolong, much less save, life.[106]

Decades ago, the evidence and testimony of both pro-life and pro-abortion physicians made it clear that mothers carrying their babies to term would not jeopardize the lives of their mothers regardless of the sickness or disease any mother contracted or was living with during her pregnancy. So the accusations of abortion promoters and supporters that pro-life men and women say such mothers have a duty to die to save the life of those children is a bald-faced lie. There are no such mothers. There are no such children.

Yet there are mothers who face decisions involving certain risk factors

---

105. C. Everett Koop, interview with Dick Bohrer, *Moody Monthly*, May 1980, reprinted in Dick Bohrer, *Sell Your Homework: 24 Ways to Write What You Think*, lesson 8 ("The Speech Critique") (Glory Press Books, 2005), 17.

106. "Abortion—Yesterday, Today, and Tomorrow," in *The Case for Legalized Abortion Now* (Diablo Press, 1967), 9.

connected with their lives and the lives of their babies, and we have read testimonies of such mothers choosing to put off certain medical treatments needed for their terminal illnesses because those treatments posed a threat to their baby.[107] These mothers have cried out to God for healing of their sickness so they can carry their little one to childbirth and life. Their doctor has explained that putting off treatment of their cancer, for instance, might hasten their death, but the mother refuses radiation, instead pleading with God for her own life and the life of her child. She has declined treatment rather than to risk harm to her child. She will speak of her love for her baby. She will remind those reading or listening how Jesus said no man has greater love than to lay down his life for a friend. She may recount how this statement of Jesus made the decision clear to her and her husband.

We ask ourselves if this is good or bad. Many things would have to be considered if one of us were to be faced with the same decision. The relative risk. The desire of one's husband. The number and ages of any children who would be left motherless. The counsel of the older women of the church, the pastor, and the elders. Whether the doctor was a Christian. Whether the baby was close enough to viability that holding out a couple weeks and taking her by Cesarean section would be an option, allowing radiation to start earlier. The list could go on.

Not one of us, though, would have the desire or claim the authority to take this life-and-death decision out of the mother and father's hands. Christians repeat our Lord's command to take up our cross and follow Him, but this is a far cry from one believer declaring to the pregnant Christian mother the specific cross she must take up is foregoing cancer treatment so that her unborn child will not be endangered by the radiation. None of us can imagine saying to such a Christian mother that her baby takes precedence over her, nor that foregoing radiation (for instance) is what Jesus means when He commands us to take up our cross for His sake. Rather, we would understand and agree with this mother if her treatment posed some level of risk to her baby, but she chose to proceed with that treatment.

---

107. It is also worth noting that a 2015 study in the *New England Journal of Medicine* (*NEJM*) indicated that "Prenatal exposure to maternal cancer with or without treatment did not impair the cognitive, cardiac, or general development of children in early childhood." Frédéric Amant et al., "Pediatric Outcome after Maternal Cancer Diagnosed during Pregnancy," *NEJM* 373, no. 19: 1824–1834, https://www.nejm.org/doi/full/10.1056/NEJMoa1508913.

The mother's and baby's lives are inextricably intertwined, and there are times when to save the mother's health and life is to save the baby's health and life. There are also times when treatments to save the mother's health and life pose an equal risk to herself and her baby, yet the decision will be made to proceed with that treatment recognizing that if the treatment ends up killing the child, this was in no way the intent of the physician or of his patient capable of full consent, the mother.[108] They both knew he had two patients and everything was considered and done to protect the well-being of both patients, but in the end the second patient, despite their best efforts to keep it from happening, died. In this case, the physician, father, and mother can all take comfort from their vigilance to protect both the mother and her child, knowing the succeeding death of the child was neither their intent nor their fault. They acted wisely and by faith in God's care for both mother and child, and God's decree was that the mother would live and the child would die. The Lord giveth, the Lord taketh; blessed be the name of the Lord (Job 1:21).

This discussion emphasizes the necessity of reminding physicians and one another that when we treat a pregnant mother, our treatment inevitably treats her child also. Pharmaceutical corporations know this very well and are vigilant to warn physicians, pharmacists, and customers of the danger their products pose to babies in the womb of the mother ingesting those products. Everyone knows pregnant mothers should not smoke or drink if they desire to protect the little child in their womb. When a child is listening to her mother's songs, feeling her mother's movements, sensing her mother's joy and pain, eating her mother's food, sharing her mother's oxygen, and swimming in her mother's amniotic fluid, her health is inseparable from her mother's health.

The doctor who prescribes medicine or treatment for the mother knows this very well, being motivated to know it by the potential of a malpractice suit if she or he prescribes a drug or treatment which produces fetal anomalies in that child, leaving the child disabled when she enters this world.

Physicians also know it because, over the course of the 1970s, amniocentesis became the standard of care for pregnant mothers older than 35

---

108. It may not need to be said, but this is the very opposite of the mother paying for an abortion. This mother takes the life of her child, almost never to save her own life or health, but to keep her future plans and lifestyle intact and unhindered.

years of age.[109] This was due to their considerably higher risk of giving birth to children with Down syndrome or aneuploidy.

Today the physician must provide their patient with the options of amniocentesis, chorionic villus sampling, or more often cell-free fetal DNA screening,[110] along with other fetal diagnostic procedures that protect the right of the parent (and yes, also the child) to exercise the option of termination of pregnancy in order to prevent what is legally referred to as "wrongful birth" and "wrongful life."

Malpractice suits are filed by both parents and children accusing physicians of neglecting to follow standards of care which would have made a diagnosis and termination of pregnancy possible, thus preventing the birth of a child of low quality of life because of a defect which might otherwise have been diagnosed in the womb.[111] In 1990, over thirty years ago, fetal testing was so common that 200,000 pregnant women were subjected to amniocentesis procedures.

Let us confess our faith by stating that we who belong to Jesus Christ abominate this practice which now results in the aborting of over 90 percent of children with Down syndrome today in North America.[112] Let us confess our faith by declaring that we Christians don't kill babies to protect ourselves from giving birth to a handicapped child. Christian physicians don't talk mothers into killing their baby in order to protect themselves from malpractice suits. In fact, no civilized person kills babies. What is the meaning of "civilization" and the "rule of law" when citizens protect their time and money by shedding the blood of their babies?

---

109. "In the United States, the current [1995] standard of care in obstetrical practice is to offer either CVS or amniocentesis to women who will be greater than or equal to 35 years of age when they give birth . . ." Richard Olney et al., "Chorionic Villus Sampling and Amniocentesis: Recommendations for Prenatal Counseling," Morbidity and Mortality Weekly Report (MMWR), CDC, July 21, 1995, https://www.cdc.gov/mmwr/preview/mmwrhtml/00038393.htm.

110. Laura Carlson and Neeta Vora, "Prenatal Diagnosis: Screening and Diagnostic Tools," *Obstetrics and Gynecology Clinics of North America* 44, no. 2 (June 2017): 245–256, https://www.ncbi.nlm.nih.gov/pmc/articles/PMC5548328/.

111. For wrongful *birth*, see, as an example, Turpin v. Sortini, 31 Cal. 3d 220 (1982), https://law.justia.com/cases/california/supreme-court/3d/31/220.html. For wrongful *life*, see, as an example, Curlender v. Bio-Science Laboratories, 106 Cal. App. 3d 814 (1980), https://law.justia.com/cases/california/court-of-appeal/3d/106/811.html. In *Curlender*, the California appellate court found *Roe v. Wade* to be "of considerable importance in defining the parameters of 'wrongful-life' litigation," because of the Supreme Court's determination "that parents have a constitutionally protected right to obtain an abortion during the first trimester of pregnancy," at 820.

112. Rebecca Lobo and Garnett Genuis, "Socially Repugnant or the Standard of Care: Is There a Distinction between Sex-Selective and Ability-Selective Abortion?" *Canadian Family Physician* 60, no. 3 (March 2014): 212–216, https://www.ncbi.nlm.nih.gov/pmc/articles/PMC3952749/.

Abortionists see only one person, the mother, and so they kill her baby. They say it forthrightly, and often. Some of them deny the babies are persons. Some deny babies are alive. Sometimes they are brutally honest, saying the mother's right to abortion is absolute, and this is "whether or not it's a life!"[113]

There will, as was pointed out above, be mothers who choose to reject treatment of their disease because the treatment poses a very serious danger to her preborn child. In such extraordinary cases, we acknowledge our Lord's declaration, "Greater love has no one than this, that one lay down his life for his friends" (John 15:13).

Clinical Callousness

Before we move on, we want to give one pastoral caution concerning the medical professionals who care for us.

Babies and pregnancy are the times of greatest vulnerability for mothers, and also fathers (to some lesser extent). For this reason, when a physician or other medical authority (and yes, they are authorities) warns us we should consider aborting our child, it shakes us to our core. Sometimes the suggestion arises from a problematic ultrasound showing the little one might have this or that anomaly indicating some potentially serious genetic disorder. Other times it arises from a serious diagnosis of the mother herself made during her pregnancy which requires a treatment that could harm or kill the baby in her womb (as in the examples mentioned above).

Regardless of the reason for the suggestion or recommendation, the simple fact is that your professional healer has just suggested or recommended to you that you kill your child. Don't let the clinical tone of the

---

113. One of us participated in a debate over abortion at the General Assembly of the Presbyterian Church (USA) in which each side was asked to summarize the other side's position. He was asked to go first and summarized the abortionists' position by saying they felt any abortion is tragic, but there are times when the circumstances of a woman's pregnancy are so harmful to the woman that having an abortion is less tragic than the alternative. Further, that since it's unclear whether or not the unborn is a real human life, choosing to have an abortion can be the moral decision. With anger, the female abortion proponent, nearly shouting, said, "No!"

The moderator responded, "No what? Are you saying this summary of your position isn't accurate?"

She responded, "Yes! We are *not* saying it's *not* a life. We are saying the woman has a right to have an abortion *whether or not it's a life!*"

suggestion throw you off guard, leaving you in shock so that you fail to react with the horror which you ought properly to feel and express. Prepare yourself beforehand so the medical professionals, who normally serve us so well, can have our help restoring their lost or attenuated instinct to protect mothers' loving solicitude towards their little ones, as well as the little ones themselves. Something like this might be said:

> What did you say? Did you really just suggest to me that I *kill* my *child*? Is my child not your patient also? Surely you weren't serious, were you? Are you so afraid of a malpractice suit that you have taken to saying such things? I'm so sorry for you. Go ahead and tell me what we can do about this problem, but don't you dare ever even in the slightest way suggest any solution to our problems that involves the death of the little one we both want to bring to term and deliver...

Something along those lines will be sufficient, and yes, it really will be helpful to many physicians who are only making the suggestion because it's a standard of practice, and not doing so can make them liable to a lawsuit if the child ends up being born with some congenital anomaly, or if carrying the little one to term contributes to the mother's death. Even if your physician reacts by sending you to another OB-GYN, rejoice that the Lord might have used you to reawaken her or his conscience, in time. Our social media generation needs to be reminded there are many things more horrible than relational or conversational awkwardness, or shame, or personally pronounced moral judgments.

Also remember that medical professionals are very limited in their knowledge, let alone ability to predict the future. If we hear the whistle of an artillery shell coming our way and are staring at mayhem all around us from previous shells that have rained down near us, it would be foolish not to take cover. But this is a far cry from reading an ultrasound and crying "wolf." Medical standards of practice might require a warning, but even as pastors, we can all recount times our sheep have come to us terror-stricken by the possible prognosis their OB-GYN just gave them, going on to suggest they consider terminating their pregnancy, after which it turned out to be a false alarm. Doctors might be required to give false alarms, but we are the children of the Great Physician for whom nothing is impossible.

Walking by faith includes pregnancy and childbirth. God loves our little ones more than we could ever love them, so even while they're still in the womb, practice entrusting them to Him.

CHAPTER 3

Applications

We now turn from the historical context, development, and spread of abortion, as well as its condemnation by nature, church history, common law, and Scripture, to the pressing question of what should be done by the church today to repent of this evil, and how God's people are to work toward restoring the liberties and freedoms of our most vulnerable and innocent neighbors. What shall we do to work toward repentance and the end of abortion?

The Duty of Civil Authorities

It's easy to summarize the duty of civil authorities in response to abortion, particularly in light of the Supreme Court's reversal of *Roe v. Wade*: They must stop it. They must forbid it by law, then punish those who break the law. They must protect and defend those God has placed under their care. They must fear and honor God by recognizing His image in every man, woman, and child. God has ordained them to punish evil and reward good. And concerning those who murder unborn children specifically, the civil authority must obey God's command, "Whoever sheds man's blood, by man his blood shall be shed, for in the image of God He made man" (Gen. 9:6).

These things are easy to write and speak, but difficult to do. Still, as with all duties commanded by God, governing with justice will yield its fruit of peace and righteousness; it will bring on both the ruler and those he rules God's approval and blessing.

The Civil Ruler and God's Law

In Romans 13, the Apostle Paul presents the clearest, most direct declaration of the civil magistrate's duties:

> Every person is to be in subjection to the governing authorities. For there is no authority except from God, and those which exist are established by God. Therefore whoever resists authority has opposed the ordinance of God; and they who have opposed will receive condemnation upon themselves. For rulers are not a cause of fear for good behavior, but for evil. Do you want to have no fear of authority? Do what is good and you will have praise from the same; for it is a minister of God to you for good. But if you do what is evil, be afraid; for it does not bear the sword for nothing; for it is a minister of God, an avenger who brings wrath on the one who practices evil. Therefore it is necessary to be in subjection, not only because of wrath, but also for conscience' sake. For because of this you also pay taxes, for rulers are servants of God, devoting themselves to this very thing. Render to all what is due them: tax to whom tax is due; custom to whom custom; fear to whom fear; honor to whom honor.
> (Rom. 13:1–7)

Note what is said about governing authorities:

1. They are from God.
2. They are appointed by God.
3. They carry out the ordinances of God.
4. They are a terror, not to good, but to evil.
5. They are God's ministers for good.
6. They are avenging ministers of God to bring God's wrath on those who do evil.
7. They are to be supported by us through taxes, customs, fear, and honor.

These statements are true of every civil magistrate no matter his particular bailiwick. The degree and scope of implementation will differ according to the office he holds. The president of the United States has a much larger sphere to govern than a city's mayor or a county councilor, yet the essence of their duties is the same. We may encapsulate these truths by focusing on the magistrate as a minister of God. In common parlance, we think of "minister" as synonymous with "pastor," but the latter is simply one species of the former.

The analogy is instructive. The pastor is a minister of God's ordinances too, but the ordinances he is to enforce are of a spiritual sort since God has delegated him authority over His church. God has not delegated him the sword, but rather the keys of His spiritual kingdom; and, in that connection, the administration of the sacraments by which the boundaries of His kingdom are made visible.

The civil ruler is a minister of God's ordinances also—but those pertaining to public life. God has granted him the ministry of authority over the public sphere of law, government, and justice. God has delegated him the sword to enforce the laws that govern his sphere. Further, those laws are not, ultimately, his own, since they flow from the eternal law of God:

> I am not now speaking of the observance of the law of nature and of the divine law, or of the law of nations; observance of these is binding upon all kings...[1]

The civil ruler has authority to promulgate and administer the law, but he also has been delegated by God authority to enforce that law through punishment. This is what Scripture refers to when it designates him an "avenger" of evil, referencing the sword that he bears. Not only does he have the ability, authority, and right to punish evil; he has the *duty* to do so. This is part of the ministry he has received from God, and he may not lawfully divest himself of it.

Moreover, the obligation of the civil ruler to enforce God's law is inseparable from his duty to discern who is violating the law. As with rulers of other spheres, the civil ruler must discern good from evil. Some

---

1. Hugo Grotius, *De Jure Belli ac Pacis Libri Tres*, 121 (1.3.16).

understanding of good and evil can be gained from natural law, but full knowledge can only come from divine revelation:

> Yet undoubtedly the revealed law is (humanly speaking) of infinitely more authority than what we generally call the natural law. Because one is the law of nature, expressly declared so to be by God himself; the other is only what, by the assistance of human reason, we imagine to be that law. If we could be as certain of the latter as we are of the former, both would have an equal authority; but, till then, they can never be put in any competition together.
>
> Upon these two foundations, the law of nature and the law of revelation, depend all human laws; that is to say, no human laws should be suffered to contradict these.[2]

Enforcing and administering the laws also has reciprocal elements. Just as the Seventh Commandment does not simply forbid adultery, but also enjoins love and fidelity toward one's wife,[3] so also the ruler's obligation to punish evil requires him to promote good. The ruler who cultivates good relations with foreign nations but refuses to commit arms to stopping an invasion is in violation of his duty. The city councilor who encourages citizens to vote but does not punish voter fraud is a failure.

Similarly, concerning abortion, the civil magistrate must understand he is a minister of God's command that those who shed the blood of man shall suffer the same. He must bear the sword of God's wrath against the one who murders His image-bearers, carrying out His sentence of death. The ruler's own background, history, opinions, sentiments, compunctions, feelings, and so on are, in one sense, immaterial. As with any other murder, the injunction against child murder comes from the Chief Lawgiver, and each subordinate lawgiver He has established has a duty to carry out the law established by His authority.

Neither the law nor the authority is, in fact, the minister's own; they are delegated to him for a specific function which is, in its negative dimension, to stop the evil of child murder. In its positive dimension, he is commanded

---

2. 1 William Blackstone, *Commentaries* *42.
3. See Westminster Larger Catechism, question 138, https://evangelpresbytery.com/westminster-larger-catechism/#Law.

to do all he can to value, honor, and care for the life of mankind as God has ordained and established it under His rule.

Thus the civil authority is required by God to defend the unborn by criminalizing abortion to the end that our little ones may be restored to the protection of the rule of law. In enforcing laws against mothers killing their babies, the civil ruler must beware of the temptation to profess he has more tenderness and compassion than God Himself. In America, our civil authorities formerly forbade abortion. Those laws must be restored.

In doing so, the overturning of *Roe* is a necessary and long-desired step. But, as we said earlier, joy in the downfall of *Roe* must not blind Christians to what is glaringly absent in the majority opinion of *Dobbs*: the recognition of the personhood of the unborn child. It is well for us to argue on the basis of federalism that the national government may not force abortion on the states, on the basis of strict constructionism that no constitutional right to abortion exists, or on the basis of originalism that the founders envisioned no such right—but all such arguments pale before the foundational issue: that, by God's decree, no man may lawfully destroy the image of God placed in man. So long as we in our laws continue to see originalism as the only proper basis for opposing abortion, we fall short of God's requirements. We act as Constitutionalists but not as Christians. May the end of *Roe* be only the *first* step in restoring God's rule of law to our nation.

Moreover, it will not be enough merely to restore pre-*Roe* legal frameworks. At that time, the law was inconsistent in its application. State and local laws permitted exceptions while not making those who procured abortions liable for the crime of murder. Even those who performed abortions were not punished for murder. The Supreme Court in *Roe v. Wade* noticed this inconsistency and decided this abolished the argument that preborn children are persons with due process afforded to them in the Constitution. The court said:

> When Texas urges that a fetus is entitled to Fourteenth Amendment protection as a person, it faces a dilemma. Neither in Texas nor in any other State are all abortions prohibited. Despite broad proscription, an exception always exists. The exception contained in Art. 1196, for an abortion procured or attempted by medical advice for the purpose of saving the life of the mother, is typical. But if the fetus is a person who is not to be deprived

of life without due process of law, and if the mother's condition is the sole determinant, does not the Texas exception appear to be out of line with the Amendment's command?

There are other inconsistencies between Fourteenth Amendment status and the typical abortion statute. It has already been pointed out . . . that in Texas the woman is not a principal or an accomplice with respect to an abortion upon her. If the fetus is a person, why is the woman not a principal or an accomplice? Further, the penalty for criminal abortion specified by Art. 1195 is significantly less than the maximum penalty for murder prescribed by Art. 1257 of the Texas Penal Code. If the fetus is a person, may the penalties be different?

A preborn baby *is* a person, and just as civil magistrates should work to overthrow all laws and policies that allow and promote abortion, they must do so with God's law as their standard. Abortion is murder according to God and should be treated as such by the civil magistrate.

Such a commitment to the law would not simply deter this great evil, but it would also serve a teaching function much needed now when it has become a habit to speak and think of little babies as "wanted" or "unwanted," "planned" or "unplanned"; when it has become our habit to dehumanize these little ones by referring to them as "fetuses," "fetal tissue," and "the products of conception."

Another element of this teaching work has already begun in some states. When a child's life ended in miscarriage or stillbirth, for many years the "fetus" was disposed of by hospitals and doctors. In fact, mothers and fathers were often forbidden by law from taking their dead child to bury and mourn. Such laws teach falsely that unborn children are not human beings, and that their loss is nothing to mourn. Recently, however, in some places the law now requires doctors and hospitals to offer mothers and fathers the opportunity to take their child's body, regardless of how old or young he may have been.[4] Laws such as this remind everybody involved that a miscarriage or stillbirth is not simply the loss of "fetal tissue," but the death of a child.

From conception, every little one created by God bears His image and

---

4. See, e.g., Indiana Code § 16-21-11-4, which recognizes parents' right to determine final disposition of the body of their little one lost to miscarriage.

likeness, so that to shed his blood is to destroy God's glory in him. Child-killing is an act of warfare against God Himself, and the civil ruler is required by God to execute His wrath upon all those committing this awful crime.

Keeping Our Eye on the Ball: Understanding the Dangers of Incrementalism

Civil magistrates must also be attentive to the current context of abortion, noting where their action is most needed. Presently, as we have noted, pro-lifers' and anti-abortionists' attention is fixed on surgical abortion. It is assumed that success on the surgical front will be a substantive victory toward the suppression of abortion overall. And, to be sure, we rejoice in the present decline of surgical abortions. It is God's blessing that, as technologies such as ultrasound shove our noses in the gore of our surgical child murders, many citizens and rulers could no longer countenance such an obvious moral monstrosity. Reforming our infant holocaust must start somewhere, so it is good there is some movement in the laws of our land outlawing a few of the more horrendous parts of this bloodshed. It is also good for the ghouls of Planned Parenthood and the National Abortion Rights Action League to see progress in laws against abortion, and to have a growing fear that society will condemn, outlaw, and punish their bloodlust.

On the other hand, while it is true that politics is the art of the possible, the people of God must let our voices be heard when pro-life legislation is proposed and passed which forestalls the abolition of abortion. We must fight against this bloodshed until all those profiting from it personally, financially, and politically are brought down from power and the lives of our little ones are brought back under the law's protection; until all the institutional forces protecting this bloodshed repent or yield up their authority in an unconditional surrender.

Laws outlawing this or that more limited aspect of our baby holocaust can be harmful if they diminish our zeal in opposing this holocaust itself. Incrementalism can have unintended consequences that are harmful to the larger goal. Eating away at the edges of our bloodletting may become a sort of medieval morality play that confirms our feelings of moral superiority while demoralizing us so we take no larger step towards the entire outlawing of abortion.

APPLICATIONS

Today, the overturning of *Roe* is a prime example of both the benefits and the limits of incrementalism. On the one hand, *Roe* was birthed in a long twilight of gradual compromises and defeats. It represented not the initial salvo from the Evil One against the unborn, but rather the culmination of decay in our marriages, churches, and societies for some one hundred years previous. And so, as *Roe* happened by incremental decay, so its downfall happened by gradual progress. Much of this has been noted in this document. The awakening of the (Protestant) Christian conscience. The development of ultrasound technology. The political awakening of Christians and their recognition of abortion as a bedrock issue. The pushing of laws to restrict abortion. The attempt to close abortion "clinics" by creative means. The election of presidents committed to appointing SCOTUS justices who would overturn *Roe*. For reasons known only to Himself, God chose to bring *Roe* down, not suddenly, but by the gradual work of faithful Christians.

Yet gradual success brings with it its own dangers. Having toiled for so long to achieve even a small victory, we rest on our laurels and take our ease. Having crossed the Jordan and defeated Jericho, we content ourselves with the land already taken by our fathers, and fail to achieve the victories and gain the ground given us by the Lord. And when a man with faith challenges us to fulfill the mission we've been given, we think him foolish. We mistake faithlessness for prudence, sloth for judiciousness, and think God incapable of working if not according to our conceptions. Faced with Goliaths on every bloody front, we quash the Davids in our midst, calling their zeal presumption and their courage recklessness.

Then, too, success tempts us to think more highly of ourselves than we ought. We become enamored with our wisdom, our strategies, our understanding of the body politic, our compassion for women, and so on—forgetting that the One who has called us to fight abortion is the same One whose thoughts are far above our own:

> Do you not know? Have you not heard?
> The Everlasting God, the Lord, the Creator of the ends of the earth
> Does not become weary or tired.
> His understanding is inscrutable.
>
> (Isa. 40:28)

There are also practical matters to consider. In particular, the civil authority should consider that anti-abortion bills that are limited in scope can have unintended consequences. Remember that the law is a teaching mechanism. As noted earlier, one unintended consequence of the pro-life focus on surgical abortions—say, for instance, twenty-week abortion bans and heartbeat bills—is that abortion moves to younger ages not impacted by these laws. An exclusive focus on surgical abortions may well entrench the murder of children at increasingly younger ages—ages it is more difficult to marshal political opposition to.

Worst of all, victory on one front can cause us to redefine the command and counsel of God. Having labored for many years against the most obvious symbol of abortion in our land, we begin to confine God's commands to it. Unable in our strength to abolish abortion completely, we satisfy ourselves that overturning *Roe* is surely enough work, and surely will please God enough. And in so doing, we circumscribe the law of God, justifying ourselves by our paltry works and omitting what we cannot achieve:

> Woe to you, scribes and Pharisees, hypocrites! For you tithe mint and dill and cummin, and have neglected the weightier provisions of the law: justice and mercy and faithfulness; but these are the things you should have done without neglecting the others. (Matt. 23:23)

Indeed, our tendency to focus on the less painful parts of reform is obvious. For example, observe how pro-lifers focus almost exclusively on surgical abortions. For a number of reasons, it's much more difficult to oppose and pass laws against chemical abortions, yet chemical abortions (what abortionists refer to as "medication abortions") are now the majority of abortions. It may be possible to focus on some aspects of chemical abortions without outlawing them entirely at first, but we must be honest with our arguments, never misleading the babies' murderers to the end that they think they can manipulate the Christian vote and retain their authority by occasionally fiddling around the edges of this ongoing slaughter. In all cases, we must be clear that the Christian conscience is principled—not pragmatic; and that its driving principle can never be stated either personally or in legal code as anything less than "Whoever sheds man's blood, by man his blood shall be shed, for in the image of God He made man."

Thus, to the extent that *Roe* is now overturned and some aspects of law concerning preborn human life return to pre-*Roe* frameworks, we should be glad, and should take stock of the means that led to this success. Yet we may never content ourselves by seeing *Roe* as the limit of our opposition to abortion. Its undoing is something that we *ought to have done*, but we may not leave *undone* the work of abolishing the countless remaining manifestations of abortion. IUDs, RU-486, Plan B, hormonal birth control—all these remain and are growing, and they are an enemy as deadly and entangled with us as *Roe* ever was.

Christians must therefore not regard any victory in the battle as the end of the war. Even with *Roe* overturned, no state has yet completely banned abortion (Oklahoma has come closest), and children younger than six weeks will continue to be killed even in states where abortion is curtailed. A generation ago, godly Christians might have seen overturning *Roe* as the final goal in ending abortion, but the truth has now become clearer. The end of *Roe* is not the end of abortion, nor even the beginning of the end, but rather—perhaps—the end of the beginning.[5]

Zeal Tempered by Knowledge: Prudent Policies

Scripture demonstrates that zeal for God's law and character is a constant feature of civil authorities who are praiseworthy. One is hard-pressed to find Scripture ever condemning a man for zeal for God's glory. Yet zeal alone doth not a just ruler make. Zeal must be tempered by knowledge:

> For I testify about them that they have a zeal for God, but not in accordance with knowledge. (Rom. 10:2)

Our Lord Himself warned against undertaking a task we lack the resources to complete:

> For which one of you, when he wants to build a tower, does not first sit down and calculate the cost to see if he has enough to complete it?

---

5. See Winston Churchill, in a 1942 speech commenting on the battle of El Alamein. "Autumn 1942 (Age 68)," International Churchill Society, March 12, 2015, https://winstonchurchill.org/the-life-of-churchill/war-leader/1940-1942/autumn-1942-age-68/.

> Otherwise, when he has laid a foundation and is not able to finish, all who observe it begin to ridicule him, saying, "This man began to build and was not able to finish." Or what king, when he sets out to meet another king in battle, will not first sit down and consider whether he is strong enough with ten thousand men to encounter the one coming against him with twenty thousand? Or else, while the other is still far away, he sends a delegation and asks for terms of peace. (Luke 14:28–32)

Assembling resources, developing strategies and tactics, assessing our opponent's resources, strategies, and tactics, and carefully considering possible collateral damage—in all these things we must temper our zeal with knowledge. Civil authorities willing to join this battle must consider not just the ultimate goal of abolishing abortion, but the means and resources God has supplied. We must evaluate the condition our fellow Christians' hearts with respect to abortion. Do those we must depend upon in this battle—our brothers and sisters in Christ—truly understand the nature of this killing in all its sordid details? Do they have the will to call their neighbors and rulers to repentance, or are they aiming simply at repeating shibboleths of the pro-life movement?

We see the sort of hostilities and dangers we will face from fellow believers as we read the history of the kings of Israel. Beginning with Solomon, Scripture records a relentless decline in the faithfulness of God's people, and this decline was represented and led by Israel's faithless and wicked kings. We have already noted some of the worst of these: Manasseh was the king of God's covenant people when he led them in sacrificing their little covenant children to the demon god of Molech.

Yet Israel was also led by godly kings such as Jehoshaphat, Hezekiah, and Josiah. The hearts of these men were toward God, and thus they sought to end the gross wickedness of their predecessors and the people they ruled.

It is noteworthy that Scripture is not absolutist toward even these godly kings, but faithfully documents both the good and evil of their leadership:

> He [Jehoshaphat] walked in the way of his father Asa and did not depart from it, doing right in the sight of the Lord. The high places, however, were not removed; the people had not yet directed their hearts to the God of their fathers. (2 Chron. 20:32–33)

This is the refrain of many a righteous king: he "did what was right in the sight of the Lord," yet "the high places were not taken away." In this and many similar passages, the Holy Spirit does not tell us *why* they were not taken away. We can imagine any number of reasons. The king had no desire himself to remove the high places. Or maybe he wanted to, but it was inexpedient or politically impossible. Maybe his advisors opposed him in it. It could well be that he was worried what his queen would think (à la Solomon).

In one sense, the reason doesn't matter; it was evil that the high places remained, and this was a blot on the soul of the king and his nation. Yet note how this failure is not the focus of the summary of the king's life.[6] It's important enough to mention, but does not dominate. It is possible to read this as a direct condemnation of the king, yet also possible to read it as more an assessment of the spiritual state of the nation and the attending realities.

So why were the high places not removed? Well, in Jehoshaphat's case, we're told why: "The people had not directed their hearts to the God of their fathers." Certainly, they ought to have; but they hadn't. They were not yet at that point in their repentance.

Our nation and its bloodshed are much like this. We have kings and rulers who resemble the kings of Israel who worshiped the true God without tearing down the idols and high places. Some of our rulers are devoted to abortion's bloodshed, while others are apathetic. Some rulers oppose abortion's bloodshed, but do so timidly. Only a very few have shown zeal in working to bring this genocide to an end.

Depending upon which sort of rulers we are governed by, we can see a variety of strategies and intentions motivating this or that policy initiative or law restricting abortion. One ruler supports an anti-abortion initiative for his own political advantage; another does so because he has some commitment to morality; and yet another because he truly fears God and honors His moral law. Still, this and similar leadership motivated by any even minimal desire to end abortion that leads to fewer infants being killed is something to rejoice over. And if we do have a ruler who fears God, we can rejoice all the more.

---

6. It may also be instructive that, in each such case, the words shift from active to passive voice: the deeds of the king (for good or for ill) are expressed in active voice, while the persistence of the high places is shifted into passive voice ("were not taken away"). This may represent a lower-level criticism of the king.

Recognize, though, that having the blessing of being governed by a ruler who fears God and trembles at the bloodshed of babies does not make the way forward totally clear. Even then, not all those who fear God and pray for the abolition of abortion will see strategy and tactics in the same way.

What some promote as a daring sortie testifying to faith and zeal will be condemned by others as a Pyrrhic victory that will result, not in less bloodshed, but more, because the zealot did not take into account all the factors: the probable response of the watching world, the stiffening of resolve on the part of godless rulers, or the effect of their action on the people of God themselves. Every calculation of how many babies will be saved each year when, by God's power, abortion has finally been criminalized, must be accompanied by a parallel calculation of how many babies will be lost. Remember, politics is the art of the possible. Our principled and absolute opposition to all abortion must not give birth to zeal without knowledge which causes even more bloodshed of the preborn.

With this in mind, civil rulers must temper zeal with wisdom from on high. We must sympathize with them in the difficulty of their decisions, praying that God will give them wisdom. In whatever station and with whatever gifting God has given them, civil rulers should work toward stopping abortion as quickly and as completely as possible. In some cases (e.g., as has been done with *Roe v. Wade*), this will mean supporting a law directly challenging a decision, policy, or law that upholds abortion in our land. In other cases, prudence may require a ruler to prioritize a strategy offering the most long-term benefits for ending the bloodshed. This may cause him to expend more energy on a bill or policy less direct in its challenge to abortion because he believes doing so has more potential to hamper the bloodshed in the future. Remember that *Roe v. Wade* did not draw its legal foundation from blunt preestablished "rights" to abortion, but from the subtle expansions of rights of "privacy" that had wound their way through earlier decisions such as *Griswold v. Connecticut*. The direct attack is not always the best path to victory. All that glitters is not gold.

For all the above reasons we renew our commitment to the truth that it is not the office of the church to dictate exactly how the civil magistrate must do his work. If complete abolition of abortion is not politically feasible in a given polity at a given time, it is still godly for the civil authority to save as many lives as possible through efforts short of complete abolition—always keeping firmly in mind that complete abolition is God's decretive standard and must remain the ruler's final objective.

The Accountability of Civil Rulers

Thus we remind every ruler that he will face accountability for how he has stewarded his authority from God. Some of his accountability will be to higher magistrates and some to those who elected him.

Nevertheless, his final accounting will be to God. He will give account to God for how he fulfilled his duty to punish evil and reward good. He will not be judged according to what he or his subjects think is evil or good, but according to what God's moral law declares evil and good. Whether he acknowledges it or not, the day is quickly coming when he will stand at the bar of the Almighty, and on that day no excuses will avail for his refusals to carry out the duties of his God-ordained station.

Every civil ruler will be judged by God for honoring or abandoning the defense of life, and especially the defense of lives weak or powerless because they live at the margins of society. This is the most fundamental God-given duty of a civil magistrate. In other ways, a particular ruler's administration of law might be commendable: he may have lowered taxes, cleaned out corporate corruption, balanced the budget, conserved natural resources, reduced government tyranny, and enhanced religious freedom across his domain; yet if he has turned a blind eye to the bloodshed of those living at the margins of his domain and not striven to bring it to an end, his administration has failed at the most basic duty God has delegated to him. The bloodguilt must be removed from the land, and he is the one charged by God with the responsibility of doing so.

Knowing God's requirements, yet being aware of our own inability, we are tempted to make only token efforts, only perfunctory attempts we know will accomplish little. Concerning abortion, we all have observed how often politicians play games with the lives of these little ones. Not having the courage to stand on principle, politicians run on being "pro-life"; they write pro-life commitments into their party platforms, then spend almost none of their political capital defending the little ones. Announcing that they are "pro-life" is a political ruse more for getting out the vote and raising campaign contributions than for ending abortion. For this reason, those who oppose abortion commonly lament, "Fool me once, shame on you. Fool me twice, shame on me. Fool me three times, I'm a Republican."

Still, despite all the promises our rulers have left unfulfilled, knowing our God's arm is mighty in behalf of the widow, the orphan, and the sojourner in our midst, by faith we rejoice in the sure and certain truth that God sees, God knows, and will bring every deed into judgment.

Apathy, half measures, and unfaithfulness are not exclusive to rulers, of course; they are common to man. Yet Scripture is clear that with authority comes greater accountability. The Apostle James warned teachers, "Let not many of you become teachers, . . . knowing that as such we will incur a stricter judgment" (James 3:1). If our teachers will be judged by God more strictly, what of His judgment of civil rulers whose raison d'être is judgment and punishment? Of all offices in God's economy, the civil ruler is the only one given expansive powers of temporal and physical penalties. He is the only one given the power of the sword, the only one authorized to compel financial support, the only one authorized to make war. God has made him steward of great power and authority, and has directed him to use it to serve and protect his citizens. The civil authority must fear God and His judgment:

> And the Lord said, "Who then is the faithful and sensible steward, whom his master will put in charge of his servants, to give them their rations at the proper time? Blessed is that slave whom his master finds so doing when he comes. Truly I say to you that he will put him in charge of all his possessions. But if that slave says in his heart, 'My master will be a long time in coming,' and begins to beat the slaves, both men and women, and to eat and drink and get drunk; the master of that slave will come on a day when he does not expect him and at an hour he does not know, and will cut him in pieces, and assign him a place with the unbelievers. And that slave who knew his master's will and did not get ready or act in accord with his will, will receive many lashes, but the one who did not know it, and committed deeds worthy of a flogging, will receive but few. From everyone who has been given much, much will be required; and to whom they entrusted much, of him they will ask all the more." (Luke 12:42–48)

Hearing this high calling might cause any man to despair. Seeing the corruption of their own hearts and the corruption of those under their authority, many rulers have thrown in the towel. Yet those suffering this temptation should remember that, though God is perfectly just and holy, He also knows His sons are not. He knows our frame and remembers that we are dust (Ps. 103:14).

Yes, this is the command given by Jesus: "You are to be perfect, as your heavenly Father is perfect" (Matt. 5:48). God doesn't dream or wish we were perfect in our exercise of authority: He commands us to be so. His standards are perfection. This is a fundamental gospel truth because the hopelessness of perfection in ourselves and our subjects causes us to despair of ourselves and live by faith in Jesus Christ, the Savior of the whole world to whom God the Father has delegated all authority in heaven and on earth (Matt. 28:18).

So then, we are to honor and keep His commandments, but we do so by faith in the Lordship of Jesus Christ, knowing that this faith has already overcome the world, making His commandments not grievous to us:

> For this is the love of God, that we keep His commandments; and His commandments are not burdensome. For whatever is born of God overcomes the world; and this is the victory that has overcome the world—our faith.
>
> (1 John 5:3–4)

This work of governing requires wisdom, care, and the ministry of the Holy Spirit. No ruler, nor any one of us, is sufficient for these things (2 Cor. 2:16), and it is only through the power of God and the fellowship of His church that any ruler may hope to honor God, particularly in his defense of the unborn. That defense may or may not result in great and epic advances against the evil of abortion, but no better epitaph for a magistrate's efforts could be given than this one given by our Lord: "She has done what she could" (Mark 14:8).

The Duty of Church Authorities

The Church and Abortion: Success Followed by Failure

In *Moby Dick*, Herman Melville makes the simple observation, "The pulpit leads the world." He adds, "Yes, the world's a ship on its passage out, and not a voyage complete; and the pulpit is its prow."[7] Jesus said He would build His church, and He promised the gates of hell would not prevail against her.

The Christian church is always to be on the offensive. After His resurrection, our Lord declared, "All authority has been given to me in heaven and on earth." It is His—not our own—authority we carry to the ends of the earth, teaching all men to do what He has commanded. We are His church militant.

God delegated the keys of His kingdom to the officers of His church. Thus pastors and elders lead the world through the proclamation of His Word, yes, but also through their exercise of these keys in their practice of church discipline. Immediately following our Lord's ascension, the power and authority of the King of kings and Lord of lords was carried by the church and her officers across the Roman Empire.

The New Testament church was born and grew in a world of infanticide, abortion, and fruitlessness. Through the pulpit, then, the early church proclaimed and practiced the protection of the weak and vulnerable, as well as the restoration of fruitfulness to the marriage bed. The church rescued unwanted, exposed infants left to die in the garbage heaps of Roman cities. The church protected the aged and infirm. As the church spread through Asia Minor, North Africa, and the Roman Empire, obedience to God's law spread. Contraception dwindled and abortion became unthinkable. Church fathers did not cease condemning the slaughter of the preborn, as well as all attempts to remove fruitfulness from marriage. Even when the church adopted unbiblical views of sex and celibacy, it did not alter its witness to these basic divine truths concerning procreation and the wickedness of abortion.

It is a terrible tragedy, then, that it was the twentieth-century church and her officers who led the West into the legalization and widespread practice first, of birth control and contraception, and then abortion. It was the early part of the twentieth century when the first major denomination announced that artificial birth control was an acceptable practice.

In August of 1930, breaking with all Christendom, the officers of the Anglican Church announced at their decennial Lambeth Conference their repudiation of their historic condemnation of intentional prevention of pregnancy.[8] A few months later, the Federal Council of Churches followed

---

7. Herman Melville, *Moby Dick*, ch. 8.
8. See Resolution 15 from The Lambeth Conference, 1930, Anglican Communion, https://www.anglicancommunion.org/resources/document-library/lambeth-conference/1930/resolution-15-the-life-and-witness-of-the-christian-community-marriage.aspx.

suit, endorsing "the careful and restrained use of contraceptives by married people."[9]

Those unaware of the uniform condemnation of contraception and abortion by Christendom will find instructive this March 22, 1931, editorial by the *Washington Post* written in response to the Anglican pronouncement:

> It is impossible to reconcile the doctrine of the divine institution of marriage with any modernistic plan for the mechanical regulation or suppression of human birth. The church must either reject the plain teachings of the Bible or reject schemes for the "scientific" production of human souls. Carried to its logical conclusion, the committee's report if carried into effect would sound the death-knell of marriage as a holy institution, by establishing degrading practices which would encourage indiscriminate immorality. The suggestion that the use of legalized contraceptives would be "careful and restrained" is preposterous.[10]

The Anglicans' reversal was not in response to some new discovery in the Bible or any advancement in theological understanding. Rather, it seems evident the change of doctrinal standards followed the practice of the pastors in their own lives.

For instance, an actuarial survey of the professional and upper classes in the UK during 1875 showed clergymen had an average of 5.2 children.[11] This was on par with the UK's national average. Yet when the 1911 census was taken, this figure had dropped to 2.8 children. Meanwhile, the national average remained at 3.7. Two decades before announcing their change in doctrine, the men of the pulpit had already changed their practice so that, inevitably, their personal practices changed their preaching.

To return to the *Washington Post*, it was only a matter of time until the Anglican bishops' talking point "careful and restrained" vanished, just as Planned Parenthood, the Religious Coalition for Abortion Rights, and the National Abortion Rights Action League's talking point about keeping

---

9. "Protestants Endorse Birth Control," *Birth Control Review* 15, no. 4 (April 1931): 102.

10. Quoted in Howard Kainz, "Failing to Connect the Dots on Contraception," *First Things*, February 8, 2012, https://www.firstthings.com/web-exclusives/2012/02/gop-fails-to-connect-the-dots-on-contraception.

11. As reported by Richard Soloway, *Birth Control and the Population Question in England, 1877–1930* (University of North Carolina Press, 1982), 103.

abortion "safe, legal, and rare" has also vanished. It took a mere thirty years for the "careful and restrained use" of contraception to give way to the National Council of Churches' full embrace of abortion. It was February 23, 1961, when the National Council of Churches endorsed abortion—twelve years before the Supreme Court legalized infant murder in 1973.

Ten years after *Roe v. Wade*, the Presbyterian Church (USA) declared abortion "an act of faithfulness before God":

> Protestants have long affirmed the use of contraception as a responsible exercise of stewardship of life. To prevent pregnancy when it is not desired is to be a responsible steward of human life. However, in the exceptional case in which a woman is pregnant and judges that it would be irresponsible to bring a child into the world, given the limitations of her situation, it can be an act of faithfulness before God to intervene in the natural process of pregnancy and terminate it.[12]

In 1970, three years prior to the Supreme Court's *Roe v. Wade* ruling, the Baptist Sunday School Board (now known as Lifeway) conducted a poll which found that 70 percent of Southern Baptist pastors supported abortion to protect, not just the physical health of a mother, but also her mental health; and that 64 percent of Southern Baptist pastors supported abortion in the case of a fetal disability. One year later (1971), the Southern Baptist Convention (the largest Protestant denomination in the US) at their annual national meeting passed a resolution stating:

> We call upon Southern Baptists to work for legislation that will allow the possibility of abortion under such conditions as rape, incest, clear evidence of fetal deformity, and carefully ascertained evidence of the likelihood of damage to the emotional, mental, and physical health of the mother.[13]

Two years later, a poll conducted by the *Baptist Standard* found that 90 percent of Texas Baptists believed their state's abortion laws were too

---

12. "Covenant and Creation: Theological Reflections on Contraception and Abortion," report delivered to the 195th General Assembly (1983) of the Presbyterian Church (USA), 17. The GA received this report and adopted its policy statements and recommendations.
13. David Roach, "How Southern Baptists Became Pro-Life," *Baptist Press*, January 16, 2015, https://www.baptistpress.com/resource-library/news/how-southern-baptists-became-pro-life/.

restrictive. Here again, the pulpit led the world, removing moral censures against the slaughter of little ones in the womb. The world followed the church's leadership, and one year later the Supreme Court issued its bloody decree.

In subsequent years, the Southern Baptist Convention went through a "conservative resurgence," and by God's grace moved back from its former advocacy of abortion. Yet the damage had been done.

Today, we have some hope that opinion polls within conservative Christian denominations would not resemble those of the 1970s. There are many pastors faithfully working to awaken Southern Baptists' consciences to the horror of the slaughter of children. We appreciate this work in any denomination, and yet still today the most conservative Christian churches and congregations neglect or even refuse to give the souls under their charge biblical moral instruction concerning these matters.

For example, in 2019, the Pew Research Center analyzed nearly 50,000 sermons shared online by more than 6,000 US churches during the second quarter of the year, and they found that abortion was mentioned in only 4 percent of those sermons. Pew Research noted that, even when abortion was mentioned, it was rarely the focus of the sermon:

> When sermons are broken into smaller segments of 250 words (the median sermon runs 5,502 words), three-quarters of all sermons that mention abortion do so in just one segment. As a result, only 1% of all sermons across the whole database discuss abortion in more than one segment.[14]

Given pastors' avoidance of these matters, it's no surprise researchers find more than 4 out of 10 women who have had an abortion are churchgoers,[15] nor is it any surprise 54 percent of members of the Presbyterian Church in America believe abortion should be legal.[16]

---

14. Dennis Quinn, "Few U.S. Sermons Mention Abortion, Though Discussion Varies by Religious Affiliation and Congregation Size," Pew Research Center, April 29, 2020, https://www.pewresearch.org/fact-tank/2020/04/29/few-u-s-sermons-mention-abortion-though-discussion-varies-by-religious-affiliation-and-congregation-size/.
15. Lisa Cannon Green, "Survey: Women Go Silently from Church to Abortion Clinic," Focus on the Family, August 17, 2021, https://www.focusonthefamily.com/pro-life/survey-women-go-silently-from-church-to-abortion-clinic/.
16. David Masci, "American Religious Groups Vary Widely in Their Views of Abortion," Pew Research Center, January 22, 2018, https://www.pewresearch.org/fact-tank/2018/01/22/american-religious-groups-vary-widely-in-their-views-of-abortion/.

The Church's Bloodguilt

We, the people of God, must confess our bloodguilt. As it was with Israel and Judah in the times of the Old Testament prophets, the people of God today have our children's blood on our hands.

We don't know how many of their lives we have sacrificed, and we're relieved not to know. At times we have used methods of birth control which have an abortifacient agency knowing full well we were doing so. At other times we have assuaged our consciences by telling ourselves we'll never know whether our method of birth control killed our child; and anyhow, it's more likely our birth control prevented conception than that it killed any little one God had created and placed in our wife's womb. We dampen down our consciences with self-talk of risk being an everyday part of life. It was not our intent to kill our little one. Surely any bloodshed we commit from a desire to provide our already-born children a college education and greater socioeconomic stability justifies any risk we take with our birth control.

It must be stated clearly that, among the people of God, the bloodguilt doesn't rest on fathers and mothers alone, but also physicians, nurses, and pharmacists who are brothers and sisters in Christ and who neglected to inform us that our birth control has an abortifacient agency. Among the people of God, many physicians, nurses, and pharmacists answered our questions with equivocations and lies concerning the medical choices they helped us make.

Listen to this command given by God to His covenant people, noting His warning against their pleading ignorance:

> Then the LORD spoke to Moses, saying, "You shall also say to the sons of Israel:
>
> 'Any man from the sons of Israel or from the aliens sojourning in Israel who gives any of his offspring to Molech, shall surely be put to death; the people of the land shall stone him with stones. I will also set My face against that man and will cut him off from among his people, because he has given some of his offspring to Molech, so as to defile My sanctuary and to profane My holy name. If the people of the land, however, should ever disregard that man when he gives any of his offspring to Molech, so as not to put him to death, then I Myself will set My face against that man and

against his family, and I will cut off from among their people both him and all those who play the harlot after him, by playing the harlot after Molech.'"

(Lev. 20:1–5)

Bloodguilt is everywhere among God's people in the Western world today, especially here in North America where there still remains such a treasure of Christian faith and witness. Having been given much, our guilt is that much greater. God commanded Moses to warn His people against child slaughter. Who warns the people of God today?

God has set apart pastors and other church officers to preach and teach His Word today. In connection with intimate matters related to women and their life-givingness, it is the particular calling of our congregation's "older women" to instruct the women of the church in these life-and-death matters. Older women are called to teach godliness to the congregation's younger women; and specifically to teach the younger women to "love their children."[17]

Would it not be the most basic fulfillment of this calling for older women to warn young brides and mothers against the horror of child sacrifice practiced all around us by the pagans? Yes, pastors must give this instruction and provide these warnings in premarital counseling also; but how can an older woman of God instruct a younger woman to love her children without warning her not to kill her children?

It is good and right for our older women to teach the younger women to read the Bible and pray, to keep a rein on their irritation at their little ones and not lash out in anger at them, to respect their husbands, to read the Bible to their little ones, to be patient with a child who is difficult to nurse, and so on. But does their obligation to lead the younger women of God not include speaking to them about the sanctity of the marriage bed and its fruit?

In the final analysis, though, none among the people of God have greater responsibility for the pervasiveness of the bloodshed of our children than the shepherds of Christ's church. The Apostle Paul testified to those he

---

[17]. "Older women likewise are to be reverent in their behavior, not malicious gossips nor enslaved to much wine, teaching what is good, so that they may encourage the young women to love their husbands, to love their children, to be sensible, pure, workers at home, kind, being subject to their own husbands, so that the word of God will not be dishonored." Titus 2:3–5.

had shepherded in Ephesus that none of their "blood" was on his "hands." How had he acquitted himself of any bloodguilt?

> For I did not shrink from declaring to you the whole purpose of God.
> (Acts 20:27)

Today, pastors shrink and run from declaring to their sheep the whole counsel of God concerning sexuality, marriage, and God's blessing of children. Pastors have not warned their sheep against subverting God's purpose in the womb by shedding the blood of those children He Himself has placed there. Pastors in their pulpits, in their offices during marital and premarital counseling, and in every part of church life—as well as elders, deacons, and older women in their congregations—are neither teaching nor warning their sheep against the wiles of the Evil One who loves death, particularly the death of little ones who have just been created by our heavenly Father.

It's an awful truth that those we worship with who are marked by the sign of God's covenant continue to do obeisance to the pagans' demon gods of choice, self-determination, convenience, academic degrees, wealth, comfort, and a whole host of other idols, even joining them in their child sacrifices. God blesses us, entrusting the womb of our wives with new life for the propagation of His godly seed,[18] and Christian wives leave His worship, drive home with their husband and children, eat dinner, and later go up to their bathroom and murder this little blessing He's given.

Do God's prophets warn them against this sin?

No. As in the days of the prophet Isaiah, so in our own day:

> His watchmen are blind,
> All of them know nothing.
> All of them are mute dogs unable to bark,
> Dreamers lying down, who love to slumber;
> And the dogs are greedy, they are not satisfied.
> And they are shepherds who have no understanding;

---

18. "But not one has done so who has a remnant of the Spirit. And what did that one do while he was seeking a godly offspring? Take heed then to your spirit, and let no one deal treacherously against the wife of your youth." Malachi 2:15.

> They have all turned to their own way,
> Each one to his unjust gain, to the last one.
> "Come," they say, "let us get wine, and let us drink heavily of strong drink;
> And tomorrow will be like today, only more so."
>
> (Isa. 56:10–12)

Within the church today, God makes husband and wife one for the propagation of a godly seed; He blesses the husband and wife by creating a child in the womb of the wife; and we respond by practicing pregnancy prevention using hormones that regularly kill a child God has created and sent to us as His blessing.

Thus God's covenant people today commit the same sin as God's covenant people in the time of Manasseh and Solomon. Where is our King Josiah whose reform included forbidding and stopping the child sacrifices practiced by God's people?

> He [Josiah] also defiled Topheth, which is in the valley of the son of Hinnom, that no man might make his son or his daughter pass through the fire for Molech. (2 Kings 23:10)

The Necessity of Repentance

Repentance is the only path back to the grace of God, but how shall pastors lead this repentance?

First, repentance must be preached. As they stand in their pulpits proclaiming God's Word, God's servants must not avert their eyes from the most helpless of lambs being taken away to the slaughter. Remember our Lord's parable of the religious leaders who walked past the victim lying injured in the road?

God has called us to rescue those being led away to death; to hold back those who are staggering to the slaughter (Prov. 24:11). Will our shepherds continue to close their eyes to the blood that stains the ground of our villages, cities, states, and nations? Will our shepherds continue to pretend they don't know about these deaths of the lambs of their flock?

Nothing is hidden from God, and He will repay according to what has been done and left undone, what pastors have said and left unsaid. From the ground, the blood of these little ones cries out to Him.

This is not a political issue, nor should pastors relegate the defense of these littles ones to a single pro-life Sunday each January. Nor should pastors preach as if the abortions are all done "out there" by others—and only at Planned Parenthood's clinics. One Sunday each year with condemnation only of outsiders is a betrayal of the pastoral office.

Shepherds must repent of their self-censorship which arises from a desire to avoid offending their people. The souls under the care of shepherds are sheep. Sheep must be taught and rebuked and led to confession of their sins by faithful shepherds watching over their souls, regardless of whether their sheep want to be rebuked and called to repentance.

If the response is that some things are impolite to speak of in mixed company, keep in mind that eternity and judgment are drawing near. How could it ever be impolite for men who are shepherds to call women to repentance for murdering their children—nor any less their husbands who are eager for, and complicit in, their decisions?

Women pay for abortion procedures and drugs. Some of our own mothers, wives, and daughters have committed abortion. Women we love and are called to instruct and protect should not lack shepherds who will speak truthfully, leading them into a biblical understanding and a true spiritual remorse for what they have done. Women who have committed abortions need the wounding of God's law so they may confess their crimes, and by faith alongside David, find forgiveness and have the joy of their salvation restored to them:

> Deliver me from bloodguiltiness, O God, the God of my salvation;
> Then my tongue will joyfully sing of Your righteousness.
> (Ps. 51:14)

In all the work of the pastor, he must keep this warning in mind:

> Now as for you, son of man, I have appointed you a watchman for the house of Israel; so you will hear a message from My mouth and give them warning from Me. When I say to the wicked, "O wicked man, you will surely die," and you do not speak to warn the wicked from his way, that wicked man

shall die in his iniquity, but his blood I will require from your hand. But if you on your part warn a wicked man to turn from his way and he does not turn from his way, he will die in his iniquity, but you have delivered your life. (Ezek. 33:7–9)

True gospel ministry never consists of God's yes without His no.

The Church's Public Witness against the Killing

As our Lord said, it was God who "from the beginning made them male and female" (Matt. 19:4). Sex is a station assigned each of us by God. We have no individuality that is not marked by God's call of each of us to the station of either man or woman. We cannot live by faith without doing so as men and women who, by faith, fulfill our sex biblically.

Given the pervasive rebellion of individuals today repudiating God's creation of each person as man or woman, the beginning of repentance and the first steps of faith will often be defined within the church by men and women rediscovering, learning to love, and fulfilling their God-given sexuality. One certain and joyful side effect of such a resurgence of biblical sexuality is that pastors who preach and teach with application to men as men and women as women will lead the way toward the abolition of abortion.

When pastors lead their people to rejoice in their God-given sexuality and to desire a godly seed (Mal. 2:15), this will awaken the consciences of the people of God to the horror of abortion's slaughter. Pastors who are fearful of the reaction of their sheep, and thus inclined to avoid serving as the instruments of this sexual awakening, may take encouragement and be strengthened by the Apostle Paul's exhortation: "Speak and exhort with all authority. Let no one disregard you" (Titus 2:15).

Men and women of God who discover the blessing of manhood and womanhood, marital love, and children will also certainly come to realize the wickedness of abortion and express a desire to witness against this great evil. This is particularly true of women who, prior to coming to faith or a truly biblical understanding of the blessing of unborn life, have aborted their little ones. Naturally, those who have repented of their own abortions will desire to find women considering abortion and awaken these women to the beauty of life and the terrible sin of killing our Lord's little ones, truly "the least of these":

But when the Son of Man comes in His glory, and all the angels with Him, then He will sit on His glorious throne. All the nations will be gathered before Him; and He will separate them from one another, as the shepherd separates the sheep from the goats; and He will put the sheep on His right, and the goats on the left.

Then the King will say to those on His right, "Come, you who are blessed of My Father, inherit the kingdom prepared for you from the foundation of the world. For I was hungry, and you gave Me something to eat; I was thirsty, and you gave Me something to drink; I was a stranger, and you invited Me in; naked, and you clothed Me; I was sick, and you visited Me; I was in prison, and you came to Me." Then the righteous will answer Him, "Lord, when did we see You hungry, and feed You, or thirsty, and give You something to drink? And when did we see You a stranger, and invite You in, or naked, and clothe You? When did we see You sick, or in prison, and come to You?" The King will answer and say to them, "Truly I say to you, to the extent that you did it to one of these brothers of Mine, even the least of them, you did it to Me."

Then He will also say to those on His left, "Depart from Me, accursed ones, into the eternal fire which has been prepared for the devil and his angels; for I was hungry, and you gave Me nothing to eat; I was thirsty, and you gave Me nothing to drink; I was a stranger, and you did not invite Me in; naked, and you did not clothe Me; sick, and in prison, and you did not visit Me." Then they themselves also will answer, "Lord, when did we see You hungry, or thirsty, or a stranger, or naked, or sick, or in prison, and did not take care of You?" Then He will answer them, "Truly I say to you, to the extent that you did not do it to one of the least of these, you did not do it to Me." These will go away into eternal punishment, but the righteous into eternal life. (Matt. 25:31–46)

Men too, discovering not only the blessing of manhood and womanhood, marital love, and children, but also their manly biblical duty[19] to protect the lives woman presents the race, will ask how they can help restrain and end this bloodshed. It is right for men and women to ask these

---

19. For more, see "Man's Duty to Protect Woman," Majority Report of the Presbyterian Church in America's General Assembly Ad Interim Study Committee on Women in the Military, 2001, https://www.pcahistory.org/pca/studies/01-278.html.

questions and seek to stand up against the slaughter of the unborn. We will all seek to love and protect the least of these, and the officers of Christ's church will be called upon to give wise counsel concerning how to best witness against this horror.

While not every church is located within driving distance of a surgical abortion "clinic," many are, and it is a work of justice and love to go and bear witness against the bloodletting as those inside their mother's wombs are being led to the slaughter. Even though pharmacies dispensing murderous drugs are fast becoming the primary battleground, the abortuary remains a place of bloodshed, and there are Christian men and women who will desire to present a Christian witness there. This work should be supported by the wise counsel of their church officers. Examining how best to undertake this work is particularly necessary given the physical, legal, and spiritual dangers that attend any Christian witness at these killing places.

Other ways and places to witness against the bloodshed are best considered under the wise counsel of those officers congregants have vowed submission to. This is no light matter and should not be entered into unadvisedly. Standing against the massive murder of our little ones, though, is righteous, and where the officers of a particular church are uninterested in preaching against it as well as supporting public anti-abortion witness by their counsel and presence, it remains a Christian duty which will weigh heavy on the consciences of God's faithful. It is no sin for them to commend their conscience to God by such public witness.

Some churches will decide to witness against abortion publicly outside the abortuary on its killing days. Some will have no abortuary to provide sidewalk counseling to and may choose to picket their local supermarket pharmacies. Other churches will go together with fellow believers of neighboring congregations to picket the city's United Way offices where the community's charitable contributions are used to support Planned Parenthood. Some churches will call their members to attend county and city council hearings related to the zoning and support of the killing places. Other congregations will have pastors, elders, and deacons gifted for open-air preaching who will ask their people to come and support that preaching outside the abortuaries, pharmacies, and supermarkets, or at the county courthouse and inside the state capital.

Some churches will focus on social media forms of witness. Other churches will join together to write a doctrinal witness and teaching tool similar to this one that can be shared among their denominational churches, officers, and members. Other churches will start and support crisis pregnancy ministries, or provide financial support to couples in the congregation who adopt children—or embryos left in the "concentration can" of in vitro businesses.[20]

Churches may provide an effective witness against abortion in countless ways. What is important is to be creative in providing men and women opportunities to speak up in defense of these little ones created by God; and, where possible, to provide this witness under the wise counsel and direction of the shepherds God has provided us in His church.

For Christians to undertake calling those killing their children to repentance is a gospel witness, not merely a political demonstration. But as we bear this witness, church members and officers must exercise caution and wisdom in this work, guarding against schism and division among God's people, as well as any needless scandal in the wider community.

Still, it must be said that any witness against the slaughter will inevitably give rise to scandal among those covered in blood and unwilling to repent. Truth is often scandalous, particularly when it exposes the bloodshed of the innocents. The mere fact of scandal in the community attendant to the church's witness against abortion may be the most clear evidence of the effectiveness of that witness.

In addition, all churches can and should be regularly praying for the end of abortion. Prayer doesn't take the place of these other forms of action but prayer itself is not passive. It is one of the main weapons of warfare that Jesus has given us. In sacred Scripture, the prayers of God's people are described as rising to the heavens like a pleasing aroma of incense. The fire of this incense is then hurled back to the earth in God's judgment on the enemies of Christ.[21] Christ hears the cry of those who suffer, and He is the great Defender of the orphan. Churches should not forget the power of prayer, and they should pray for God's mercy on little ones and judgment upon those who oppress them without repentance.

---

20. For more information on embryo adoption, see the website of the National Embryo Donation Center, https://www.embryodonation.org/; or the website of Nightlight Christian Adoption's "Snowflakes" program, https://nightlight.org/snowflakes-embryo-adoption-donation/.

21. See Revelation 8.

Remember that the church, God's house, is to be a house of prayer for the nations (Isa. 56:7). The Apostle Paul instructed the church to offer entreaties *and* prayers, petitions *and* thanksgivings, on behalf of all people including those in civil authority (1 Tim. 2:1–2). Surely, the little children in the womb are among those who are of the nations that we ought to pray on behalf of. Prayer and thanksgiving for these children and their mothers ought to be a normal part of the intercessory work of the church. Pray that God would turn the hearts of the fathers and mothers toward their children. Pray that God would move the hearts of our civil authorities. Pray that all our efforts to bear witness will be used by God for His glory, the souls of mothers, and the lives of the preborn.

Instructing the Civil Magistrate

Pastors are not simply called to shepherd God's flock. That is their primary call, but by that call they are also responsible to serve as God's servants commissioned to proclaim His law and gospel to the nations. Pastors today are God's servants, the prophets.

The gospel of Jesus Christ always and necessarily proclaims God's law. Calling men to repent and believe is no private Christian work, and this is our Lord's Great Commission:

> All authority has been given to Me in heaven and on earth. Go therefore and make disciples of all the nations, baptizing them in the name of the Father and the Son and the Holy Spirit, teaching them to observe all that I commanded you; and lo, I am with you always, even to the end of the age. (Matt. 28:18–20)

Add to this statement our Lord's call to His followers to be His witnesses to the world:

> You are the salt of the earth; but if the salt has become tasteless, how can it be made salty again? It is no longer good for anything, except to be thrown out and trampled under foot by men.
>
> You are the light of the world. A city set on a hill cannot be hidden; nor does anyone light a lamp and put it under a basket, but on the lampstand,

and it gives light to all who are in the house. Let your light shine before men in such a way that they may see your good works, and glorify your Father who is in heaven.

Do not think that I came to abolish the Law or the Prophets; I did not come to abolish but to fulfill. For truly I say to you, until heaven and earth pass away, not the smallest letter or stroke shall pass from the Law until all is accomplished. (Matt. 5:13–18)

Christian pastors are to heed and obey our Lord's order that we make disciples of "all nations," that we be "the salt of the earth," that we remain "salty," that we provide "the light of the world," and that we serve as His "city on a hill" which "cannot be hidden." We are not to hide our light under a basket, but to lift it up on a lampstand for all to see.

The Apostle Paul is simply reiterating these commands, emphasizing this responsibility of pastors and their congregations to serve as witnesses to our wicked world when he writes to Timothy that the Christian church is "the pillar and support of the truth" (1 Tim. 3:15).

When pastors censor themselves, justifying it by talk of "being gospel-centered" or pontificating on "two-kingdom theology," we betray our calling. When we are silent, refusing to expose and condemn the bloodlust and slaughter we are drowning in today, we betray our commission. Why would anyone repent of abortion who has not been confronted with God's terrible condemnations of child sacrifice?

Understanding why we are petrified to proclaim those condemnations is not difficult.

Given how intensely the state supports the bloodshed of our little ones, it's important to say that Christians' prophetic witness against abortion must begin with proclaiming the truth to the rich, powerful, and strong, particularly the civil magistrate. Yes, it is true that ministers are church—not civil—authorities. It is true some pastors suffer the temptation to focus on the political realm to the neglect of their calling to feed and guard their flock. Yet God's prophets must not use this first priority as an excuse for abandoning their prophetic calling. We are to call all men—including especially civil authorities—to repentance.

Pierre Viret, a minister in Calvin's company of pastors, put it this way:

Just as ministers are not bound to do what pertains to rulers and magistrates, so on the other hand if they do not sound the word, and do not speak to the rulers and magistrates with all frankness according to their calling, they will be guilty of grave guilt. For they would then be included in the number of dumb dogs which Isaiah speaks of. For their office requires them to call the rulers and magistrates to do their duty according to the Law of God.[22]

The historic church has always proclaimed God's law to civil magistrates. John Calvin addressed his *Institutes of the Christian Religion* to the civil magistrate. Luther was relentless in challenging the princes of Germany. A thousand years earlier, John Chrysostom enraged the empress with his rebukes of her luxurious lifestyle, and was exiled for his work. The early church apologists directed their works to the civil magistrates, calling them to repent and believe on Jesus Christ.

Here, church fathers are only following the biblical example. The Old Testament prophets rebuked kings to their faces, both Israelite and gentile kings. These same prophets proclaimed the coming salvation of the nations in the time of the New Covenant, foretelling that kings would be nursing maids to the church. Psalm 2 explicitly commands rulers to "kiss the Son," warning of the consequences if they refused.

Do we remember that John the Baptist lost his head for rebuking the civil ruler, Herod, for violating God's law? Jesus told His disciples they would stand before kings, and so they did, preaching to civil authorities, some of whom were converted. There was the proconsul Sergius Paulus (Acts 13) and Dionysius the Areopagite (Acts 17). The book of Acts concludes with Paul's journey to the capital of the Roman Empire, leaving the reader with the anticipation of his encounter with its leaders. Even Theophilus, the man addressed by Luke in both his gospel and the book of Acts, is thought by some to have been a civil magistrate.

It involves no admixture or denial of the discrete nature of the two kingdoms to command civil rulers in God's name to punish abortion as a fundamental violation of God's law. It's an old tactic here in the United

---

22. Pierre Viret, *The Christian and the Magistrate: Roles, Responsibilities, and Jurisdictions*, trans. R. A. Sheats (Psalm 78 Ministries, 2015), ch. 7, Kindle.

States to maintain the canard of the separation of church and state in order to silence those prophesying against injustice and oppression. Both ecclesiastical and civil rulers are agreed that the church should shut up.

Here in the United States, this is nothing new. Note this lament by President Lincoln:

> You say that you think slavery is wrong, but you denounce all attempts to restrain it. Is there anything else that you think wrong, that you are not willing to deal with as a wrong? Why are you so careful, so tender of this one wrong and no other? You will not let us *do* a single thing as if it was wrong; there is no place where you will allow it to be even *called* wrong! We must not call it wrong . . . in politics because that is bringing morality into politics, and we must not call it wrong in the pulpit because that is bringing politics into religion . . . and there is no single place, according to you, where this wrong thing can be properly called wrong![23]

Pastors are not to allow God's prophetic words to be gagged in the public square. Right there at the heart of our towns and cities, pastors are to preach against the evils of our day, condemning those evils as well as civil magistrates who live by them electorally. Of course pastors must not abandon their flock to become political hacks. And yes, this is a danger when the sheep feel impotent in the face of pagan culture warriors and desire that a champion be raised up representing their side. Many pastors choose to be their flock's hero rather than their shepherd. It is enticing, and shepherds must resist this temptation.

Still, pastors have a duty to serve as prophets to the civil rulers. They can only fulfill their duty to rule by the law of God if they heard that law proclaimed.

The Civil Authority and the Power of the Keys

This responsibility is even more imperative when, as is so often the case here in North America, the civil ruler is a Christian who has vowed submission

---

23. Speech at New Haven, Connecticut, March 6, 1860, *Collected Works of Abraham Lincoln*, vol. 4 (University of Michigan Digital Library Production Services, 2001), 21, http://name.umdl.umich.edu/lincoln4. Emphases original.

to his shepherds and sits with the people of God each week under the preaching of God's Word, then communing with them at the Table of our Lord. In such cases, pastors must preach and teach this ruler; but if he refuses to honor his shepherds calling him to submission to God's law, they must exercise the tools of discipline given them by God. Civil rulers who bow the knee to Molech and refuse admonitions and rebukes concerning their promotion of bloody sacrifices to demons must, in time, be barred from the Lord's Table. No one who is complicit and unrepentant in spilling the blood of the innocent should be allowed to continue to commune with God's people. He is not discerning the body and blood of our Lord.

Walking alongside Our Sheep in the Death of the Unborn

Finally, pastors testify against abortion by being tender with those in their flock who have lost their little ones. Despite improvements in technology, the death of children in utero is still a regular sadness felt by many of our sheep. Yet, too often, God's people do not know how to grieve the loss of the unborn, because pastors, church officers, and the older women of the church have not been examples to them in these things, nor instructed them. In light of the massive numbers of abortions the past half century, as well as the dwindling love of fruitfulness within the church the past full century now, it's no surprise the church has grown insensitive to the grief of mothers, fathers, and children mourning the deaths of their unborn and stillborn babies.

Families should not be left to suffer this grief hidden and alone. Shepherds and their wives can lead the way in helping and comforting those who grieve the deaths of our lambs. Shepherds and their wives can lead the way, showing the flock the beauty and relief of mourning these little ones with the eyes of faith fixed on the resurrection of Jesus Christ. King David himself taught us how to do so, mourning the loss of his little one (2 Sam. 12:23).

A number of our modern practices surrounding death are unhelpful in this regard. Our forced cheerful and happy-clappy posture toward death today inside and outside the church is a betrayal of the Fall and its awful consequences which seek to drown us in grief and sadness. Mutual conspiracies to deny death's terrible weight are no good.

The church should be led back to our former heavy and truthful liturgies of death and mourning testifying to our hope in the resurrection of our Lord. These liturgies will be so helpful directing families in their grief (over the deaths of adults *or* babies), and this is particularly the case following the loss of their little child—when it does seem awkward to grieve someone so very tiny whom we have never seen.

This leadership of the pastor and church will be particularly helpful to mothers who have carried these little ones and known them intimately, sometimes for a full nine months; who with great expectation have been singing to them, praying for them, talking to them, and naming them. We provide a safe place for the mother and father's grief when we give a homily, pray, sing, and help bury their lambs at the end of funerals and committal services.

It is not absurd to have a funeral for a child. It is not foolishly sentimental to bury him. It is not wrong to love him before he has lived outside his mother's womb.

God's flock needs shepherds who will join the ewes in grieving over their little lost lambs. It will be difficult to know precisely when and how to provide such ministry in this or that circumstance and with this or that family. Immediately questions will come up concerning what age to begin, and whether or not to have any service if there is no body to bury. These questions will need pastoral sensitivity and the guidance of the Holy Spirit.

What is crucial, though, is that the church recover the uniquely Christian way of life and death. Pastors who lead that recovery will be blessed by the deepening love and trust of their sheep—particularly the mothers. But more, these pastors will have the supreme good of the approval of our Chief Shepherd.

APPLICATIONS

The Duty of Individuals

> For if God . . . did not spare the ancient world, but preserved Noah, a preacher of righteousness, with seven others, when He brought a flood upon the world of the ungodly . . .　　　　　　　　(2 Pet. 2:4, 5)

Have we followed Noah, preaching righteousness against the bloodguilt we live amidst? Or rather, have we participated ourselves in the wickedness by paying for a surgical abortion, encouraging or sympathizing with others who have paid for one, or using an abortifacient drug regimen or hormonal birth control?

God's hatred of the bloodshed of innocents is repeated many places in Scripture, but the shedding of the blood of one's own little ones is a particular horror. There is no more terrible pollution of the land:

> They even sacrificed their sons and their daughters to the demons,
> And shed innocent blood,
> The blood of their sons and their daughters,
> Whom they sacrificed to the idols of Canaan;
> And the land was polluted with the blood.
>
> 　　　　　　　　　　　　　　　　　　　　(Ps. 106:37–38)

At its core, abortion is an act of idolatry. Sacrificing one's own children must necessarily be the most intensely religious act. Sacrificing one's own child is the bloody confession of faith in demons. It is a denial of faith in the only true God who closes and opens the womb. It is a denial of faith in God's provision for His own and the blessings He sends them. It is a final irreversible declaration concerning one's own child that God is wrong in His creation.

But prior to this horror, what can be said about lust? Lust permeates the Christian church and home, the Christian computer and phone. Christian men and women tend their idols, consuming the naked flesh of strangers. God will judge us for this.

Many reading this paper have somberly nodded along up to this point, reassuring ourselves of our innocence. We haven't killed our own children. We've protected them. We haven't paid for an abortion. We haven't committed adultery. We haven't even used the Pill. But even in such cases, we lack knowledge of our own lust and the ways it contributes to the sin of abortion among the idolatrous objects of that lust.

We also lack understanding of our responsibility for our neighbors. We may object that we can't be held accountable for what wicked men and women do, but responding this way, we demonstrate our normal thought process is the denial we are our neighbor's keeper. Do we not feel the weight of the example Noah should be to us today in his preaching of righteousness to his own neighbors?

Abortion is the violation of the Sixth Commandment, "Thou shalt not kill." The Westminster Larger Catechism expounds on what this commandment requires of us positively:

> All careful studies, and lawful endeavors, to preserve the life of ourselves and others by resisting all thoughts and purposes, subduing all passions, and avoiding all occasions, temptations, and practices, which tend to the unjust taking away the life of any; . . . just defense thereof against violence . . . ; comforting and succoring the distressed, and protecting and defending the innocent.[24]

God deals with men representationally and corporately. God judges nations for the sins prevalent among them. Even if there are people of God today who have not participated directly in the sin of abortion, we cannot claim clean hands and hearts. We live in a nation committed to the bloodshed of children, and God is just to judge our nation corporately, showering His holy wrath upon us all.

When the day comes when God's judgment falls upon the bloodshed of our nations, will there be men of God among us we have seen and heard stand and preach as righteous Noah preached righteousness to his own generation?

Male Leadership in Fighting Abortion

In modern discussions of abortion, it is not uncommon to hear the claim that men should keep silent on the issue. Since men can't get pregnant,

---

24. Westminster Larger Catechism, question 135.

the argument goes, the issue doesn't pertain to them. Abortion is a deeply personal issue for women, and men have no right to tell women what to do with their bodies.

To the contrary, murder is everyone's business—particularly men. It is the nature of the male of the species to guard and protect life. Men are the first ones we expect to step up and protect a woman who is being beaten, a child who is being slapped around, a black man with a rogue law enforcement officer kneeling on his neck, a mentally handicapped person who is being mocked, or a homeless person being beaten up by a gang of punks. In the same way, it is men we expect to step up and protect little babies from being aborted. It is a glorious fulfillment of his nature for the male of the species to do so.

But what about when women oppose them doing so? What if even pro-life women try to shush men working to defend the babies, saying things like:

No woman about to have an abortion is going to listen to any man's warnings. Men don't understand the difficulties women face during pregnancy. Let us do the talking.

One of us made a habit of picketing a Planned Parenthood abortuary in his city with his young daughters some years back, and one day an angry woman from the abortion side of things walked up to him and, having asked if he was married and where his wife was ("at home taking care of our other children"), she rebuked him: "You should go home and take care of the children yourself, and let your wife do the picketing!"

Initially, the man thought, "That's a good point. Why am I here, and not my wife?" But almost as quickly, the truth of God's creation order hit him and he responded to her, "Defending life is the man's job. My wife is home taking care of our other children, and that's what God has called her to do."

Readers likely are shuddering. Was this man trying to be as offensive as he possibly could be? Why on earth would he take such a volatile situation as an opportunity to start an argument with the woman over what men should do and what women should do? It was only going to infuriate the woman, and how does that help?

It's interesting, then, to record here that his response left the woman nonplussed. It didn't anger her more, but it seemed to take the edge off her anger. She was silent for some seconds, seemingly wondering what to say. Then she uttered something like "Oh" almost under her breath, and wandered back inside.

Who was it who raised this matter of what is man's and what is woman's work? It wasn't the pro-life man, but the pro-abortion woman. The man simply answered her question by calmly testifying to the biblical truth that God has called man to defend women and children.

In truth, such arguments are not peculiar to the work opposing abortion. They permeate life today in the home, church, and society. Men are told not to take leadership of anyone but themselves, and even in their leadership of themselves, men are warned to submit to the women of their lives so they will be kept from their naturally bad inclinations and desires. Never mind women's equally bad inclinations and desires—we're talking men here, and everyone knows they're a piece of work.

It may well be true that, given our track record, men today lack any moral authority. And certainly Christians should not ignore strategic concerns. But shall we turn from our distinctly male calling to defend the vulnerable and rescue the perishing? Remember righteous Job's description of his own godliness:

> I delivered the poor who cried for help,
> And the orphan who had no helper.
> The blessing of the one ready to perish came upon me,
> And I made the widow's heart sing for joy.
> I put on righteousness, and it clothed me;
> My justice was like a robe and a turban.
> I was eyes to the blind
> And feet to the lame.
> I was a father to the needy,
> And I investigated the case which I did not know.
> I broke the jaws of the wicked
> And snatched the prey from his teeth.
>
> (Job 29:12–17)

The duty of man is clear. God's fatherhood is written into human society. That fatherhood is present from the individual household up to the kingdom, from the newly married husband up to the king or president. God places men in authority and holds men accountable for themselves and for those they are in authority over. Just as God dealt with Adam and Eve, so He continues to deal with us today. Yes, being made equally in the image and likeness of God, women are moral agents alongside men, but as Adam was responsible for Eve and the race in his Fall, so God to this day still requires each man to answer for those under his care, starting with his wife and children. The husband and father is to guard and protect his wife and children. The first chapters of Genesis could not reveal and demonstrate this fundamental truth of God's creation order with greater clarity.

> Deliver those who are being taken away to death,
> And those who are staggering to slaughter, Oh hold them back.
> If you say, "See, we did not know this,"
> Does He not consider it who weighs the hearts?
> And does He not know it who keeps your soul?
> And will He not render to man according to his work?
>
> (Prov. 24:11–12)

Consider the understanding of our fathers who fought, bled and died to win and defend life. They knew it was the man's job, though the cost was great. Will we honor those men, putting wreaths on their tombs while refusing to protect lives today?

Men must recognize the slaughter of the little ones is no "women's issue." It is a justice issue. It is a murder issue, and bloodguilt hangs in the balance.

Of course, we do not deny women can and should also be Christian witnesses standing against abortion. Yet Christian men have the greater duty. Christian men must lead the opposition to this great wickedness.

Christian Witness at the Killing Places

One weakness of the church in our time is the tendency believers have to think godliness simply consists of keeping our own hands clean. Note our habit of focusing on the first half of the following command given by the Apostle Paul to the church in Ephesus, while neglecting the second half:

> Do not participate in the unfruitful deeds of darkness, but instead even expose them. (Eph. 5:11)

It is not enough to avoid the unfruitful deeds of darkness. We must also expose them, which is quite costly by comparison. Naming the sin of abortion "murder," "child sacrifice," "slaughter," "genocide," and a "holocaust" elicits hostile responses such as:

Don't you dare tell me what I can and can't do with my own body!
Jesus said judge not lest you be judged. I thought you were a Christian!
Keep your religion out of politics.
Why don't you shut your mouth!

It's possible to hide while keeping oneself from wickedness personally, but it's not possible to hide while exposing wickedness. Yet the God's command is not simply to have nothing to do with the unfruitful deeds of darkness, but rather to expose them.

So how do we do this? What are we to do as individuals living in this bloodthirsty land? How can we expose this shameful deed of abortion done in darkness? How do we awake the sleepers and help them arise from the dead (Eph. 5:14)? These are difficult questions, and the application will necessarily differ country by country, state by state, city by city, church by church, and person by person.

Some of us live in red states, some blue states. Some congregations have an abortuary in their city, some don't. Some churches have a strong ethnic or denominational commitment to fruitfulness which trains husbands and wives to accept however many children God blesses them with, while other churches made up of a more transient membership and lacking a strong ethnic element are largely middle-class families intent on limiting their fruitfulness. Their priority is not fruitfulness, but a superior education and the socioeconomic improvement of their family. Obviously, the first sort of family will need little exhortation to turn away from killing their children while the second will be sorely tempted so that witness against the bloodshed of infants will necessarily begin within the church herself.

Outside of the church, each locale has unique factors that inoculate the populace at large against abortion; or oppositely, promote it. Some of our cities and towns are within the former manufacturing centers with a heavy

Roman Catholic presence, while other cities and towns live in the shadow of large research universities. Some of us work in the fields of medicine, education, and law, and we see thunderheads on the horizon. We easily anticipate special challenges coming toward us which will likely jeopardize our ability to work in our current job field. We know there are growing ethical conflicts that may soon become unavoidable. In fact, it is a simple and necessary observation that some fellow believers are set apart to bear heavy responsibility in the fight, while others are not.

Again, it is imperative that we make gentle and charitable assessments of brothers and sisters in Christ as we head into the future conflict over abortion, but also a host of other moral and ethical conflicts resulting from the wickedness of our cultural repudiation of Christendom and resultant reversion to paganism. We may have two physicians in our congregation, one working in trauma and emergency care and the other in obstetrics and gynecology, and one of them will soon be denied hospital privileges while the other will continue to work in that same hospital. One of our lawyers might practice family law and find herself brought up before the state bar association's legal ethics committee while another has a practice in probate law and is able to avoid most ethical conflicts.

Context is a much-abused word in mainstream evangelical culture, but context does matter—personal, familial, educational, provincial, spiritual, and otherwise. We do not forget that one of the most important personal contexts of all is our own particular weaknesses, temptations, and sins. For example, some men may not be fit to protest at an abortuary because they are hotheaded. Some men are guilty of sexual sins which open their public protest against abortion up to charges of hypocrisy from their wife, children, church, or the community at large. Some women who have suffered sexual abuse might be cautioned to stay away from the scene of our present holocaust, since it might be too harmful to them emotionally. Some women have had many abortions, and having come to faith in Christ and repented, they might be particularly effective in public protests, while other women who mourn their inability to have any children thus far might be tempted to sinful anger and bitterness.

Showing up at the killing fields and protesting remains a fundamental way of protecting those without a voice. Asking the counsel of their pastors and elders, Christians ought to consider whether they are called to this ministry. The weapons we have from God are powerful for tearing down strongholds so that when Christians show up at the killing fields, darkness is put on notice and sometimes individual children are saved from death.

Those who do become engaged in public ministry at these killing places need to be aware of the dangers. While we are promised the gates of hell will not prevail against the church, this does not mean the church and her people will not suffer the hatred and attack of pagans drowning in their bloodlust. Exposing the deeds of darkness is always a dangerous work.

Other dangers arise, not from others, but ourselves—dangers such as pharisaism, spiritual pride, bitterness, and parading our righteous deeds on social media. We must not become proud in our work of public witness. But for the grace of God, we would be the ones walking into the abortuary.

We particularly need to avoid giving ourselves over to disappointment. People will reject our plea, leaving us vulnerable to becoming jaded. We will want every member of our church to show up and protest with us, and when they don't, we will be tempted to condemn those who, in our judgment, have no good reason for their absence.

Whatever form of witness we choose, we must keep in mind that the abortion "clinic" is no longer the main place of killing. Today, that place is hidden. The evil deed is done in complete privacy. It is done silently there behind the bathroom door of our homes—and not just the homes of worldlings, but also our own homes and the homes of our brothers and sisters in Christ. Today, our child sacrifices are done in our own homes so that no one will know when we commit our murders. No one ever catches a glimpse of the lifeless bodies of little ones murdered by their mothers there at home.

Often these murders are hidden by the mother even from her own husband—the little one's father. We mention protesting outside pharmacies alongside protesting outside Planned Parenthood abortuaries because of the prevalence of over-the-counter drugs in killing our unborn children today. Increasingly, the main killing place is an individual woman's conscience and her bathroom. Exposing this darkness requires entirely different tactics than the tactics used for decades in protests outside surgical abortuaries.

As the battlefield shifts, we need to do the work of informing ourselves and others concerning the abortifacient agencies of what are falsely labeled "contraceptives." Not simply the obviously abortifacient mifepristone-and-misoprostol regimen, but stealth agents such as the Pill and Plan B. We need not present ourselves as one more internet expert. It's enough for us to know and communicate the basics to others, taking special care to counteract the lies of the media and medical professionals who assure women that their drugs are *absolutely not* abortifacients.

As we do this work, we should speak from humility, remembering Scripture's warning that "we all stumble in many ways" (James 3:2).

Christian Witness on the Job

In opposing abortion in our individual callings, the tactics we use must be tuned to the present context. Increasingly, the movement of abortion from surgical and public to chemical and private will require a retooling of our methods. Some older methods of witness may still have some utility, but others will no longer be useful. Still, each calling has its own unique contributions to make.

We need pro-life state legislators, particularly as *Roe v. Wade* is overturned and the battle is returned to each state. We need physicians who will warn their patients against abortifacient drugs. We need pharmacists who will inform their customers. We need physicians, physician's assistants, nurses, and pharmacists who will decline any involvement in the bloody trade in poisons that kill the preborn child; who will declare to their ethics committee that, still at this late date, they retain medicine's historic commitment to the Hippocratic Oath:

> Neither will I administer a poison [*pharmakon*] to anybody when asked to do so, nor will I suggest such a course. Similarly, I will not give to a woman a pessary to cause abortion.

We need judges who use every tool at their disposal to end this genocide perpetrated against the little ones. We need writers to produce *Uncle Tom's Cabin* for the unborn. We need artists to depict the horror visually. We need musicians to compose songs[25] and symphonies[26] lamenting our lost little ones. We need drivers to transport needy mothers to their ultrasound. We need carpenters, drywallers, and painters to build homes for poor families.

We need soldiers in every last job and calling who will fight using the weapons of God:

> For though we walk in the flesh, we do not war according to the flesh, for the weapons of our warfare are not of the flesh, but divinely powerful for the destruction of fortresses. We are destroying speculations and every lofty thing raised up against the knowledge of God, and we are taking every thought captive to the obedience of Christ. (2 Cor. 10:3–5)

Christian Witness in the Public Square

The Old Testament repeatedly records God's people giving themselves to bloodshed, particularly through child sacrifice. If 1 and 2 Corinthians teach us anything, it is the vulnerability of God's people to the temptation

---

25. See Michael Card's 1984 song, "Spirit of the Age":

> I thought that I heard crying coming through my door.
> Was it Rachel weeping for her sons who were no more?
> Could it have been the babies crying for themselves,
> Never understanding that they died for someone else?
>
> A voice is heard of weeping and of wailing.
> History speaks of it on every page:
> Of innocent and helpless little babies,
> Offerings to the spirit of the age.
>
> No way of understanding this sad and painful sign;
> Whenever Satan rears his head, there comes a tragic time.
> If he could crush the cradle, then that would stop the cross;
> He knew that once the Light was born, his every hope was lost.
>
> Now every age has heard it, this voice that speaks from hell:
> "Sacrifice your children and for you it will be well."
> The subtle serpent's lying, his dark and ruthless rage;
> Behold, it is revealed to be the spirit of the age.
>
> Soon all the ones who seemed to die for nothing
> Will stand beside the Ancient of Days.
> With joy we'll see that Infant from a manger
> Come and crush the spirit of the age.

26. One example of such is David DeBoor Canfield's "Sighs and Sorrows," Sonata No. 2 for Violin and Piano (1987; rev. 2010), a work protesting abortion.

APPLICATIONS

to ape the culture around them, making the sins of their pagan neighbors their own sins also.

What a betrayal of our Lord Jesus who resisted Satan's temptations to go along to get along. To "fit in." God commands us to be "blameless and innocent, children of God above repraoch in the midst of a crooked and perverse generation, among whom [we] shine as lights in the world" (Phil. 2:15). Our citizenship is not here on earth, but above in heaven. Fixing our eyes on our Lord and setting ourselves on pilgrimage to His heavenlies, we will no longer fear man, nor will we be ashamed of Him and His words. With respect to this gross and bloody horror of baby killing, we'll be intransigent in our opposition to the act itself, as well as to those covered in its blood. Fearing God, we will not fear man:

> Abortion and euthanasia are . . . crimes which no human law can claim to legitimize. There is no obligation in conscience to obey such laws; instead there is a grave and clear obligation to oppose them by conscientious objection. From the very beginnings of the Church, the apostolic preaching reminded Christians of their duty to obey legitimately constituted public authorities (cf. Rom. 13:1–7; 1 Pet. 2:13–14), but at the same time it firmly warned that "we must obey God rather than men" (Acts 5:29). In the Old Testament, precisely in regard to threats against life, we find a significant example of resistance to the unjust command of those in authority. After Pharaoh ordered the killing of all newborn males, the Hebrew midwives refused. "They did not do as the king of Egypt commanded them, but let the male children live" (Exod. 1:17). But the ultimate reason for their action should be noted: "the midwives feared God." It is precisely from obedience to God—to whom alone is due that fear which is acknowledgment of his absolute sovereignty—that the strength and the courage to resist unjust human laws are born. It is the strength and the courage of those prepared even to be imprisoned or put to the sword, in the certainty that this is what makes for "the endurance and faith of the saints" (Rev. 13:10).
>
> In the case of an intrinsically unjust law, such as a law permitting abortion or euthanasia, it is therefore never licit to obey it, or to "take part in a propaganda campaign in favour of such a law, or vote for it."[27]

---

27. John Paul II, *Evangelium Vitae*, § 73. The concluding quote is from *Declaration on Procured Abortion*, § 22.

Still, recognizing our subordinate earthly citizenship, we must call our elected officials to defend life by stopping any and all abortions. Further, we must vote accordingly. Further still, as citizens of a democratic republic, we have obligations past generations of Christians did not have, most notably the obligation to create and advance policies through our elected representatives. This is a tool ancient Israel did not possess, nor did God's people possess it under the reigns of Herod or Nero. With democracy comes individual responsibilities. The bloody condition of our Union came about not through hostile foreign takeovers, but hostile domestic betrayals of God's law and our Constitution by our elected officials. Harry Blackmun wrote the abominable ruling in *Roe v. Wade*, but it was two Republican presidents, Dwight Eisenhower and Richard Nixon, who promoted him to the Supreme Court of the United States, while Christians stood by, either unaware or in support.

Yet the awakening of the (especially Protestant) Christian conscience did bear political fruit. It was Republican president Ronald Reagan who initiated the "Mexico City" policy prohibiting taxpayer money from funding abortions overseas. And it was also Ronald Reagan who nominated Antonin Scalia to the Court, and subsequent Republican presidents' appointments which have resulted in SCOTUS being willing to impair or overturn *Roe*: Clarence Thomas (George H. W. Bush); Samuel Alito (George W. Bush); and Neil Gorsuch, Brett Kavanaugh, and Amy Coney Barrett (Donald Trump).[28] Indeed, attacking *Roe* by reclaiming the courts is a strategy born over forty years ago,[29] which only now has borne its most visible fruit—and it has largely been Christian electoral calculus that has made that strategy bear fruit. So votes do matter, and though politics must never be our final hope, the Christian who neglects his democratic responsibilities abdicates his authority delegated him by God.

For centuries, Scripture was the bedrock of Christendom's rule of law, such that there was broad agreement concerning that law's fundamentals, and those fundamentals transcended political sectarianism. The heart of

---

28. On the other hand, Republican presidents have also been responsible for a number of disappointments on abortion: e.g., Sandra Day O'Conner, Anthony Kennedy, and David Souter.

29. As but one example, the Federalist Society, an organization that advocates for originalism in constitutional interpretation, was founded in 1982. In recent elections, Republican candidates (especially Donald Trump) have made a cornerstone of their platform a commitment to choosing judges that are approved by the Federalist Society.

those fundamentals was the law's duty to protect the vulnerable—those at the margins of society because of poverty, handicap, age, race, or lack of citizenship.

That time is gone. The Democratic party now holds as its most sacred principles its commitments to promote sodomy, to deny God's creation of male and female; and, worst of all, its bloodthirsty pursuit of the death of preborn children, even to the point of rabidly demanding this slaughter be subsidized by every last taxpayer.[30] Back in 1973, a third of Democrats opposed abortion, but now, pro-life Democrats are extinct.

This is not to extol the Republican party. Republicans did not begin to oppose abortion until the 1980s, and still today, many who vote Republican deny the preborn have any right to life under our Constitution. Yet if hypocrisy is the tribute vice pays to virtue,[31] we must honor this tribute the Republican party keeps paying to the law of God by producing party platforms which claim to be "pro-life."

How do Christians determine who gets their vote?

Read *World* magazine, emails from Friday Fax[32] and National Right to Life, Personhood Alliance, Operation Save America, and/or Catholic Vote. Read the blog posts and listen to the podcasts of orthodox Protestant pastors and elders. Read news from a variety of sources, including mainstream media. (Reading mainstream media will keep us informed concerning our enemies' strategies, a highly effective form of espionage.) Vote in every election you're eligible for, and vote knowing which candidates are determined to end our present genocidal holocaust. Don't vote for a county dogcatcher if she's not pro-life.

---

30. From the 2020 Democratic party platform:

> We believe unequivocally, like the majority of Americans, that every woman should be able to access high-quality reproductive health care services, including safe and legal abortion. We will repeal the Title X domestic gag rule and restore federal funding for Planned Parenthood, which provides vital preventive and reproductive health care for millions of people, especially low-income people, and people of color, and LGBTQ+ people, including in underserved areas.
>
> Democrats oppose and will fight to overturn federal and state laws that create barriers to reproductive health and rights. We will repeal the Hyde Amendment, and protect and codify the right to reproductive freedom.

"Achieving Universal, Affordable, Quality Health Care," Democrats.org, accessed June 21, 2022, https://democrats.org/where-we-stand/party-platform/achieving-universal-affordable-quality-health-care/.

31. François de La Rochefoucauld, *Maxims*, no. 218.

32. This publication is by the Center for Family and Human Rights, covering life and social policy issues at the United Nations and other international entities.

Get rid of judges who traffic in the blood of infants. And if, like us, you have a hard time keeping up on the various candidates, find a brother or sister in Christ who has kept up, and circulate their recommendations within the body of Christ.

Once the election is over and our rulers have taken office, bear witness in behalf of the little ones at times set aside for the public to address their rulers. There are Christians in some cities who have worked to get their local government to pass sanctuary laws that abolish abortion in their city. State legislators, too, provide times for meeting with their constituents. Allow your children to write their state legislators, respectfully requesting that they outlaw abortion.

Indeed, much good work has been done recently at the state level. Legislators in states such as Texas, Mississippi, and (most notably) Oklahoma have done good work in bringing down *Roe* and striving to end legal abortion. If you're in a state that hasn't done so, push for this to happen in writing, through calls, and at the ballot box. And if you are in a state that's taken even small steps in this direction, thank your officials who have had a part; and keep encouraging them to press on. Remember the downfall of *Roe* represents only the beginning of the work.

Some of us will even run for office. Yet our purpose here is not to outline every way in which a Christian can meet his obligation as a citizen, but rather, to exhort Christians to do what is good and right for each of us in our own particular situation.

What about the Babies of Pagans?

Some Christians speak and write, suggesting Christians chill out over the pagans aborting their own babies, and should just concern themselves with not killing their own children. But this is, in fact, what pagans have always done.

Brothers and sisters, let us not commit the sin of Cain. We *are* our brother's keeper.

True, we must not participate in the unfruitful works of darkness, but the godly alternative to this is not to withdraw from society, but to expose those deeds and to reprove those committing them. Do we really feel no compassion and recognize no obligation to rescue those little ones being murdered?

Like Job, we are to take responsibility for "widows and orphans in their distress" (James 1:27). The Apostle James places this injunction upon us, and it is not simply widows of the Christian community he is referring to. His day was similar to our own. Men and women were killing children without any slightest remorse. This was the context in which the church became known for saving the baby girls exposed on the hillsides—girls born to the very pagans who persecuted the Christians rescuing their little ones.

Why such concern among the early Christians? Didn't they realize their actions failed any cost-benefit analysis? Didn't they know demography was on their side because they were the ones allowing their children to be born and live? Didn't they know the future belonged to Christians?

Yes, but they also remembered their heavenly Father sends rain upon both the just and the unjust. The children of pagans are not simply objects of punishment, but fellow men made in the image of God. They are children of His hand (Acts 17:28), and therefore proper objects of Christian compassion.

We must never turn a blind eye to the slaughter of the preborn, especially those who belong to the pagans around us. They too bear the image and likeness of God. They are our neighbors, and we are commanded to love our neighbors as we love ourselves.

Dedication to Life in the Face of Congenital Anomalies and Disabilities

Information from diagnostic testing for birth defects and genetic abnormalities is often a blessing. It helps fathers and mothers prepare spiritually and mentally to care for their child and allows nurses and doctors to spring into action upon the child's birth. Yet, because of the heartless ease with which life is disposed of today, it is the general expectation that hardship will be avoided at any cost so that positive tests often lead parents to kill their child. This tendency is particularly awful when we consider that the best diagnostic methods—maternal blood screens,[33] fetal echocardiogram,

---

33. These analyze fetal DNA in the mother's bloodstream.

ultrasound, chorionic villus sampling,[34] and amniocentesis[35]—often give false positives.[36]

When a fetal anomaly is predicted, fathers and mothers face immense pressure to "terminate the pregnancy." The very fear of caring for a child with structural or genetic abnormalities may lead to the temptation to kill the child. Add the counsel of parents, friends, and doctors to that fear, and many parents become convinced killing their child is the only humane option. No one's reminding them how often the results of the screening tests are wrong.

Even if diagnoses could be made with 100 percent accuracy and a particular diagnosis is troublesome, is it not a fundamental of Christian faith that each child in the womb is God's creation? The presence of an extra or mutated chromosome, the lack of a limb or an eye, the deformity of an organ or blood cells—none of these eviscerate any son or daughter of the image and likeness of God.

---

34. A piece of the placenta is removed and tested.

35. Amniotic fluid from the area surrounding the baby is withdrawn and tested.

36. Maternal blood tests are frequently used to screen for Down syndrome, trisomy 18 and trisomy 13. The Mayo Clinic reports that 15 percent of women receive a false negative and 5 percent receive a false positive for Down syndrome ("First Trimester Screening," Mayo Clinic, https://www.mayoclinic.org/tests-procedures/first-trimester-screening/about/pac-20394169). More recently, these non-invasive prenatal screenings (NIPS) have been used for other genetic micro-deletions. A 2017 study concluded that the false positive rate for the detection of some of the micro-deletion syndromes could be as high as 90 percent (Henna Advani et al., "Challenges in Non-invasive Prenatal Screening for Sub-chromosomal Copy Number Variations Using Cell-Free DNA," *Prenatal Diagnosis* 37, no. 11 [November 2017]: 1067–1075, https://doi.org/10.1002/pd.5161). Even the *New York Times* found this news troubling (Sarah Kliff and Aatish Bhatia, "When They Warn of Rare Disorders, These Prenatal Tests Are Usually Wrong," *The Upshot* (blog), *New York Times*, January 1, 2022, https://www.nytimes.com/2022/01/01/upshot/pregnancy-birth-genetic-testing.html). A 2014 study in France determined that ultrasounds yielded a false positive rate of 8.8 percent and a misclassification rate of 9.2 percent (Anne Debost-Legrand et al., "False Positive Morphologic Diagnoses at the Anomaly Scan: Marginal or Real Problem, A Population-Based Cohort Study," *BMC Pregnancy and Childbirth* 14, art. no. 112, March 24, 2014, https://doi.org/10.1186/1471-2393-14-112). Chorionic villus sampling (CVS) and amniocentesis are generally recommended only after an abnormality is indicated by means of less invasive maternal blood tests or ultrasounds. Neither of these methods is foolproof: "A false positive rate was reported to be 3.6% for early amniocentesis and 8% for mid-trimester amniocentesis" (Zarko Alfirevic, Faris Mujezinovic, and Karin Sundberg, "Amniocentesis and Chorionic Villus Sampling for Prenatal Diagnosis," *Cochrane Database of Systematic Reviews* 2003, no. 3, https://doi.org/10.1002/14651858.CD003252). Both CVS and amniocentesis can lead to the death of the baby in the womb; for pregnant women at least 35 years old, the risk of the baby dying from amniocentesis is the same as the risk of the child having, for example, Down syndrome (Susan Pauker and Stephen Pauker, "Prenatal Diagnosis—Why Is 35 a Magic Number?" *NEJM* 330, no. 16 [April 21, 1994]: 1151–1152, https://doi.org/10.1056/nejm199404213301610). For CVS the rate of the baby dying after the procedure was around 2.5 percent (Laird Jackson et al., "A Randomized Comparison of Transcervical and Transabdominal Chorionic-Villus Sampling," *NEJM* 327, no. 9 [August 27, 1992]: 594–598, https://doi.org/10.1056/NEJM199208273270903).

The real question is whether or not we are willing to accept from God both prosperity and adversity (Eccles. 7:14). Whether we recognize it is God who sends us handicaps and deformities:

> Who has made man's mouth? Or who makes him mute or deaf, or seeing or blind? Is it not I, the Lord? (Exod. 4:11)

Any defect of any child does not in any slightest way negate the image of God in him, nor does it negate his absolute right to be defended against those determined to kill him. The difficulties of our lives do not justify murder, whether that murder is committed by ourselves or another.

Two Challenges

As we draw to an end, two challenges before us need to be examined. In both cases, the difficulty of our task of calling God's people to repentance over abortion may lead us to throw up our hands with despair, turning aside from the work because we had not counted the cost or difficulty of that task beforehand. These two challenges then need to be clarified so we may be wise in carrying out our prophetic work.

Challenge 1: Restoring Our Depleted Understanding of the Image of God in Man

Watching the selectivity of moderns choosing their objects of compassion, the Christian soon comes to the necessary conclusion that compassion now is based on feelings, and those feelings are awakened only by finding oneself identifying with a victim personally. The compassion of moderns is reserved for those who tug on their heartstrings, and wokeism is our parading those heartstrings.

This superficiality of modern compassion is the center of our inability to awaken the people of God to the horror of murdering our little ones by means of hormonal birth control. The two-day-old child is hard for anyone to feel empathy towards,[37] so he awakens no one's compassion. What we're left with, then, is the objective fact of his bearing the image of God. This is his ironclad claim to life, but this doctrinal truth does not tug heartstrings.

Can it really be true that, concerning bloodshed, the church today has turned from truth to feelings?

Again, if 1 and 2 Corinthians teach us anything, it is that the church is never immune to the sins of the surrounding culture, and this is particularly true concerning the bloodshed of innocents. The Lutheran Church in the time of the Third Reich and the Evangelical Christians of Rwanda in the time of their genocide mark this truth with an exclamation point. So today, the selectivity of our compassion and concern for life has reached a level best described as lunacy.

Stop for a second and think about the laws protecting dolphins and the eggs of bald eagles. Think about the national outpourings of anguish over whether or not the newborn panda bear at this or that zoo will survive. Think about the regular headlines and pictures of cats trapped in trees, and firefighters' attempts to rescue them. Think about the compassion of social justice warriors opposing racism and human trafficking and the effect of climate change on unborn generations.

There is no end to the masses' riots of indignation and demands for government action on behalf of Mother Nature, almost every sort of animal, and endless oppressed people groups. Many never stop shouting down others over these things. The parading of one's moral superiority in such matters may well be the central theme of social media. The discovery of a new people group or species suffering some new, heretofore unrecognized,

---

37. We are aware this concept of "empathy" has become controversial in some parts of the church recently. No question false empathy is abroad and social media is the perfect breeding ground. While conceding that the word can be abused, the abuse of a thing does not invalidate its proper use. The *Oxford English Dictionary* defines "empathy" as "the ability to understand and share the feelings of another." Thus empathy is a critical component of the character of Christian charity:

> For we do not have a high priest who cannot sympathize with our weaknesses, but One who has been tempted in all things as we are, yet without sin. (Heb. 4:15)

> When Jesus therefore saw her weeping, and the Jews who came with her also weeping, He was deeply moved in spirit and was troubled, and said, "Where have you laid him?" They said to Him, "Lord, come and see." Jesus wept. (John 11:33–35)

> And if one member suffers, all the members suffer with it; if one member is honored, all the members rejoice with it. (1 Cor. 12:26)

injustice is a vein of riches greater than any found during the Klondike Gold Rush.

But why do these waves of discovery of injustice and compassion toward a succession of victims never extend to the unborn? Even among Christians whose compassion does extend to the unborn killed surgically later in pregnancy, why does this compassion for *some* preborn not continue backwards to the little one trying to implant in her mother's womb shortly after conception? Surely she deserves some small benefit from our much-ballyhooed tenderness for the weak and oppressed?

Once we have the wisdom to question the eliciting of our compassion today, and its relevance to our battle against abortion, the answer becomes clear. Preborn children don't tug at our heartstrings because their existence is hidden in the secret places, seen only by the God who created them. The mother can't see or feel these little ones in her body. Often she kills them before she is able to establish that they exist.

She has unprotected sex, she's forty and wondering if she may give birth to a child with Down syndrome, so just to be safe, she takes an ECP. The mother is a junior in college and has a boyfriend she expects to marry, but they're living together and both are Christians, so they make provision for their flesh by getting on the Pill. The pastor's daughter gets drunk with the son of an elder at a party one night and they copulate. The next morning, though, filled with horror, the daughter runs to the Kroger pharmacy and asks the pharmacist for the morning-after pill. The deacon and his wife already have five children and have decided they can't afford a Christian education for those five if they have any more, so she pays her OB-GYN to insert an IUD.

In each of these cases, there's plausible deniability of any knowledge of pregnancy, so the act of hormonal birth control seems morally unremarkable. Note that word "seems." Add to this the small percentage of the abortifacient agency of hormonal methods of birth control, and it's no wonder the people of God feel no pangs of conscience when they use these methods. "Everything in life involves risk," they say.

However, move the timeline forward: the mother's period is late, she feels sick to her stomach and takes a pregnancy test and it's positive. See then how that mother reacts to a casual offer of a smoke or her girlfriends getting together for drinks or her family telling her to take a ride on the roller coaster at King's Island. This woman has turned into a whole different person called "mother," so no thank you, no thank you, and thank you very much—but no. Move the timeline forward a few weeks more after the baby has woken this mother up with shifting and kicking her womb, and try again the smoke, the drink, or the roller coaster. Oh my, there is nothing and no one more intense than a mother whose newborn has quickened. She is hardwired to die protecting her little one now.

What has changed?

The mother knows she has a baby now, and she has bonded with that baby physically and emotionally. In other words, her perceptions of the life God has created within her are acute, and they tug at every one of her heartstrings. This is her precious child!

But was the child precious before the pregnancy test? Before he moved and kicked? To put it another way, is the child's life and claim on his mother's protection a function of her personal perceptions of his value? Or is it the simple fact of God's creation of this little one in His own image?

Every Christian knows the truth. Man's value is not a function of his ability to elicit empathy or sympathy from others, but the prior fact of his creation by God who, at the moment of conception, placed within him His own image and likeness. Thus as we have said repeatedly, this little one's murder is prohibited by God because this little one is His image-bearer.

It's understandable that pagans who flip all God's distinctions upside down would feel no guilt over killing babies they have not yet bonded with physically or emotionally. It's even understandable that they would be able to descend to that level of hell where they feel no guilt over killing their own babies *after* quickening. Such women are dead in their trespasses and sins and need to be born again by the Holy Spirit, that they might be horrified at their sin and flee to Jesus' blood and righteousness.

But Christians? What do we say to women of God and their husbands who feel no guilt over practicing birth control that has an abortifacient agency in the first days of life?

Several passages come to mind:

> And do not be conformed to this world, but be transformed by the renewing of your mind, so that you may prove what the will of God is, that which is good and acceptable and perfect. (Rom. 12:2)

APPLICATIONS

For He who said, "Do not commit adultery," also said, "Do not commit murder." Now if you do not commit adultery, but do commit murder, you have become a transgressor of the law. (James 2:11)

Do not participate in the unfruitful deeds of darkness, but instead even expose them; for it is disgraceful even to speak of the things which are done by them in secret. But all things become visible when they are exposed by the light, for everything that becomes visible is light. For this reason it says,

> "Awake, sleeper,
> And arise from the dead,
> And Christ will shine on you."

(Eph. 5:11–14)

Note that command, "expose them." This is one of the major purposes of this document—to open up the sin of this violation of the Sixth Commandment, including opening up the sad truth that worldlings have no slightest qualms over the morality of killing living beings they can't see or feel who are incapable of eliciting any slightest empathy or sympathy from them.

Living in this culture of death, Christians need this great sin exposed to us also. We must have the degraded state of our empathy and compassion demonstrated to us. We must be reminded of the image of God in man—particularly that image in the little man or woman in our womb struggling to attach himself or herself there in order to receive his mother's protection and nurture.

Until the image of God in teeny-weeny babies is exposed once more by the light of the Word of God, there will be no repentance within the church over our ubiquitous and incessant killing of our God-given sons and daughters. We may not see any quick restoration of our ability to see and recognize and cherish His image, but this objective fact must lead us to repentance and set us free from our bloodshed.

This truth of the image of God in man from the moment of conception must be taught repeatedly, fervently, and with all authority. No other truth will do.

Challenge 2: Maintaining the Unity of the Body of Christ

The second problem we face in leading the church to repent of abortion is schism. Among the people of God within His church, calls to repentance are always divisive. How much more so, then, when we are called to repent of the sacrifice of our unborn children to the idols of our hearts. Naturally, the response will often be hostility. Brothers and sisters in Christ will accuse this call to repentance of being divisive within the church.

It's always been true that some whose consciences are tender repent, while some with consciences that are seared or hardened refuse and attack those who preach to them. Our Lord spoke this tender lament:

> Jerusalem, Jerusalem, who kills the prophets and stones those who are sent to her! How often I wanted to gather your children together, the way a hen gathers her chicks under her wings, and you were unwilling. Behold, your house is being left to you desolate! (Matt. 23:37–38)

During His week of passion, our Lord prayed for His people that we would be one as He and His Father are One. He said our unity would show the world His Father had sent Him (John 17:21). Much is at stake with the unity of the body of Christ, but this unity is not a simple or straightforward thing.

Five centuries ago, the Protestant reformers sought to restore the gospel of regeneration in the power of the Holy Spirit to the Christian church. The response of Rome to the reformers who condemned the selling of indulgences was to threaten their lives, then excommunicate them. Rome's priests never stopped condemning the reformers for schism, and the reformers never stopped defending themselves against this charge.

Similarly, one century ago, J. Gresham Machen strongly condemned the denial of the gospel and many fundamental doctrines of Scripture by missionaries and church officers of his time. Calling for the restoration of biblical Christianity to the church and God's sheep, he wrote his classic *Christianity and Liberalism*, whose call for division is resident in that very title. His message was that the liberalism of the Presbyterian church at the time was a different religion than Christianity, and that the church must separate from liberals who called themselves Christians.

APPLICATIONS

Much of the church's history in North America across the twentieth century is simply the outworking of Machen's clarion call for reform implemented in mission after mission, denomination after denomination, church after church, carried in waves across the continent in city, town, and village. In time, those dividing from liberals came to be known broadly as "Evangelicals," regardless of their denominational or doctrinal affiliation, and those liberals who refused to repent were cut off.

The reigning religious authorities of the time accused these reformers of schism, but were they truly schismatics? Who was responsible for the division of the church at the time of the Reformation? Rome, or reformers such as Martin Luther and John Calvin? Who caused schism in the battle over liberalism? The liberal pastors and seminary professors of the Presbyterian church, or J. Gresham Machen whom they condemned and defrocked?

In Galatians, the Apostle Paul did not hesitate to divide the church by his denouncements and anathemas against those within the church calling for the Gentiles to be circumcised. If we believe Paul did so under his apostolic authority and his words here are inspired by the Holy Spirit, we acknowledge the rightness of his divisive statements such as:

> I am amazed that you are so quickly deserting Him who called you by the grace of Christ, for a different gospel; which is really not another; only there are some who are disturbing you and want to distort the gospel of Christ. But even if we, or an angel from heaven, should preach to you a gospel contrary to what we have preached to you, he is to be accursed! As we have said before, so I say again now, if any man is preaching to you a gospel contrary to what you received, he is to be accursed! (Gal. 1:6–9)

Strong words, those, and they are fully justified by what is at stake, which was the preaching of a different gospel which was no gospel at all. If the people of God in the church of Galatia allowed themselves to be circumcised, they were turning aside and following preachers the Apostle Paul said were to be damned.

There are many other places in Scripture where God's servants called for division from false preachers and prophets, and they did so not because they were seeking to please their listeners and readers, but because they loved the unity of the bride of Christ and knew the false teachers' assaults on the purity of the doctrine of salvation was destroying that unity. John the Baptist, Jesus, the Apostle Paul, Luther, Calvin, Bucer, Knox, and Machen are all alike in this.

We must grow in our discernment concerning the nature of the church's unity, so that we can distinguish between reformers and schismatics. After all, every schismatic claims to be a reformer. The Judaizers of the New Testament church preached another gospel as restorationists, as prophets, as the only men truly concerned for the unity of the body of Christ. They said they had to preach circumcision in order to restore unity in God's truth among God's people.

There are no false prophets, false apostles, false preachers, or false shepherds dividing the church with false doctrine who neglect to claim they are the true healers of Christ's body, restoring the unity of ages past through what in truth is their schism.

First then, the unity of the church is protected by distinguishing between true shepherds and false shepherds, the true church and the false church. Any work of reform must be recognized as an effort, not at division of the true church, but the reform of this church. The church reformed must always continue pursuing that reformation.

Those who condemn the exposure of false ethics and doctrine because of the divisive nature of that exposure must keep in mind John Calvin's warning:

> "Peace" is certainly a pleasing word; but cursed is the peace that is obtained at so great a cost that there is lost to us the doctrine of Christ, by which alone we grow together into a godly and holy unity.[38]

There is a godly unity, but also an ungodly unity. What ought we to call that unity that defends the practice of hormonal birth control by denying the image of God in the unborn present from the moment of conception? What ought we to call that unity that condemns those who call for repentance in this matter, claiming they are schismatic?

This brings us to another consideration, though, which must be thought through carefully.

---

38. John Calvin, comments on Acts 15:2, *The Acts of the Apostles 14–28*, trans. John W. Fraser, ed. David W. Torrance and Thomas F. Torrance (Eerdmans, 1995), 27.

The Apostle Paul condemned those false preachers who called for the Gentile believers to be circumcised, and he sought to expel them from the body of Christ, but at the same time he also condemned the division in the body of Christ over meat sacrificed to idols. This second division over meat was a matter of "weaker" and "stronger brothers," and while making it clear that one group was "stronger," he nevertheless commanded both sides to "accept one another." It was not that there was no truth in the matter, but that this doctrinal disagreement was not to divide the people of God.

There have been innumerable divisions in the history of the church of a similar nature, where one group is properly called "strong" and the other "weak." Is the division between those who do and those who do not use hormonal birth control of such a nature that it is right to label those who condemn these early methods of birth control "weaker brothers" and those who use them "stronger brothers"? Maybe it's unfair to word it that way? Maybe it should be left up to the individual church or family whether to label those who repent of hormonal birth control "weaker" or "stronger"?

As we come to the end of this document, it is obvious those who have adopted this call to the church to repent of abortion do not believe abortion is properly spoken of as a secondary or tertiary matter in which Christians should agree to disagree. Abortion is a matter of life and death, and not the life and death of dolphins or cats or the murderer on death row, but the life and death of our own precious sons and daughters made in the image and likeness of God.

In this connection, keep in mind God's command to the sons of Israel not to "play the harlot" with those sacrificing their children to Molech by disregarding this heinous crime committed by their neighbors. Keep in mind His warning that the penalty of this disregard will be His cutting them off from the people of God:

> If the people of the land, however, should ever disregard that man when he gives any of his offspring to Molech, so as not to put him to death, then I Myself will set My face against that man and against his family, and I will cut off from among their people both him and all those who play the harlot after him, by playing the harlot after Molech. (Lev. 20:4–5)

But what if, as in Solomon's time, the people of God have become inured to the horror and wickedness of child sacrifice? Is this not the case today, and does this necessitate the same sort of radical act Ezra commanded when he demanded the Jewish husbands cast out their idolatrous pagan wives?

In other words, should the church divide over abortion? Should the church divide over surgical abortion? Should the church divide over late-first-trimester abortion by mifepristone and misoprostol? Should the church divide over early-first-trimester abortion through IUDs and other hormonal methods of birth control?

Is there a simple answer to this question? Those who have adopted this paper do not speak with apostolic authority. We are not familiar with every cultural context of those who will read it, and we do not know the condition and vulnerabilities of each church that readers are members of. In one sense, we believe the division of denominations and churches over abortion is necessary, yet the challenge is in the details, so we make no overarching claim about how and when that division should be accomplished.

There are many questions related to this division that require great wisdom in pastoral application. Is there a member of the church who is paid for performing abortions? Is there someone in the congregation who works for United Way or Planned Parenthood? Is there a representative serving in state government who has voted in favor of lifting restrictions on hormonal birth control methods, approving their distribution on the internet and over-the-counter in pharmacies? Is there an engaged couple who tell the pastor during their premarital counseling that they plan to use a hormonal method of birth control for the first couple of years so they can save up a down payment on a house? So they can minister in a Muslim part of the world without worrying about having a child? Is there an ER physician or physician's assistant who is required to care for rape victims by providing them an ECP? Is there a public school teacher who is responsible to teach a sex education module which presents drugs with an abortifacient agency as "contraceptives" which "do not cause an abortion"?

The list of such challenges to any simple call for church division over abortion could be multiplied, going on for pages. The meaning of the Sixth Commandment is clearly opened and explained in many doctrinal statements of the church adopted over many centuries since the Reformation, one helpful example being the Westminster Larger Catechism cited above. Even the penalty for breaking the Sixth Commandment and the divine rationale for that penalty is recorded in Scripture concisely and precisely. We have worked hard to make it clear how abortion in all its forms is a violation of this Sixth Commandment, and that Scripture, church history, and genetics speak in unison concerning this violation.

Still, the pastoral instruction, preaching, and application of these truths to God's flock and sheep never may disregard our necessary commitment to uphold the purity of God's truth while also seeking the peace of Christ's church. Sometimes division is the necessary tool of restoring the church's peace. Sometimes not. Making this determination is not something pastors, deacons, elders (and the older women of the church who teach the younger women under the authority of those officers) may avoid. We must not shirk this responsibility. We must have faith and make pastoral decisions in light of the coming judgment of our Chief Shepherd. Jesus calls each of us to lead in such a way that we can join the Apostle Paul in stating to our sheep that we have none of their blood on our hands (Acts 20:26).

It is undeniable that even the most biblical of churches today living in the midst of this growing holocaust are unfaithful in condemning all the forms of abortion practiced in our congregations. This must end, and it must end now! Pastors must preach and teach against abortion in all its forms, doing so with love and patience, but also authority and boldness.

On the other hand, each of us will have our own way and timing of turning the ship of the church towards this repentance, but difference in timing and method must not lead us to condemn those also committed to calling for repentance from this bloodshed.

We may put it this way: the pursuit of the church's repentance over abortion is an act of love for God and our neighbor, and that love should be obvious, even and especially when it divides those who claim the name of Christ. This is not an impossible goal. Let us give ourselves to it.

The End of Abortion: Reclaiming God's Blessing of Fruitfulness

And so, many thousands of words later, we bring this jeremiad against the slaughter of children to a conclusion. What will be the end of abortion?

God alone will most certainly bring about the end of abortion, but when and how will He do so?

We believe in the power of God to end oppression and bloodshed. Those of us alive at the time of the fall of the Soviet Union remember well how astounding this great change was to the entire world. Many heroic men had been laboring to this end, but no one anywhere predicted what happened, and the shock was heard around the world. Christians rejoiced in this wonderful act of God, even though, in retrospect, the crumbling of the foundations was clarified so that natural causes seemed sufficient for the explanation. But natural causes are never the whole, and not even most, of the story in the eternal conflict between good and evil, life and death.

Having surveyed this monstrous genocidal holocaust, we wonder what work we can do to hasten its demise. Preaching, prayer, and our own repentance are the first things we give ourselves to. There's no question that, here as always, we wrestle not with "flesh and blood, but against the rulers, against the powers, against the world forces of this darkness, against the spiritual forces of wickedness in the heavenly places" (Eph. 6:12).

The Evil One never ceases in his attack upon little ones. Hating and seeking to destroy life, he inspired Pharaoh to slaughter the Hebrew baby boys. He led generations of the people of God in both kingdoms of Israel and Judah to sacrifice their little ones to Molech. He led Herod to murder all the sons of Bethlehem born within two years of our Lord. Then, finally, we have this prophecy given through the Apostle John, recorded in Revelation 12:

> A great sign appeared in heaven: a woman clothed with the sun, and the moon under her feet, and on her head a crown of twelve stars; and she was with child; and she cried out, being in labor and in pain to give birth.
>
> Then another sign appeared in heaven: and behold, a great red dragon having seven heads and ten horns, and on his heads were seven diadems. And his tail swept away a third of the stars of heaven and threw them to the earth. And the dragon stood before the woman who was about to give birth, so that when she gave birth he might devour her child.
>
> And she gave birth to a son, a male child, who is to rule all the nations with a rod of iron; and her child was caught up to God and to His throne. Then the woman fled into the wilderness where she had a place prepared

by God, so that there she would be nourished for one thousand two hundred and sixty days.

And there was war in heaven, Michael and his angels waging war with the dragon. The dragon and his angels waged war, and they were not strong enough, and there was no longer a place found for them in heaven. And the great dragon was thrown down, the serpent of old who is called the devil and Satan, who deceives the whole world; he was thrown down to the earth, and his angels were thrown down with him. Then I heard a loud voice in heaven, saying,

"Now the salvation, and the power, and the kingdom of our God and the authority of His Christ have come, for the accuser of our brethren has been thrown down, he who accuses them before our God day and night. And they overcame him because of the blood of the Lamb and because of the word of their testimony, and they did not love their life even when faced with death. For this reason, rejoice, O heavens and you who dwell in them. Woe to the earth and the sea, because the devil has come down to you, having great wrath, knowing that he has only a short time."

And when the dragon saw that he was thrown down to the earth, he persecuted the woman who gave birth to the male child. But the two wings of the great eagle were given to the woman, so that she could fly into the wilderness to her place, where she was nourished for a time and times and half a time, from the presence of the serpent. And the serpent poured water like a river out of his mouth after the woman, so that he might cause her to be swept away with the flood. But the earth helped the woman, and the earth opened its mouth and drank up the river which the dragon poured out of his mouth. So the dragon was enraged with the woman, and went off to make war with the rest of her children, who keep the commandments of God and hold to the testimony of Jesus.

What a terrible account of the Evil One's attempt to destroy our Savior and His mother, but what a wonderful account of God's justice and mercy, throwing him down and protecting our Lord, as well as His mother in the moment of her womanly vulnerability and labor as life-giver!

Satan is forevermore standing before woman in childbirth, seeking to devour the precious life of her child. Yet God is seated on His throne, building His kingdom generation after generation to the very end, with victory sure and certain. We must note the glorious theme of the miraculous births of little ones predestined to be the servants and saviors of His plan of salvation.

Think of the promise He made to Abraham and Sarah fulfilled in the miraculous conception and birth of Isaac. Think of His miraculous protection of the infant Moses. Think of His promise to Zacharias and Elizabeth fulfilled in the miraculous conception and birth of John the Baptist. Remember the response of the blessed Virgin Mary when she was told she would give birth to the Savior of her people. In innocence, she responded, "How can this be, since I am a virgin?"

> The angel answered and said to her, "The Holy Spirit will come upon you, and the power of the Most High will overshadow you; and for that reason the holy Child shall be called the Son of God." (Luke 1:34–35)

Mothers giving birth to saviors promised and protected by God is a central theme of salvation history. This history never denigrates or dismisses women's work and contribution to that history. Surely it is in large part these accounts of God's work in and through women's life-givingnesss that have borne the fruit of the equality of women and men which, among the world's religions and ideologies, is uniquely Christian.

Then also, we remember our Lord's promise concerning these little ones, whose mothers look on and listen with joy. Note the men. Note the children. Meditate on the response of the women present:

> Then some children were brought to Him so that He might lay His hands on them and pray; and the disciples rebuked them. But Jesus said, "Let the children alone, and do not hinder them from coming to Me; for the kingdom of heaven belongs to such as these." After laying His hands on them, He departed from there. (Matt. 19:13–15)

This document can be understood as our work seeking to restore the beauty of womanhood and childbirth to the church, because without that restoration, no negative attempt to expose and oppose the bloodshed of babies will get any purchase among us, let alone the pagans.

Necessarily so, much of this statement has been negatively focused. We have spent much time showing God's no—His condemnation of abortion, His judgments upon bloodshed, and our own sin that has brought it about. We have labored to show the need to speak truly about this evil, from our courts, our pulpits, and now from our own lips as men and women claiming Christ's name. We have shown why "pro-life" must never be defined so as to exclude or hide "anti-abortion."

But we have also shown that God's commandments are always reciprocal. Where God says yes to something, He also says no to its opposite. When God forbids something, He encourages its opposite. And so must we. The opposite of abortion is childbearing. It is painful, but it is life-giving. The opposite of death is life, and as God creates life, so we must love life. But not simply generic "life," but this and that newborn child and this and that preborn child, back to the moment of his or her conception. And as we shall see below, even before his conception.

God has made His world fruitful. Fruitfulness is creation's DNA.

We see the early spring bulbs. We gaze on snowdrops bursting through the snow in their glee for spring. We see the roses full of color, changing in shade with the temperature, so full of petals they can't hold themselves up. We see the apple and peach trees so laden with fruit that they can't bring it all to harvest. And then there are the animals that fill our world. The cardinals outside our windows, diligently pecking through the snow to find their food. The coyotes we hear at night, glorifying God by the howls they share one with another. And the tenderness and delicacy of newborn kittens, full of unchecked curiosity and jaunty in their play.

Today, it's commonplace to talk of how best to conserve this life. We understand that proper conservation involves not just stopping threats to creation, but also working positively to undo the damage done. We know that if the wolves on Isle Royale are lost because of man's mismanagement, repairing the problem may involve reestablishing them. That if the fish are depleted in our waters because our effluent is full of hormones from the Pill, we must not only purify the waters but also replenish the fish. And that repairing land whose soil is eroded because of clear-cutting involves not just stopping the harvesting, but reforesting it. Caring for creation means not just stopping its destruction, but promoting its prosperity—its fruitfulness.

The same is true concerning abortion. Ending abortion means not just hating abortion but loving the life God gives us as His blessing. We have

ABORTION AND THE CHURCH

shown how the civil magistrate must have a commitment to this, in fostering and protecting the lives of those he rules. We have seen how pastors and elders and churchmen as a whole must pursue this, in both disciplining the sins of those under their care and also encouraging them towards obedience in caring for children, born and preborn. And so, we conclude by exhorting each of us to rekindle our commitment to gratitude toward God for every one of His blessings.

Consider the wonder and privilege He has bestowed on woman to bring into this world children made in His own image and likeness. Let our love for woman as God made her fire our hatred of snuffing out those lives He blesses her with—and also those of us privileged to be her husband and lover through all the days, months, and years of her self-sacrifice as the mother of all the living. We are to be romanced and inspired by the fruitfulness God placed at the heart of all His creation, glorying particularly in woman's gift of this fruitfulness to us all.

Being moralists, it is tempting to think negatively. Strangely, as hard as it is for many of us to speak God's no publicly, we sometimes have no difficulty allowing it to be the extent of how we define our faithfulness, and this is particularly so concerning abortion. After all, we reassure ourselves that we have been firm where it counts. We've stood outside of the abortuary and condemned the ghoulish "escorts" leading women into the killing chamber to kill her child. We linger on Facebook, ready and waiting to thunder against the wickedness of child murder. We relish every opportunity to prove our intellectual acumen and godliness by dispatching all the craven arguments of postmodern pagans in support of the slaughter of the innocents. We have rebuked our congressmen, calling down God's wrath on him for his hatred of life. We declare that we won't vote for him. Pompously, we denounce our governor publicly, informing him that he has no claim to authority because he hasn't shut down Planned Parenthood's "clinics."[39]

And yet, does our defense of the babies extend to embracing them?

---

39. A clinic, properly called, is a place where the healing arts are practiced—not a place presided over by an executioner of the innocent and defenseless. From the *Online Etymology Dictionary*: "1620s, 'bedridden person, one confined to his bed by sickness,' from French *clinique* (17c.), from Latin *clinicus* 'physician that visits patients in their beds,' from Greek *klinike* (*techne*) '(practice) at the sickbed,' from *klinikos* 'of the bed,' from *kline* 'bed, couch, that on which one lies,' from suffixed form of PIE root *klei-* 'to lean.'" Accessed April 10, 2022, https://www.etymonline.com/word/clinic.

Yes, this is the canard every escort shouts at us: "If you love babies so much, why don't you try *having* one!" they yell derisively at godly men walking the sidewalk with signs that say "Love life!"

Sure, they're hardhearted and scornful, but their mocking presents us an opportunity for self-examination. Do we love children, or do we simply love our own moral superiority? This is the question every preacher knows too well. Sure, I warn the people of God against sin and am faithful to preach against abortion, but do I love my neighbor? Do I love life?

> If I speak with the tongues of men and of angels, but do not have love, I have become a noisy gong or a clanging cymbal. If I have the gift of prophecy . . . but do not have love, I am nothing. (1 Cor. 13:1–2)

The last fifty years of Evangelicalism have been so soft, so cloyingly sentimental, so opposed to any proclamation of God's judgment, that our repentance from these things has not been easy to do ourselves, nor to call others to. Proclaiming God's no as well as His yes, we are tempted to reassure ourselves that we practice and preach repentance, and thus are superior to those who do not. Opposing abortion is so seductive to the growth of spiritual pride, but love casts out pride. Love leads us to give ourselves to vulnerability and self-sacrifice.

Are we willing to become childlike? Remember Jesus' words: "Truly I say to you, whoever does not receive the kingdom of God like a child will not enter it at all" (Mark 10:15).

Protecting life without loving life is absurd. Protecting children without loving and coming to resemble them in childlike faith falls short of the kingdom of God. The godly love life and children.

"Well, of course," we say, "a more obvious truth has never been written."

Then, if it's so easy, why did the people of God in Israel and Judah sacrifice their sons and daughters? Why do we ourselves sacrifice our own sons and daughters?

The reason Scripture commands Christians to love is that it is very difficult. Were it easy, the commands would not be so constant across the New Testament. Let us recognize that the core of child murder is a desire not to be inconvenienced by the burdens of another. Lovelessness is the seedbed of child sacrifice, although this lovelessness is strengthened by our resolve not to allow ourselves to become the subject of God's sovereignty in creating life within us and within our wife. Lovelessness combined with rebellion against God's sovereignty and a refusal to thank God for His creation and gift of life are a toxic triad that corrupts many of our marriages and families. We have even passed these sins on to the next generations.

Our precious children see and hear how often we think and speak of them as an inconvenience to us. Maybe it's when our daughter comes in while we're writing about the evil of abortion and the precious gift of life, and she asks us to look at her drawing. Maybe it's when our son interrupts our train of thought, wanting to tell us (in never-ending detail) about the snowman he just made outside. Maybe it's when we can't take that vacation to Europe we'd like because the airfare for seven is as ridiculous as having seven children in the first place in our modern dissipated world. How would we manage traveling across countries devoid of children with our own brood needing potty breaks and diaper stops every hour?[40]

Or think of how knowledgeable your children are of your irritation at God for His blessings of little ones. You wanted to finish that degree, but couldn't because you had to provide for that new mother and baby—and you have made no effort to hide or put to death your continuing bitterness and the lethargy in your fatherhood and leadership. You resent the fact that you couldn't take that high-paying job because it would have left you no time for your children, and your children live with the awareness that they are a perpetual pain to you. Your five-year plan was perfectly on track, but then your fifth or sixth child was born with special needs and you take no joy in him.

Is it any wonder that our wives hanker after jobs and more spending money and the positive affirmation they receive working outside the home where their bosses and coworkers never stop telling them how great a gadget inventor and gadget maker and gadget marketer and gadget seller and gadget improver and gadget-maker human resources manager they are?

---

40. A note of encouragement on this. One married couple of our congregation traveled across Europe a couple years ago with a brood of four, ages 1, 2, 6, and 8. They reported: "We walked out of our Airbnb as a family of 6, and a very old Italian woman looked at our kids and her eyes filled with tears and she said, 'Bella! Bella! Bella familia!' On more than one occasion we had waiters go out of their way to serve us because they were so thrilled that we were out and about with so many small children. The Italians were smitten, and even the French were accommodating to an extreme."

APPLICATIONS

Is there any better way to kill our wife's femininity, motherly instinct, and life-givingness than daily displaying our bitterness at the burden of the children she has presented us? Woman is made by God to be the glory of man. Why join the world in trashing her glory?

Our negative reactions and bitterness at the outpouring of life God sends us as His blessing are obvious to all, and our wives are acutely and painfully sensitive to it. By the will of our Father, even men and women as evil as we are have been given the gift of new life, both spiritually and physically. He has allowed us to share our lives with those born from our own bodies, sharing our own genes, and often sharing our interests and hobbies also. He has privileged us to take part in the propagation of the human race and the calling of men into His kingdom—two of the profoundest mysteries of existence. Yet we are ungrateful. Often we loathe our tiresome duties toward our children. We even commit murder in our hearts as we wickedly wish that God had never given us these blessings.

Truthfully, how different are we from worldlings who kill their children? By God's grace, His Spirit keeps us from going *that* far, although often we think the same thoughts, have the same motivations, display the same ingratitude. Brothers and sisters, as sons and daughters of our heavenly Father, this must not be. It is these sins of our hearts we must recognize, bring captive to the power of the Holy Spirit, repent of, and destroy. At the core of ending abortion is not just *opposing* those who would kill children, but *becoming* those who welcome and love them—which begins by loving our wife as *mother*, as *life-giver*, as *Eve*.

Loving children and motherhood includes loving the children we haven't yet been given. On the surface, this statement may sound like nonsense. How can we love a child we haven't been blessed with? How can we have affection for someone whose face we haven't seen, whose personality is yet unknown, whose habits and quirks and even sins are (as Melville put it) a lipless, unfeatured blank to us?[41] How can we love children God has not blessed us with yet; children He has not yet created?

The question itself reveals part of the problem: we think highly of our thoughts, and lowly of God's. We live in an age that prizes empiricism and scientific discovery, and we are self-assured in our understanding of what

---

41. Herman Melville, *Moby Dick*, ch. 134.

life is and how it begins. Ultrasounds and DNA research *have* been instrumental in reinforcing the truth that life begins at conception, but pro-lifers celebrating and using these tools to defend little ones must not fall into thinking we have unveiled the mysteries of life's beginnings.

We can love our wife's womanly fecundity and her future children even while God has not yet granted her any child. Is this not the meaning of Otis Redding singing, "When a man loves a woman"? Woman is life. Woman is fruitfulness. Woman is fecundity and this cannot be separated from her being. The love of a man for his woman is not simply love of her personhood, but love of her womanhood which will ache with longing until it is satisfied by God's gift of a child.

In God's economy, our unborn children who are the coming fruit of our lovemaking *do* exist. The same Psalmist who tells us we're formed *in* our mother's womb goes on to speak of things even more mysterious:

> My frame was not hidden from You,
> When I was made in secret,
> And skillfully wrought in the depths of the earth;
> Your eyes have seen my unformed substance;
> And in Your book were all written
> The days that were ordained for me,
> When as yet there was not one of them.
> (Ps. 139:15–16)

There are, indeed, more things in heaven and earth than are dreamt of in our philosophy. When we begin to preen ourselves on our understanding of biology, we must remember Scripture records that Levi gave the tithe to Melchizedek while he was still in the loins of Abraham:

> And, so to speak, through Abraham even Levi, who received tithes, paid tithes, for he was still in the loins of his father when Melchizedek met him.
> (Heb. 7:9)

And the Apostle Paul tells us a perhaps even greater mystery: God the Father "chose us in [Christ] before the foundation of the world" (Eph. 1:4)!

Remember that several of our church fathers speak of killing a child

APPLICATIONS

before he exists[42]—and they were not ignorant of the law of non-contradiction. Still today, it is a great mystery when and how soul and body are joined together by God. Deep truths are open, and infinity is finite, to God.[43] It is no absurdity to talk of cherishing our wife's fecundity, her life-givingness and the coming little ones we hope and pray for, while we have not yet heard or seen them. This is the center of man loving woman.

Pornography's eroticism is woman's life-giving body parts put on display for men who hate life, who hate fruitfulness. The world is full of men incapable of loving woman as woman. Refusing the responsibility and celebration at the heart of true manhood, these men remain dead in their trespasses and sins, giving themselves over to their infantile desires and lusts, and dying with little or no seed. Their particular taste in erotic images might differ from the sodomites, but the essence of sodomy is sex denuded of fertility; it is sex robbed of life-givingness. One may use one's wife for such lust, or one may use another man, but the essence of the thing is identical. What's love got to do with it? What's woman got to do with it? What's life got to do with it?

---

42. Cf., e.g., Augustine, *On Marriage and Concupiscence* 1.15.17 (AD 419–420): "Indeed, sometimes this lustful cruelty or cruel lust [*libidinosa crudelitas vel libido crudelis*] extends so far that it obtains poisons of sterility [*sterilitatis venena*]; and, if nothing else works, [it] snuffs out and breaks up by some means the offspring conceived in the womb, preferring its own offspring to perish before it lives [*prius interire quam vivere*]; or, if it was already living in the womb, to be killed before being born [*occidi antequam nasci*]."

Cf. also John Chrysostom (AD 391): "Why do you sow where the field is eager to destroy the fruit, where there are medicines of sterility? Where there is murder before birth? You do not even let a harlot remain only a harlot, but you make her a murderess as well.... Indeed, it is something worse than murder, and I do not know what to call it; for she does not kill what is formed but prevents its formation. What then? Do you condemn the gift of God and fight with his [natural] laws?... Yet such turpitude... the matter still seems indifferent to many men—even to many men having wives. In this indifference of the married men there is greater evil filth; for then poisons are prepared, not against the womb of a prostitute, but against your injured wife. Against her are these innumerable tricks." *Homilies on Romans* 24, trans. J. Walker, J. Sheppard, and H. Browne.

43. "Far be it, then, from us to doubt that all number is known to Him 'whose understanding,' according to the Psalmist, 'is infinite.' The infinity of number, though there be no numbering of infinite numbers, is yet not incomprehensible by Him whose understanding is infinite. And thus, if everything which is comprehended is defined or made finite by the comprehension of him who knows it, then all infinity is in some ineffable way made finite to God, for it is comprehensible by His knowledge. Wherefore, if the infinity of numbers cannot be infinite to the knowledge of God, by which it is comprehended, what are we poor creatures that we should presume to fix limits to His knowledge, and say that unless the same temporal thing be repeated by the same periodic revolutions, God cannot either foreknow His creatures that He may make them, or know them when He has made them? God, whose knowledge is simply manifold, and uniform in its variety, comprehends all incomprehensibles with so incomprehensible a comprehension, that though He willed always to make His later works novel and unlike what went before them, He could not produce them without order and foresight, nor conceive them suddenly, but by His eternal foreknowledge." *City of God* 12.18, trans. Marcus Dods.

So now, again: Do we love life? Do we love that life not yet placed in the wombs of our wives? In faith we may do so. By faith we love what He has promised to give us according to His will. We not only hate the murder of children, but we also agree with the Psalmist that they are a heritage from the Lord. That the fruit of the womb is His reward, and that God is pleased to give good things to His children.

And so, for our part, we commit ourselves to loving children past, present, and future, trusting God with the fruitfulness of our marriage beds. We choose faith for the lives God gives us as His blessings, welcoming not just some of the lives He sends in a timely way, but also those He sends in what we might think an untimely way.

And when we choose to offer our fruitfulness to God as Christians before the twentieth century did, we do so fully aware of how many of our fellow believers will mock us; or worse, will accuse us of being Quiverfullists who are ignorant, presumptuous, foolish, patriarchal, and irresponsible. They will tell one another that our motivation is pride.

Brothers in Christ may characterize us as legalists who think God requires us to have as many children as possible. They will never understand the truth that we have simply become committed to loving life, and that this love has led us to openness to God blessing our lovemaking as He chooses, by faith receiving with joy all the fruit He may bestow on it. No, nothing so joyful will cloud the judgments of the loveless and coldhearted Christian who speaks of childbearing (and even abortion) as merely a question of stewardship.[44] Fellow Christians will say we are in bondage to some law of multiplication of the species that will grow our tribe and take us to a higher level of heaven, and we're sure we'll have more crowns there. They'll claim we believe God requires us to have as many children as possible.

Truth is, though, that we believe the Lord opens and closes the womb. This is our joy, our faith, and we love trusting God with all His blessings. When the advocates of abortion scream "My body, my choice," we smile, noting that unless we recognize our bodies as His, our choices are nothing but slavery. The freedom to abort is nothing but bondage to the devil. It

---

44. One of us recalls an elder telling him that the wife of one of the staff members of the church had just found out she was pregnant. He said the staff member had come to him asking what they should do, since his wife had been on some medication that might have harmed the child and they were fearful. The elder explained he'd suggested the staff member consider abortion, explaining to his pastor, "I consider abortion a matter of stewardship."

is only when we *choose* to abandon our claims to autonomy that we have freedom to be the fathers and mothers God has made us to be. Those the Son makes free are free indeed (John 8:36).

Of course our love of life runs utterly against the grain of our culture—particularly the culture of Evangelicalism. And it's not that we can't come up with a host of reasons why we should avoid fruitfulness: Until both husband and wife get their degrees, a child would be inconvenient. Our house is too small for another child. More than one child per bedroom is irresponsible. Our wife frets over the future, and we would not be a servant-leader if we neglected her fears. Our husband's single income isn't sufficient to feed another mouth. We need to get a job. Our parents already think we're irresponsible, and another child would just confirm their judgment.

In fact, we're just as good at coming up with reasons to shut down our fruitfulness as all our friends who stopped at two. (And yes, we know some couples have valid reasons for stopping there.) Nevertheless, for the vast majority of us, our problem is not an excess of prudence, but a deficit of faith and the love that flows from it. Sure, everyone around us thinks three or four children is the outer limit of sanity. How can parents of five provide music lessons? How can they have their kids in sports? How will they be able to send their children to college, let alone graduate school? How will they pay for each of their daughters' weddings?

Some of these expenses are unlike the others, but the point is clear. These judgments of what fathers and mothers need to give their children are not a function of what pleases God and will lead to our children's godliness, but what our peers see as the minimal obligations parents have to their sons and daughters. Here as everywhere, "The Christian ideal has not been tried and found wanting. It has been found difficult; and left untried."[45]

The doubts and fears of fathers and mothers are nothing new. Every generation of Christians faces them. In fact, a good case can be made that the doubts and fears of past generations were far more substantive than our own. In a world where food was self-produced, they had to be concerned whether there would be enough food to go around come winter and spring. Whether God would provide summer rains this year after last year's drought. Whether locusts would swarm in and destroy their crops.

---

45. G. K. Chesterton, "The Unfinished Temple," ch. 5 in *What's Wrong with the World*, https://www.gutenberg.org/files/1717/1717-h/1717-h.htm.

In a world without Walmart, Goodwill, and eBay—a world where clothing was ten times the relative cost of clothing today—they didn't know if they could afford to clothe their children. Technological and economic development have put so many of these fears to rest, today, yet we manufacture new ones like whether or not we can afford a piano or guitar for our musically gifted children, a kit for our budding soccer player, private school tuition, or college tuition for all of them.

To those of little faith, the Christian family's resources are always a fixed pie, with each new child depleting the share of those who came before. Whereas anyone who has grown up in a large family, or any father and mother blessed by God with one, knows this is a lie. To those of little faith, every last act of faith is way too costly and must be carefully weighed by those who understand that judiciousness is next to godliness.

What if we trusted God? What if we truly believed the promise of Romans 8:28, that God is ultimately causing all things to work together for good to those who love God—including antibiotics, vaccines, farming techniques that massively increase yield, NICU advancements, and on and on. God's providence has made it much easier to fulfill the command to be fruitful and multiply, and yet we balk. Does God still rule His world? He has orchestrated many, many technological mercies in this world so that the church might grow with godly seed to the praise of His glory. With all the benefits and blessings He's given us in the modern world, can we not still rest upon the same promises our fathers and mothers in the faith did?

> For this reason I say to you, do not be worried about your life, as to what you will eat or what you will drink; nor for your body, as to what you will put on. Is not life more than food, and the body more than clothing? Look at the birds of the air, that they do not sow, nor reap nor gather into barns, and yet your heavenly Father feeds them. Are you not worth much more than they? And who of you by being worried can add a single hour to his life? And why are you worried about clothing? Observe how the lilies of the field grow; they do not toil nor do they spin, yet I say to you that not even Solomon in all his glory clothed himself like one of these. But if God so clothes the grass of the field, which is alive today and tomorrow is thrown into the furnace, will He not much more clothe you? You of little faith! Do not worry then, saying, "What will we eat?" or "What will we drink?" or

"What will we wear for clothing?" For the Gentiles eagerly seek all these things; for your heavenly Father knows that you need all these things. But seek first His kingdom and His righteousness, and all these things will be added to you.

So do not worry about tomorrow; for tomorrow will care for itself. Each day has enough trouble of its own. (Matt. 6:25–34)

Early Christians knew these promises, and took them to heart. Their world was filled with sin: with child abuse and neglect, abortion, exposure, and infanticide; with poverty, rampant injustice and oppression, and terrible cruelty. Life expectancy was around 40, and more than half their children and mothers died in childbirth. Persecution was constant. There were many physical and spiritual threats to their children. The greatest minds and philosophers of their time had concluded it was better not to bring children into a world of such difficulty, cruelty, and bloodshed. There was a pervasive cynicism about marriage, children, and family, and it caused Greco-Roman birth rates to plummet even as standards of living improved. Their world was our world.

But their response was not ours. Amid a Roman population in decline, the population of Christians was on the increase.[46] In the face of realities that, to the natural mind, argued for moderation, the church fathers became, if anything, *more* adamant against abortion and contraception. And as the Christian population increased, demographic change continued. The Christians who had more children became the Christians who loved more children, and the Christians who loved more children sought to ensure that the children of their persecutors were cared for as well. This continued throughout periods of war, famine, and persecution.

Finally, in God's good providence, the magistrates themselves began to change. But it took time and went in fits and starts. It would be glorious to

---

46. Hard data on Roman fertility in general, let alone Christian Roman fertility, is lacking. But Stark, *The Rise of Christianity: A Sociologist Reconsiders History* (Princeton University Press, 1996), 122–128, considering the available evidence, lays out a compelling argument for a healthy increase in the Christian fertility rate in the late Roman world, pointing in particular to the following advantages held by Christians in comparison to pagans: (1) abhorrence of abortion and infanticide, (2) objections to contraception, (3) a positive view of marriage (even in cases of mixed marriage), and (4) a high percentage of women of childbearing age. There is also some testimony from primary sources of the time. Noting this, Stark comments, "Differential fertility was taken as fact by the ancients," and quotes Minucius Felix approvingly: "Day by day the number of us is increased [because of] [our] fair mode of life" (122).

imagine that, when Constantine marked Rome with the cross, abortion was done and gone, but the reality was messy. Abortion's demise proceeded by gradual steps of law. First to be proscribed was abortion that deprived a husband of offspring.[47] Then came banning of child exposure and infanticide.[48]

Finally, some 450 years after our Lord sanctified childbirth by His incarnation, Emperor Leo banned abortion outright.[49] Yes, the legal end of abortion was brought about through wars, politics, protests, prayers, and schemes,[50] but all of it was the providence of God, and He worked through simple Christians who loved their children, and who rescued and adopted babies left to die on the hillsides. In doing so, they heaped coals of fire on the heads of their enemies (Rom. 12:20).

This is our hope. It is the hope that has undergirded countless Christians working to protect the widow, the fatherless, and the unborn, ever since the Evil One set his sights on them. It is the hope that has carried us through the dark days of *Griswold*, *Roe*, and *Casey*, knowing that the cause of righteousness proceeds in fits and starts. It is the hope that gives meaning to every small act of courage: every man who refuses to kill his child to hide his sin; every woman who chooses to let her little one live despite the cost to her reputation, her relationship with her parents, or her career prospects; every downtrodden protestor who stands alone in the rain with nothing to show for it; and every legislator or magistrate who defends the unborn at the cost of his own position. And it is the hope that must abide even with the downfall of *Roe*, since only this hope can sustain the pro-life struggle in the terra incognita of a post-*Roe* landscape.

We have spent much time and many words unpacking the wicked state of our land. We have shown how, to our utter shame, we the people of

---

47. Put in place by Emperor Septimius Severus (193–211): "A woman who intentionally induces an abortion is to be sentenced by the Governor to temporary exile; for it can be considered dishonorable for a woman to defraud a husband of his children with impunity." *Digesta* 47.11.4.

48. Particularly under Theodosius II (408–450): "If anyone commit the crime of killing an infant, this evil shall constitute a capital offense." *Codex Theodosianus* 9.14.1.

49. "Two laws have been enacted, one against a woman who, through dislike to her husband, takes pains to produce an abortion upon herself, and accomplishes the death of her unborn child, and another enacted against the husband requiring him to repudiate a woman who has been guilty of such an outrage." Leo later says that such a woman "has committed a crime which is an outrage ... against Nature." *The New Constitutions of the Emperor Leo* 31, trans. S. P. Scott, https://droitromain.univ-grenoble-alpes.fr/Anglica/NL31_Scott.htm.

50. This does not mean that the practice of abortion ended immediately, of course. Indeed, child murder was apparently slow to decline. Law, as all else, is bound by God's decrees, but law cannot in itself change hearts.

APPLICATIONS

God have also given ourselves to the bloodshed of our infants. We have recounted God's condemnation of abortion writ large across creation and throughout Scripture and church history. We have begun to open up what we can do to end the bloodshed—as magistrates, churchmen, and men and women of God.

Finally, though, our hope for the end of abortion isn't a matter of historical insight, proper argument, or wise application. The only end of abortion will be born through the preaching of the gospel of Jesus Christ which alone produces the fruit of repentance. This repentance must begin within the church of the Living God, but it will not end until it has spread throughout the earth.

This repentance from abortion is no abstract thing. It will be a living, breathing reality that is produced in the power of the Holy Spirit, and it will lay claim to every part of our lives, most especially our marriages and lovemaking. It seems almost unfathomable that God graces man with His very image and likeness. It seems unfathomable that, despite Adam's sin and our own multiplied transgressions adding to it, our heavenly Father continues to shower both the righteous and unrighteous with the gift of life, with the gift of children—the fruit of our lovemaking.

This extravagance from God should never be taken for granted or despised. He owes us death and hell, and shall we despise His gifts of love and life? Do we hear His warning?

> Do not be deceived, my beloved brethren. Every good thing given and every perfect gift is from above, coming down from the Father of lights, with whom there is no variation or shifting shadow. In the exercise of His will He brought us forth by the word of truth, so that we would be a kind of first fruits among His creatures. (James 1:16–18)

We are a kind of first fruits sent down from above by our heavenly Father. He has blessed His creation with such endless fruitfulness! Let us commit ourselves to being the instruments of His fruitfulness. Let us propagate a godly seed to serve in His courts of praise, giving Him glory forevermore.

Yes, doing so will require sacrifice. But the reality of sacrifice is built into creation. Into the little strawberry plants, which even in their first year will try to produce as much fruit as they can, stunting their own growth. Into the apple or peach tree which will bear so much fruit that their branches, laden with fruit, will break and fall. Into the salmon of Alaska, which travel a thousand miles upstream, expending all their energy to lay their eggs and then die. Of course, also, into our wonderful wives, who will endure the indignities of pregnancy, the pains of labor, the resulting stretch marks and varicose veins and bouts of depression, and on and on—who, in infinite ways, die so their child (*our* child) may live.

The cross is unavoidable. The only question is who will bear it and to what end. Will the cross be borne by fathers and mothers who sacrifice time, labor, money, and convenience—and in the mother's case, even their own bodies—so our children may live? Or, oppositely, will fathers and mothers demand the cross be carried by their children? Will fathers and mothers demand of their children their death, without even asking them if they're willing? Will fathers and mothers demand of their sons and daughters this last measure of devotion, which they hope will enable them to live an unencumbered life, not bothered by their children's needs, free to pile up wealth and possessions with no thought for anyone's needs but their own?

Will we call these little ones to die for us, or will we die for them? Every man and woman ever conceived has faced this choice, and each answer reveals to the watching world faith or unbelief in the King of kings and Lord of lords.

When God's people are fruitful, bearing, loving, and disciplining our own and others' children (through adoption), we testify to our rulers as well as the watching world of the kindness, mercy, and love of the heavenly Father. When we respond to ridicule not with cynicism or anger but by entrusting ourselves to Him who judges righteously (1 Pet. 2:23), we follow the Apostle in showing our gentleness to all men, knowing "the Lord is near" (Phil. 4:5). When our pastors and elders condemn oppression and injustice, particularly that terrible injustice of the murder of little ones awaiting birth, we tread the path our own fathers and mothers trod two millennia ago, thus changing the Roman Empire.

It will not happen overnight. *Roe* stood for half a century, and its debris is everywhere. But abortion *will* in God's time be brought down; and so let us here declare it simply: to embrace the fruit of the womb is to prove ourselves true sons of our heavenly Father. To care for the soul of every little one is to see in that life the image of God Himself and of our Lord, made man for us. And to love children, ours and our neighbors', is not to burden the world, but to exercise godly care by tending to our own corner of it. Or, as J. R. R. Tolkien put it:

> It is not our part to master all the tides of the world, but to do what is in us for the succour of those years wherein we are set, uprooting the evil in the fields that we know, so that those who live after may have clean earth to till.[51]

This, then, is our hope. That our pastors and elders, legislators and magistrates, will lead us toward repentance and a return to God and His law. That as our own hearts bear new life, so we as fathers and mothers will have the blessing of the fruit of the womb that is the Lord's reward. And that, day by day, this joy will provoke our neighbors to jealousy—our repentance leading theirs, so that, finally, our eyes may see the day when this mighty scourge of evil shall speedily pass away.

Until that day, we persevere in hope—not a hope of chimera or fancy, but of faith and certainty, that when abortion is all past and the blood of Abel altogether purged, it will be by the sovereign hand of the Almighty as He turns our hearts once again to repentance.

The final verse of the Old Testament proclaims the wonderful fruit of this repentance:

> He will restore the hearts of the fathers to their children and the hearts of the children to their fathers, so that I will not come and smite the land with a curse. (Mal. 4:6)

Even so, come, Lord Jesus.

---

[51]. J. R. R. Tolkien, "The Last Debate," ch. 9 in bk. 1 of *The Lord of the Rings: The Return of the King*.

Epilogue

A valiant warrior for the faith who never ceased opposing abortion and all evils metastasizing from it was lost to the battle back in 2009. He was the late Richard John Neuhaus, and a few months before his death, he presented the concluding message of the 2008 annual convention of National Right to Life.

He ended his speech with these words:

> We do not know, we do not need to know, how the battle for the dignity of the human person will be resolved. God knows, and that is enough. As Mother Teresa of Calcutta and saints beyond numbering have taught us, our task is not to be successful but to be faithful. Yet in that faithfulness is the lively hope of success. We are the stronger because we are unburdened by delusions. We know that in a sinful world, far short of the promised Kingdom of God, there will always be great evils. The principalities and powers will continue to rage, but they will not prevail.
>
> In the midst of the encroaching darkness of the culture of death, we have heard the voice of Him who said, "In the world you will have trouble. But fear not, I have overcome the world." Because He has overcome, we shall overcome. We do not know when; we do not know how. God knows, and that is enough. We know the justice of our cause, we trust in the faithfulness of His promise, and therefore we shall not weary, we shall not rest.
>
> Whether, in this great contest between the culture of life and the culture

of death, we were recruited many years ago or whether we were recruited only yesterday, we have been recruited for the duration. We go from this convention refreshed in our resolve to fight the good fight. We go from this convention trusting in the words of the prophet Isaiah that "they who wait upon the Lord will renew their strength, they will mount up with wings like eagles, they will run and not be weary, they will walk and not be faint."

The journey has been long, and there are miles and miles to go. But from this convention the word is carried to every neighborhood, every house of worship, every congressional office, every state house, every precinct of this our beloved country—from this convention the word is carried that, until every human being created in the image and likeness of God—no matter how small or how weak, no matter how old or how burdensome—until every human being created in the image and likeness of God is protected in law and cared for in life, we shall not weary, we shall not rest. And, in this the great human rights struggle of our time and all times, we shall overcome.[1]

---

1. Richard John Neuhaus, "We Shall Not Weary, We Shall Not Rest," speech given at the conclusion of the 2008 annual convention of National Right to Life, July 5, 2008, as published on July 11, 2008, in *First Things*, https://www.firstthings.com/web-exclusives/2008/07/we-shall-not-weary-we-shall-not-rest.

Electronic versions of this book are available for free online at
abortion.evangelpresbytery.com

Listen for free at
abortion-and-the-church.transistor.fm

The paperback edition can be purchased online at
warhornmedia.com

For more information on Evangel Presbytery, please visit
evangelpresbytery.com